The Royal Seed

Why the Genealogy of Jesus Is Important to You Today

Judd F. Allen

WESTBOW
PRESS®
A DIVISION OF THOMAS NELSON
& ZONDERVAN

WestBow Press books may be ordered through booksellers or by contacting:

WestBow Press
A Division of Thomas Nelson & Zondervan
1663 Liberty Drive
Bloomington, IN 47403
www.westbowpress.com
1 (866) 928-1240

ISBN: 978-1-5127-0912-4 (sc)
ISBN: 978-1-5127-0913-1 (e)

Library of Congress Control Number: 2015913585

Print information available on the last page.

WestBow Press rev. date: 10/21/2015

Contents

Epigraph

And when Athaliah the mother of King Ahaziah saw that her son was dead, she arose and destroyed all the *royal seed*. (2 Kings 11:1)

Preface

As a youngster and a young adult, I could not understand why the Bible includes all those boring . . . Boring . . . BORING chapters of hard to pronounce names. What purpose do they serve? They must not be very important because they are not mentioned anywhere else in the Bible. Why are they relevant in the twenty-first century? Is anyone inspired by reading a list of "begats" or kings? Nevertheless, the spark to write this book was ignited by my half-century long interest in genealogies.

It will soon be evident: I am just a layman. I have never had one Bible course. I was encouraged to write this book when I realized Jonah, Habakkuk, Matthew, and Jude never attended seminary. I have read through the Bible multiple times. In fact, it was by my reading the Bible sequentially that the Holy Spirit ignited my interest. The more I poked around and cross-referenced, the clearer my focus became. I have written this book in an attempt to reconcile various texts in the Bible into a uniform synopsis of just one of the Bible's many truths. I believe the Bible to be trustworthy, dependable, inerrant, and infallible. Where discrepancies occur, it is due to our being humans and our lack of Godly wisdom and not because God or His inspired authors made mistakes.

As an older adult, I began to study the Bible more intently and with more purpose. When doing daily Bible readings in a sequential fashion, what I read on Tuesday reminded me of what I had studied the prior Wednesday or Friday. From the Old Testament to the New Testament or from Genesis to Galatians, it really became an exciting path. This was a search for hidden treasures in the Bible. Millions will ignore, scan, or casually skip over these jewels lying right in plain view. I hope you will enjoy this journey of discovery as we extract these treasures from the Bible.

Acknowledgements

First and foremost, I am thankful for the guidance and direction of the Holy Spirit in urging me to attempt this task. I pray the Holy Spirit is pleased with the result.

Beginning in 2009, Coach Jerry Moore began to nudge me to undertake this endeavor. Thanks, Coach. Regina bought me a gift at the 1981 World's Fair, which has been an invaluable resource. Thanks, Regina, for your vital assistance, thirty years in the making. Two ladies I'm deeply indebted to are Barbara Beach and Vivien McMahon. Barbara spent many hours reworking my feeble efforts, correcting my many errors, and doing a wonderful job of hiding her impatience with my irrational requests. Vivien helped to further edit this into a more manageable manuscript. Also, I thank the members in my Sunday school class who have prayed for this book to come to fruition. Special thanks to Linda, Jim, Karen, Joe, Judy, Elizabeth, and Doug. Church members Roger, Denise, Scott, Steve, Travis, Deb, and Danny also were encouragers. Fellow travelers Ruth, Helen, Jan, Elsie, and Linda lent prayer support as well. My long term friend Ted was an encourager. Macklyn and Jim offered professional, wise criticism and counsel. And thanks to my friend Genelle who told me some time ago she wanted a copy of this book. Her untimely death spurred me on to complete my efforts. Lastly, I dedicate this book to my only sibling, Rev. Jerry Y. Allen, who passed into eternity May 26, 2015. To each of you—thank you so very much for your support, assistance, and prayers.

Introduction

Royalty. For most people, that one word evokes a wide array of thoughts about castles, kings, princes, moats, jousting, King Arthur, armor, shields, Friar Tuck, dungeons, serfs, wars, ladies-in-waiting, the Round Table, golden chalices, swords, regalia, pomp, Robin Hood, damsels, knights, heraldry, lords, bishops, religion, banners—enough, enough! You get the idea. Nearly everyone has a host of images that appear when they hear that one single word—*royalty*.

When studying royalty, it is also important to consider dynasty. Dynasty gives credence and legitimacy to the royalty. In a casual worldwide study of the word *dynasty*, easily upwards of three hundred dynasties can be identified. Many dynasties lasted only twenty-five, fifty, or one hundred years. A few dynasties survived two- to four-hundred years. An even more select group of dynasties prevailed for five hundred to a thousand years.

This book is about the oldest, most unique, most powerful, most authoritative dynasty the world has ever known. Other dynasties and royalty have been conquered, diminished, or dissolved. Not so with this dynasty of kings. This dynasty is unique in that it still exists, making it the oldest in all of the history of the world. Its lineage includes princes, princesses, kings, and priests. Members of its royal family are alive today. The story of this dynasty is a tale about wars, the claiming of lands, and the securing of territory. This dynasty had some interest in acquiring real estate, but that was not the primary objective—this unique dynasty was more interested in reigning not over real estate, but reigning over the hearts and souls of men.

The people of this dynasty are unusual. Rather than cowering before a heroic knight or a tyrannical conqueror, the subjects in this dynasty voluntarily submit to their King. This King has been portrayed as a lamb, but in the future He will come forth as a lion. `This King is the man the American pilgrims called "King Jesus." This King was present at the creation of the world; consequently, no dynasty is older than His dynasty. And yet this King's humble beginning probably started in what is today Iraq.

He is a good King. He has shown Himself to be true, to be honorable, to be knowledgeable, to be dependable, to be kind, and to even love His subjects. This King even provided His voluntary subjects with an instruction manual known as the Bible. The truth is, the Bible is a book about royalty.

A few years ago, most of us were fascinated with Kate Middleton's engagement to Prince William. Their wedding was broadcast and published throughout the world. Her clothes, the ring, their meeting, their dating, her trousseau, and the design of her going away outfit, all provided endless media speculation. Later, citizens of the United States were absorbed, fascinated, and preoccupied with the births of their children, Prince George and Princess Charlotte.

And let us not stop with the English. Consider the five-hundred-year reign of the Romanoffs in Russia. Or, the reigns of Queen Juliana and her daughter Queen Beatrix in the Netherlands. Even sixty years ago, the marriage of Prince Rainier of Monaco to film star Grace Kelly captivated the public. A brief study of European royalty shows the longest European dynasties have survived no more than twenty generations. The Hanover-Windsor dynasty to date has endured three-hundred years, but the four-thousand-year providence of God's plan, showing the history and dynasty of His Son, is even more worthy of study.

This book was inspired by my Bible reading. Over time and on more than one occasion, a particular name would appear. When some momentous event occurred in the Bible, there standing quietly in the shadows was this man, this man named Nahshon. When Nahshon came up a couple of times, I thought, *I have never heard of this guy. Was he a king? A bad guy? What?* After my own journey to find out who this biblical person was, I found the answer. Nevertheless, my search created even more puzzles that I wanted to solve.

Eventually, it all began to pull together into a cohesive learning experience. As a visual learner, I needed to get what I was learning down on paper, either in charts or text or maybe both. I had invested much time in learning this; I didn't want to lose it or later have to extract it all over again. It was important to make it concise, for it came from the books of Genesis, 2 Chronicles, Ruth, Zephaniah, Matthew, James, Jude, and Revelation. I wondered, *"How do I synthesize all of this?"* That's when I started thinking about how to best integrate these tidbits from such a wide variety of sources.

My conclusion was to chart it out and see if it made sense to a visual learner—and it did! [1] But the chart does not tell the narrative of the *when*, the *how*, or the *who*. I decided, *Okay, I'll make some footnotes and prompts to help me recall what I've learned.* Soon I was inundated with notes on scraps of white copy paper and still more detailed notes on yellow legal pages.

Concurrent with this time of study, I suffered some eye issues which could have led to permanent blindness, along with other health concerns. During this period, I could only think. I could not read. I could not write. I could not study. Because of prayer, today my sight is 100 percent once again. During these months of just thinking, I realized my efforts at data gathering needed to be in a readable format that I could follow. Slowly, the most farfetched, ridiculous concept came into my thought process: *This needs to be in a book. I need to write a book. But, wait a minute! I have no experience—no knowledge of how to do this. It will take a lot of time— nope, no, this is just too crazy. No. I won't do it.*

You have probably realized how the story ends. You're holding the end of this journey in your hands. While writing this book, the Holy Spirit has gently but persistently nudged this project forward. I felt unqualified, not spiritual enough, and just generally incompetent. I was recently sharing my feelings of inadequacy for this task with a spiritual friend of mine. Joedy smiled and kindly reminded me of the following verse:

"Now, when they saw the boldness of Peter and John and perceived that they were unlearned and ignorant men, they marveled and they took knowledge of them that they had been with Jesus" (Acts 4:13).

In summary, I am trying to be obedient to what I feel has been a multi-faceted, grandly designed, multi-year research project. It was the Holy Spirit who tweaked my interest to write this book. I hope it helps every reader to recognize God's master plan and how *all* the words of God contain treasures of truth. Just remember, you can blame brother Nahshon! I hope his life and those of his relatives will give you a better understanding of God's wonderful word—and the purpose of all those "hard word" names being in the Scripture. All those difficult names have a purpose; they have a message. Eventually, these names will validate Jesus as the Son of God, the only Great High Priest.

When one is on a journey, it is important to note the road signs and mile markers along the way. If a warning sign is posted three times along the road, it is more important than if only one bright orange warning sign appears. The frequency of words in the Bible also helps us to determine the importance of the topic being discussed. Shown are two lists of words that appear in their basic form or in some derivation in the Bible.

THE IMPORTANCE OF WORDS

Bible Words	Frequency of Occurrences in Bible	Bible Words	Frequency of Occurrences in Bible[2]
Belief	144	Genealogy	23
Obey	155	Royal	29
Trust	174	Generation	225
Sacrifice	218	Begat	240
Truth	237	Mother	328
Seed	279	Daughter	581
Faith	359	Name	928
Sin	448	Father	979
Holy	611	Children	1,803
Evil	613	Son	2,374
King	2,254	God	4,470

The left column contains important words to the basic tenets of faith. Yet, we tend to skip or glaze over the scriptural significance of other words, such as those listed in the right column. Is it not interesting how much more frequently words in the right column occur in the Bible than the words *sin, faith, trust,* or even the word *holy?* For example, the word *begat* occurs more often in the Bible than the word *truth.* The word *name* occurs more often than the words *belief, obey, trust, sacrifice,* and *truth* combined.

Genealogy is sprinkled throughout the Bible. Hebrews chapter 7 is entirely devoted to Melchizedek and the mystery of his ancestors. He is mentioned briefly in Genesis and again in Psalms. Yet Hebrews devotes an entire chapter to this "priest of the Most High God" (Hebrews 7:1). Genealogy was vital for determining if a male was worthy to serve as a priest. Passages in Ezra 2:62 and in Nehemiah 7:5 address this very topic. These verses provide evidence that priests had to have a holy, acceptable lineage.

In the Bible, *seed* appears more often than *belief, obey,* or *trust.* In fact, the word *seed* occurs over two hundred fifty times. In the majority of cases, *seed* refers to genealogy rather than agriculture, to human beings rather than plants. Indeed, in Old Testament language, *seed* more often refers to one's family history. For example, study the following chart:

The Genealogy of the "Seed"

Seed of Abraham	John 8:37
Seed of Isaac	Hebrews 11:18
Seed of Jacob	Isaiah 45:19
Seed of Israel	Psalms 22:23
Seed of David	Romans 1:3

Also note: the words "her seed" in Genesis 3:15 involve the original confrontation with the serpent. Flash forward to Revelation 12:17. Here we see the final war between the dragons and the "remnant of her seed."

In addition, consider the frequency of some proper names in the Bible:

THE IMPORTANCE OF WORDS

Bible Names	No. of times in Bible	Bible Names	No. of times in Bible[3]
Noah	51	Azor	2
Josiah	53	Zadok	2
Isaac	128	Matthat	2
Solomon	281	Achim	2
Abraham	311	Salathiel	4
Aaron	352	Salmon	6
Jacob	377	Nahshon	9
Moses	829	Obed	13
Jesus	983	Zerubbabel	22
David	1,139	Adam	30

We are familiar with most of the names in the left column from children's Bible stories or sermons. Notice David's name appears one hundred fifty more times than the name of Jesus. Contrast the familiar names in the left column with the column on the right. In the right column, we assume these men cannot be very significant because they are mentioned so infrequently. The first four may be mentioned twice in the Bible, but in each case, it is in the very same verse. To us, it seems safe to skip over these infrequently used names and move on to the good stuff.

Chapter 1

Genealogy and Ancestors

> Besides their genealogy of males . . . both to the genealogy of the priests . . . and the Levites . . . and to the genealogy of all their little ones, their wives, their sons, their daughters . . . for in their faithfulness, they consecrated themselves in holiness. (2 Chronicles 31:16-18)

As these verses exhibit, the ancient Israelites and the Jews appreciated their heritage. Without the Internet, television, and cell phones, the ancients had to rely on oral traditions, scrolls, testimonies, and sacred texts. Originally, God had chosen a man, Adam, and then later, He selected another particular person, Abram, with whom to covenant. Over time, Abram's family became a clan, and later, they became tribes on their way to even establishing a nation.

Before the Israelites entered the Promised Land, God stated that His purpose for Abraham's family was to make them "a peculiar special treasure unto me . . . a kingdom of priests and a holy nation (Exodus19:5-6 NASB).

This intention of creating a holy kingdom with priests persists throughout the Bible, as exhibited in Revelation 1:6 where John states that Christ ". . . hath made us kings and priests unto God." Likewise, Revelation 5:10 reads, "And hast made us unto our God kings and priests, and we shall reign on the earth." Kings and priests are a recurring theme throughout the Bible from Genesis to Revelation.

In documenting these various kings and priests, genealogies will be important to verify their claims to position, power, and authority.

Unfortunately, Bible genealogies often appear inconsistent. There are several explanations for this. Sometimes different names are used for the same person. A prime example is Jacob's name being changed to Israel. Another was Abram becoming Abraham. In some places, the man is known as Jesus, while at other times, He is known as Christ. Inconsistencies also occur when names are miscopied. It is not surprising that genealogies do not always precisely agree when scribes were copying texts over a period of two or three thousand years. Inconsistencies also occur when a passage is translated from one language into another language. For example, 1 Chronicles 6:3-11 and Ezra 7:1-5 both provide a genealogy for Aaron, the high priest. They mostly agree, but there are discrepancies.

Such differences do not discredit the Bible. At some future time, the Bridegroom will be available to answer our questions. And when He does, His infinite mind will reveal to our human, finite minds how all of creation fits so neatly together.

In a courtroom, validation occurs when two or three different sources confirm one another's testimony. Similarly, when studying genealogy, if a researcher can find two or three different sources, each serves to make the other evidence more trustworthy. Two thousand years ago, the known world consisted of just three continents: Europe, Asia, and Africa. God just happened to place His Son in Israel, which is at the very intersection of these three continents. At such a crossroads, multiple languages were spoken, many different cultures existed, and a wide variety of goods were traded.

Deuteronomy's command that two or three witnesses validate testimony is corroborated by three Gospel writers, each of whom wrote to a different audience in the melting pot known as Israel. Matthew was the hated Jewish tax collector addressing his comments to the Jews; Luke was the physician writing to the Greeks; and Mark was a missionary companion of Paul who wrote to citizens living in the Roman Empire. Here, we see three witnesses (authors) affirming the truth and existence of Jesus: One writer to the Jews. One writer to the Greeks. And still another writer to the Romans.

Another occasion to observe the principle of three witnesses is found in Luke 23:38 and John 19:19. The Roman governor Pilate had a sign placed on the cross of Jesus to claim, "This is the King of the Jews." Pilate had the message written in three different languages: Greek, the language of the sciences; Hebrew, the language of the Jews; and Latin, the language of Rome. In life, Jesus had the three biographers — Matthew, Mark, and Luke. All declared Jesus to be the Messiah. In death, Pilate's sign on the cross bore witness in the same three languages used by Matthew, Mark, and Luke—Jesus is a King.

Although Mark and John ignored genealogy, Matthew and Luke offered extensive lists of Jesus's ancestors. The two lists vary greatly. Not to be overlooked, however, is the fact *that Mary and Joseph shared the same genealogy for thirty-four generations.* Their common ancestry stopped with the birth of two of King David's sons, Solomon and Nathan. Joseph may have been a lowly carpenter or stone mason in a village; nevertheless, not only his but also Mary's heritage flowed through the centuries from the great King David. And David was descended from the tribe of Judah from whom God, in Genesis, had promised would come Israel's lawgivers and kings (Genesis 49:10; 1 Chronicles 5:2). Some have thought Matthew, in writing to the Jews, followed Joseph's line and stressed royalty and kingship, as King David is mentioned in Matthew 1:1. With a focus on kingship, royalty becomes paramount to confirm and validate the very King of Kings (Revelation 17:14, 19:16). In fact, at the beginning of Matthew, King David preempted his ancestor Abraham from thirteen generations earlier. Then quickly, Matthew mentioned Abraham because he is known as the Father of the Jews. Immediately after acknowledging the Abrahamic covenant, Matthew, the Jewish tax collector, assumed all his audience were Jewish and promptly jumped into the Davidic dynasty. The dynasty proceeded in a mostly orderly fashion with Matthew using poetic license to skip four kings and arrive at three sets of fourteen fathers.

(Jews often used such mnemonic tools to help them memorize portions of the Torah.) Matthew starts with King David and the patriarch Abraham. Thereafter, he sequentially proceeds through forty-one fathers to Joseph, Jesus's earthly father. Of those forty-one fathers, nineteen of Jesus's forefathers were kings. In the remaining portions of chapters 1 and 2, Matthew writes about Jesus's earthly father, Joseph, the wise men, and the flight into Egypt.

In contrast, Luke was a physician. His occupation and nationality led to a different focus, a unique witness, and a totally different audience. Likely, Luke traced Mary's ancestry because he was Greek and not Jewish. Luke's account starts after Jesus was baptized by John and then it works backward into antiquity all the way to the first man, Adam. Ultimately Luke concluded with God, Himself, the Creator.

Luke addressed the Greek population in places like Philippi in northern Greece. Unlike the despised tax collector, Luke was a doctor. He was a man of culture and education, as his writing and fluency of language attest. As a scientist, research and documentation were very important to him. Luke was the only Gentile author of any book in the New Testament. He lived in Philippi under a Roman government, with kingship and royalty far removed from his thinking.

Luke, the meticulous physician, possibly interviewed Mary herself, her close relatives, or maybe her neighbors during his visit to Palestine. Luke described the pains and joys of the virgin birth in more detail than any of the other gospel writers. Many scholars believe that by Luke's intimate knowledge of Mary (or those close to her), his genealogical lineage was of Mary's family, not Joseph's. In Luke, the genealogical journey concludes with God's creation of the first man on Earth, Adam. Luke, the Greek physician, had scientifically pursued his research. Luke stressed not the Jewish, or legal, or royal kingship of Jesus, but a more methodical, all-inclusive lineage study. Luke started with Mary's husband, Joseph, and proceeded to pull back the layers of genealogy for seventy-seven generations. Luke's first two chapters tell us most of what we know about John the Baptist, his parents, Mary's pregnancy, and the shepherds in the field. Jesus's lineage is not presented until Luke chapter 3.

We have two Gospel writers as witnesses of Jesus's lineage, writing to two different groups in two different languages. And Pilate, the provocateur, served as a third New Testament witness by his ordering of the sign proclaiming, in three different languages, "Jesus King of the Jews." The two contrasting genealogical lists from Matthew 1 and Luke 3 offer us a starting point. The two lineages of forty-two generations, (Matthew) and seventy-seven generations (Luke) have fourteen fathers who appear in both lists. After having the same fathers for fourteen generations, the two lists separate for twenty generations before returning to a period of two generations where they intersect once again. Then the two lineages diverge for another nineteen generations. How can this be?

That is the purpose of this book: to unlock some of the mysteries of the Bible, to show the spiritual significance (even today) of the long-ago history faithfully recorded in the Bible, and to amplify the relevance of these long, boring lists in 1 and 2 Chronicles. Trust me. They are relevant in making sense of our world even in the twenty-first century.

Let us start with a word and its derivatives that are important to our study. The word is *king*. The importance of kingship in the Bible is the fact that the word *king* and other words, such as *kingly, kingdoms,* and so forth are used over two thousand times in the Bible. Of thirty-nine Old Testament books, the word *king*, in some form, occurs in thirty-six. Except for Leviticus, Ruth and Joel, every Old Testament book mentions *kings* or *kingdoms*.

The Bible also uses the word *royal* when referring to kings in Israel's royalty and genealogy. The term *royal seed* is used in the Bible several times. Furthermore, the Bible includes such terms as *royal city, royal bounty, royal wine, royal house, royal estate, royal commandment, royal crown, royal apparel, royal throne, royal diadem, royal pavilion, royal law,* and *royal priesthood*. However, one of the most intriguing uses of royalty-type words is used by none other than Jesus himself in Matthew 6:9-13. The disciples ask Jesus how to pray. He responds with the model prayer.

Jesus recites in this model prayer: "Thy kingdom come, thy will be done, on Earth as it is in Heaven." Shortly thereafter (v. 13), Jesus uses *kingdom* once again when He says, "For thine is the kingdom, the power and the glory forever. Amen." So Jesus's model prayer is all about the *king* and the *kingdom*, with God being in heaven and on earth.

If a kingdom is coming, it simply follows that any kingdom must have a king. And when that king does come, he will reign forever, just like Handel's *Messiah* concludes with "forever and ever and ever."

The Bible even has two books named 1 Kings and 2 Kings. Today, when emphasis is placed on the New Testament and we often bypass the Old Testament, we tend to overlook kings; we focus on Jesus and His disciples. We focus on Paul and the infant New Testament churches. The four Gospels all mention kings. In three of the Gospels, Jesus himself even talks about kings. Once we pass the four Gospels and Acts, kings are infrequently mentioned in the New Testament. After the first few New Testament books, the New Testament is pretty much silent concerning kings until we get to the last seven chapters of Revelation. Suddenly, Jesus appears as the King of Saints and the King of Kings.

This book is about the slender thread of history that is twisted, warped, woven, stretched, splayed, and tattered through the millennia of peoples, nations, and kingdoms. Yes, there is a slender thread of history, a thread of royalty, a thread of kings, and a thread of "forever." The authors of the Bible weave a tapestry of faith. Those authors all validate the genealogy of Jesus, the King of all Kings. This book is a study of the greatest, longest, most powerful, most omnipotent royal dynasty the world has ever seen. This dynasty was present at creation, is present now, and will be present into forever.

Chapter 2

God

In the beginning, God. (Genesis 1:1 NASB)

I once read about a young American who was of Chinese heritage. His family had kept meticulous records of their history for generations. The young man even knew the Chinese village from which his family had immigrated to the United States. He went searching for relatives in the village and found the records of distant ancestors, causing the people to come alive in his mind. At the end of his visit, the American could document his lineage for twenty-one generations, with a family history stretching back over five hundred years.

In Luke 3, God is listed as the first father—the father of Adam, the first man on Earth. In this sense, God is the father of Jesus, seventy-seven generations into the future. Here we have Luke certifying a direct lineage from God to Jesus. It was not six generations or twenty-one generations, but *seventy-seven* generations! But the fact remains that today we have a recorded royal lineage that extends for over two thousand years.

Matthew's account follows fourteen identical ancestors for both Mary and Joseph. It then deviates at David's two sons, Solomon and Nathan. Twenty generations later, the two distinct lineages intersect at Shealtiel and Zerubbabel, only to divide once again and to rejoin twenty generations later in the union of Joseph and Mary. We tend to think of the Father, the Son, and the Holy Spirit as the Trinity, which they are. But especially in Luke 3, we note that Jesus is "the Son of God."

Chapter 3

Adam

> Then the Lord God formed man of dust from the ground and breathed into his
> nostrils the breath of life and man became a living being. (Genesis 2:7 NASB)

It is important to remember the first eleven chapters of Genesis occur in what is modern-day Iraq. This suggests the Garden of Eden may have been in the areas known in later centuries as Assyria or Babylon. Assyria was the northern portion and Babylon the southern portion of present day Iraq. In addition, the last eleven chapters of Genesis and the beginning twelve chapters of Exodus take place in Egypt. In the remainder of Exodus—plus Leviticus, Numbers, and Deuteronomy—the children of Israel are camped in the desert of the Sinai Peninsula between Egypt and Israel. Most of the Pentateuch (the first five books of the Bible, which were all written by Moses) takes place outside Israel in Iraq, Egypt, or the Sinai desert.

Approximately one thousand five hundred years later, the Israelites were held captive seventy to one hundred years in Iraq. First, they were captives in Assyria in northern Iraq. Then, the Babylonian Empire rose several decades later in central and southern Iraq and conquered the Assyrians. The Old Testament books of Jonah, Esther, Ezekiel, Daniel, Nahum, Ezra, and Nehemiah take place in today's Iraq.

The first man lived in the Garden of Eden, probably in the land of Iraq (Genesis 1:2).

Beginning in Genesis 1, God alone has been at work creating the fish and animals. In 1:26, God uses the term "us," which hints at the Trinity. This first man is the only creature created from the dirt. Adam is unique. Not only is his body not created like other animals, but he also has a soul. Later, in Genesis 35:18, death is described as the soul departing from the human, earthly body.

Adam and Eve are occupants of the garden. They live innocent, unassuming lives. I imagine them with honesty and simplicity, the trusting nature of an infant who would tend to obey almost any older child or adult. They are not inhibited, scornful, angry, or possessive people. It is tranquil. The Garden of Eden is perfect.

In Genesis 2:9, two trees are mentioned: the Tree of Life and the Tree of Knowledge of Good and Evil. We all know the story of the Tree of Knowledge of Good and Evil. Verses 9 and 16 tell us Adam and Eve can freely eat of the garden. They may eat even of the Tree of Life, but they choose not to. They are vegetarians. No animals are killed for meat, and there is no fear of animals or by animals. God has stated the couple is not to eat of the Tree of Knowledge. If they do, they will die.

Once the Serpent seduces Eve and she in turn tempts Adam, they do not physically die, but their innocence does. By eating of the Tree of Knowledge, they can discern good and evil, right and wrong. The Serpent has lied to the couple with a half-truth. Their bodies, true enough, do not die, but their souls become impaired. Their loss of innocence is verified by the fig leaves and hiding from God.

We do not hear too much about the other tree in the garden. What about that other tree? Did it fade out of the story? Because of Adam's sin in Genesis 3:22–23, the Lord God declares, "Behold the man is become as one of Us to know good and evil" and "now lest he put forth his hand and take also of the Tree of Life, and eat, and live forever," man has to suffer the consequences of his disobedience. God sends man forth from the Garden of Eden to till the ground from whence he was taken. Genesis 3:24 declares that God drives Adam and Eve from the garden. They do not want to leave. God places cherubim and a flaming sword to guard the garden to prevent Adam from returning. The end of the verse explains why God is harsh. He is not guarding the Garden of Eden as a whole; he is preventing man from eating of the Tree of Life and attaining immortality.

Two things stand out in verse 24. First, the cherubim are noted. This is significant because in Exodus 25:18 the cherubim are also chosen to guard the Ark of the Covenant and the mercy seat of God. Furthermore, Psalm 104:4 and Hebrews 1:7 list angels ministering as a "flame of fire." Second, what is even more exciting is the mention of the Tree of Life. After God mentions the Tree of Life growing in the garden, God is seen defending His Tree of Life in Genesis 2:9 and 3:22. God guards the Tree of Life from Adam and Eve by commissioning the angel and flaming sword to keep the couple from the Tree of Life.

After this event, we find scant reference to the Tree of Life. The Bible proceeds to talk mostly about the consequences of the couple having eaten from the Tree of Knowledge. Since man was banished from the Garden of Eden, for thousands of years he has been on his search for knowledge. From Nimrod and the Tower of Babel until now, man has been on this quest for more knowledge. First Corinthians 1 is nearly an entire chapter devoted to man's wisdom and quest for knowledge. Verses 25 and 27 announce God has chosen the foolish things of the world to confound the wise. Did the Corinthians of yesterday or do today's Americans stop their pursuit of knowledge?

By the way, in prior years, I was a college professor. One of America's growth industries in recent decades has been education. Students come from all over the world to America for knowledge. Yes, in the past few millennia, the Tree of Knowledge has bloomed, flowered, and reproduced exponentially. At the end times, the prophet Daniel declares knowledge will increase (Daniel 12:4). As we have continued to seek more education, we have become more intellectual and more fact-oriented and have replaced our faith with facts. Today, we do not see a need for God. Why? We now have our knowledge and our governments to protect us, to guide us, and to provide for us.

You might ask, *Whatever happened to that other little tree in the Garden of Eden? The Tree of Life—whatever became of it?* God has His agenda, His plans. Man's wisdom will not thwart God's foolishness, much less God's purpose.

After the references to the Tree of Life in Genesis 2:9, 3:22, and 3:24, the term almost disappears from the Word of God. Only wise King Solomon makes reference to a generic tree of life in Proverbs 3, 11, 13, and 15. The Tree of Life is mentioned in the second and third chapters of the entire Bible, and then the Word of God is mostly silent about it until this tree once again reappears in Revelation. Good news! The Tree of Life did not die out, it did not wither, and it did not disappear. Jesus, addressing the church at Ephesus in Revelation 2:7, promises to him who overcomes that He will "give to eat of the Tree of Life, which is in the midst of the Paradise of God." Then in the very last chapter of the Bible, Revelation 22, the Tree of Life reappears in verses 2 and 14 in the very center, no less, of the New Jerusalem. God wins! His ultimate plan is victorious!

If Eve and Adam had not disobeyed God about the Tree of Knowledge, then they would not have been tempted to partake of the Tree of Life. Adam and Eve would not have been thrust out of the Garden of Eden. We could all be living there today, avoiding the Tree of Knowledge and expectantly waiting the Tree of Life's eternal future blessings. But it was not to be—not for Adam, not for you, and not for me.

We know how this saga concludes. We know from Genesis 3 that man has been forbidden from having access to the Tree of Life. We know from Revelation that man on his own cannot gain access to the Tree of Life. The Tree of Life appears in two of the first three chapters of God's Word and then appears twice in the very last chapter of the Bible. The Tree of Life and its appearing reminds me of a sermon I once heard. The gist of the sermon was that the Bible only deals with man's perfection in the first two chapters of Genesis—and the last two chapters of Revelation.

So how does God restore the banished Adam and all mankind from tilling the ground to fellowship with Him for eternity? Well, it is all about the seed. The word *seed* occurs nearly three hundred times in the Bible. Over forty of the Bible's sixty-six books have a reference to *seed, seeds, seed time*, etc. The first occurrence of the word *seed* is in Genesis 1:11. In fact, the word *seed* occurs six times in the very first chapter of Genesis. In Genesis 1:29, man is a vegetarian. It is after Adam has sinned that the first blood is shed in Genesis 3:21, when God covers the sin of Adam and Eve with a tunic of skins. The penalty for disobedience to God's instruction is pronounced in Genesis 3:14 and 15, first to the serpent and second to Eve. But, rather than talking about agricultural seeds, it becomes animated. It becomes the serpent's seed versus the woman's seed (v. 15). The conflict of Genesis 3:15 is resolved in Revelation 3:17. In Genesis, Satan, via the serpent, makes war on the remnant of "her seed." It is the Bible's first prophecy. The phrase "her seed" is one of the very first terms in the Bible used to describe Jesus. Biologically, the use of "her seed" appears to be in error; a woman has no seed. Galatians 4:4 contains the answer: "His son made of a woman." In other words "her seed" announces a prophecy far into the future—a virgin birth. The curse of Genesis 3:14 will then be lifted. Galatians 4 and 5 teaches that the children of God are adopted by God. This adoption is described in Galatians 3:14–29 where believers are called joint heirs with Jesus and members of the royal family of God.

In Revelation 22:3, the very next verse after the Tree of Life reappears, John further states, "And there shall be no more curse." Two trees were in the first Garden. Adam was tempted to eat from the Tree of Knowledge and yielded. God removed the temptation of the Tree of Life by banishing Adam and Eve from the garden. All men will now encounter the curse of enmity with their Creator. Ultimately, when God's plan concludes, the curse will be lifted. Obedient man will enjoy the Tree of Life in eternity, enjoying a reconciliation made possible by the woman's *seed*, the virgin birth.

Why Adam is relevant to Jesus's heritage is explained in 1 Corinthians 15:45. This verse talks about the "first Adam" being a living soul and the "last Adam" being a light-giving spirit. Paul telescopes through seventy-six generations from the first Adam, to God's son, the last Adam, Jesus. From the very first man, Adam, runs a genealogy, a thread, to Jesus, to whom the Bible names the last Adam.

What did we learn about Adam?

1. He is the son of God.
2. He was in the image of his Creator.
3. He lived to be the fourth-oldest man in history.
4. He was to name and subdue animal and plant life and to rule over the world. Most importantly, obedience to God would maintain an eternal relationship with God.
5. He was happy when Eve came on the scene.
6. He listened to his wife.
7. He lied to God.
8. He felt guilty about disobeying God.
9. He was led astray by the tempter; he sinned (Romans 5:12) and was condemned to life by trials.
10. He did not want to leave the garden.
11. His two (or three) sons would provide grandchildren.
12. His descendants will also endure these trials. Just as sin entered the world by one man, likewise salvation will enter the world via one man (Romans 5:15; 1 Corinthians 15:21-22 NASB).

Adam's Relatives

Name	Relationship	APPROXIMATE Dates
God	his Creator and Father	?
All other peoples	his children	?

Chapter 4

Enoch

> And Enoch walked with God; and he was not; for God took him. (Genesis 5:24 NASB)

Adam had three sons: Cain, Abel, and Seth. Abel was dead and Cain was his murderer. After a brief genealogy of Cain's descendants in Genesis 4, they disappear forever from the Bible, but not so with Seth and his descendants. In Genesis 4:25 Eve says, "God appointed me another *seed* instead of Abel." Then verse 26 states, "Then began men to call upon the name of the Lord." Chapter 5 starts again with Adam and Adam's great-great-great-great-grandson, Enoch. Adam and his five descendants all lived about nine hundred years, yet Enoch only lived three hundred sixty-five years. Early verses in Genesis 5 make the repetitive statement "he died" about *six* of Enoch's ancestors. Genesis 5:22 makes a note about Enoch; "he is not as his ancestors." For this verse records something special about Enoch: "he walked with God."

For six generations we read that "he died;" yet verse 22 tells us Enoch walked with God—now that is special. In verse 24 we get another bit of detail about Enoch. Again the Bible repeats that Enoch "walked with God;" but in this verse it goes on to state, "he was not; for God took him." Apparently Enoch's Godly walk is very special.

To better understand Enoch's walk with God, we read chapter 11 of the book of Hebrews, which gives additional insight. Early in this chapter, the unnamed author of Hebrews mentions four men who "by faith" obediently served God: Abel, Enoch, Noah, and Abraham. We see that the author of Hebrews verifies Enoch's faith, *thirteen generations before Abraham is born*. As an ancestor of Abraham, Enoch is significant, for centuries later, God calls Abraham to be the father of the nation of Israel. Hebrews 11 acknowledges Abraham's ancestor Enoch had already "walked with God" and was exhibiting his faith centuries before Abraham believed in God (Genesis 15:6). What was special about Enoch was his faith.

Centuries before the call of Abraham, or Moses' writing the first five books of the Bible, it is evident keeping the law is not what is important. What is important is "by faith." The Bible shows that from Adam's three sons, one lineage is clearly favored—Seth's. Once Seth is identified, the following verses more fully develop the lineage of Seth's children. Seth's family is unique because it was from this clan "man began to call on the Lord," and five generations later, in this same family, "Enoch walked with the Lord."

Look at that phrase, "Enoch walked with God." It implies a fellowship, a close and personal relationship. In Leviticus 26:15, God says to the Israelites (and later to Christians): "And I will walk among you and will be your God and you shall be My people." Paul later quotes this verse in 2 Corinthians 6:16. Enoch's walk with God is a journey of faith, of fellowship, of closeness.

Besides Enoch, only one other human walked with God and never died. Second Kings 2:1-11 tells us about Elijah, who is taken up to heaven in a whirlwind. At the end of the Old Testament, in the next to last verse of Malachi (4:5) the prophet Malachi declares, "Behold, I will send you Elijah, the prophet, before the coming of the great and dreadful day of the Lord." In Matthew Jesus states, "And if ye will receive it, this is Elijah which was for to come. He that hath ears to hear, let him hear" (Matthew 11:14-15).

More about Enoch and his being a prophet is in the New Testament book of Jude. The first verse of Jude gives us an important clue as to which Jude most likely penned this text. In the first verse of the book that bears his name, he calls himself the brother of James, that is, Jesus's half-brother. A few verses later, Jude documents Enoch as the seventh generation from Adam (Jude 14-15). This passage also confirms Luke 3:37-38, where Enoch is also noted as the seventh from Adam.

Many scholars believe Elijah to be the greatest prophet in the northern kingdom. Elijah is the prophet who predicts a drought in 1 Kings 17:1 and then prays for a flood. So, what does Elijah have to do with Enoch? In Revelation 11, the Angel of God declares, "And I will give power unto my two witnesses that they should prophecy." Some scholars believe the two unnamed witnesses to be Moses, the author of the Law, and Elijah, representative of the prophets. But Deuteronomy 34:5 states "Moses died." Other Bible students think the two witnesses are Elijah and Enoch because these two are the only two humans who are "called up into heaven and were no more" (Hebrews 11:5 and 2 Kings 2:3-5). Revelation 11:6 states these two witnesses "have power to shut heaven; that it may not rain in the days of their prophecy." Verses 7 and 8 states, "The Beast shall make war against these two witnesses and overcome them and kill them. Their dead bodies shall lie in the street of the great city." Of all the human beings who have ever lived, only Enoch and Elijah never died. As for the power to shut heaven, we know Elijah did this, as already noted. But, Enoch lived before rainfall ever occurred on Earth. The floods came when "the windows of heaven were opened," but it did not rain until the time of Enoch's great-grandson, Noah.

In Revelation 11:2, John is instructed, when mentioning the temple of God, to leave out the court of the Gentiles; therefore it seems likely the two witnesses will be Messianic Jews who will witness to their fellow Jews. It seems obvious that one of the two witnesses will be Elijah. But what's intriguing is that second witness in Revelation 11. Could it be Enoch?

Go back to the passage in Jude. In verse one, Jude declares himself brother to James and Jesus. When Jude holds up Enoch as a prophet, he is also holding up his great-grandfather Enoch from sixty-eight generations earlier! Luke 3 mentions Enoch as an ancestor of Jesus. If Jesus is the coming bridegroom of the church who will appear soon after the two witnesses reveal themselves to the Jews, and if Luke 3 traces Jesus's seed all the way back to Adam, would it not be fitting in God's omnipotent power for one of the two witnesses to be Jesus's ancestor from the dynasty of *the Royal Seed*?

What did we learn about Enoch?

1. Enoch was *taken* by God.
2. He never died. (Only Elijah will have a similar experience.)
3. He may be one of the two witnesses evangelizing the Jews in the Book of Revelation.
4. Jude is his great grandson, sixty eight generations later.

Enoch's Relatives

<u>Name</u>	<u>Relationship</u>	<u>APPROXIMATE Dates</u>
Methuselah	Son	?
Noah	Great-grandson	±3000 BC
Abraham	Great-grandson, 12 generations removed	±2000 BC
David	Great-grandson, 25 generations removed	1000 BC
James	Great-grandson, 67 generations removed	AD 30
Jude	Great-grandson, 67 generations removed	AD 30
Jesus	Great-grandson, 67 generations removed	AD 30

Chapter 5

Methuselah

So all the days of Methuselah were nine hundred sixty and nine years; and he died. (Genesis 5:27 NASB)

Genesis covers a greater period of time than any other book in the in the Bible. Genesis chapter 5 alone covers ten generations.

The Begats

Name		Reference
Adam	"and he begat (had other) sons and daughters"	Genesis 5:4
Seth	"and he begat (had other) sons and daughters"	Genesis 5:7
Enosh	"and begat (had other) sons and daughters"	Genesis 5:10
Cainan	"and begat (had other) sons and daughters"	Genesis 5:12
Mahalalel	"and begat (had other) sons and daughters"	Genesis 5:16
Jared	"and begat (had other) sons and daughters"	Genesis 5:19
Enoch	"and begat (had other) sons and daughters"	Genesis 5:22
Methuselah	"and begat (had other) sons and daughters"	Genesis 5:26
Lamech	"and begat (had other) sons and daughters"	Genesis 5:30
Noah	"and he begat Shem, Ham & Japheth"	Genesis 5:32

We know none of the names of these other ten generations of "sons and daughters." The only ten names we know are the ones listed above. Of all of the "sons and daughters" in these ten generations, why does the Bible share the names of just these ten men? Why did Moses not record the names of at least some of the other "sons and daughters"?

The answer is simple. Of all the children born in these ten generations, only these ten men have something in common. These ten men in Genesis chapter 5 are the first ten ancestors of Jesus! By Genesis chapter 5, Moses has already documented the first ten forefathers of Jesus.

Turn over a few chapters in your Bible to Genesis 11. Once again we see a similar pattern.

The Begats Continued

Name		Reference
Shem	"and begat sons and daughters"	Genesis 11:11
Arphaxad[4]	"and begat sons and daughters"	Genesis 11:13
Cainan	"and begat sons and daughters"	Luke 3:36
Salah	"and begat sons and daughters"	Genesis 11:15
Eber	"and begat sons and daughters"	Genesis 11:17
Peleg	"and begat sons and daughters"	Genesis 11:19
Reu	"and begat and daughters"	Genesis 11:21
Serug	"and begat sons and daughters"	Genesis 11:23
Nahor	"and begat sons and daughters"	Genesis 11:25
Terah[5]	"and begat Abram, Nahor and Haran"	Genesis 11:26

The important thing to note is Moses has now recorded almost twenty generations of men, and we are only into the first eleven chapters of the Bible. These twenty select men are not just random men. They are the first twenty generations of Jesus's ancestors.

In Genesis 43, Joseph's eleven brothers marvel at how the Governor of Egypt has seated them in correct birth order. This is no small feat—the eleven brothers had four different mothers! In Genesis chapters 5 and 11, Moses gets nearly twenty generations of Jesus's lineage in precise, correct order. Furthermore, after Noah is born at the end of Genesis 5, another set pattern of nine generations emerges over the next thirty chapters. In the following list, of nine generations, six additional men are ancestors of Jesus. Jesus's forefathers are noted with an *asterisk*.

Generations of the Old Testament[6]

Generations of the Heavens and the earth	Genesis 2:4
The book of the generations of Adam*[7]	Genesis 5:1
The book of the generations of Noah*	Genesis 6:9
The book of the generations of the sons of Noah	Genesis 10:1
The book of the generations of Shem*	Genesis 11:10
The book of the generations of Terah*	Genesis 11:27
The book of the generations of Ishmael	Genesis 25:12
The book of the generations of Isaac*	Genesis 25:19
The book of the generations of Esau	Genesis 36:1
The book of the generations of Jacob*	Genesis 37:2

Generations of the New Testament

The book of the generations of Jesus Christ	Matthew 1:1
"Ye are a chosen generation, a royal Priesthood"	1 Peter 2:9

When Matthew begins his writing, he opens the New Testament with the identical format used by Moses in Genesis: "the book of the generations of," not of Adam, but of "the book of the generations of Jesus Christ." Matthew starts the New Testament with this same format: "the book of the generations." And later, Peter uses a similar title.

The son of Enoch was Methuselah. Although he is mentioned in the lineage of Jesus, (Luke 3:37), we have only a few verses in the Bible about him. His only claim to fame is that he lived nine hundred sixty-nine years, longer than anyone else in recorded history.

This biblical account has a specific journey and a particular destination. Just as Cain and Abel's descendants dropped from the narrative, similarly Adam's, Jared's, and Methuselah's other sons and daughters are not even named. Besides his age, Methuselah has one other claim to fame: he is the grandfather of Noah through Lamech. In verse 29, Lamech names his son Noah and declares, "Maybe he will comfort us concerning our work and toil of our hands concerning the ground which the Lord hath cursed." Lamech does not offer any reason for why God has cursed the ground (which is man's sinful nature). Genesis 5:30 mentions Lamech as it does his father, Methuselah, "and he begat sons and daughters." Likewise, of all Lamech's sons and daughters, the Bible specifically names only his son Noah. These other children disappear into the darkness of antiquity. Methuselah fathers Lamech when he is one hundred eighty-seven years old (Genesis 5:25). Lamech becomes a father at age one hundred eighty-two (Genesis 5:28). Thus, although Enoch "was no more" (living only three hundred sixty-five years), he has been gone just nine years when his great-grandson Noah is born. The dramatic event of Enoch's walking with God and being no more would still be told around the campfires and tents of Methuselah and Lamech to the impressionable young lad, Noah.

What did we learn about Methuselah?

1. Methuselah lived longer than any other human being in history.
2. His grandson, Noah, became famous for building the ark and surviving the Flood.
3. His father, Enoch, was special to God.
4. The Bible records the name of only one of his many children.
5. Through the son named Lamech, the Bible traces Methuselah's lineage to his great-grandson, Jesus, several generations later.

Methuselah's Relatives

Name	**Relationship**	**APPROXIMATE Dates**
Enoch	Father	?
Noah	Grandson	±3000 BC
Jesus	Great-grandson, 66 generations removed	AD 30

Chapter 6

Noah

> Noah was a just man and perfect in his generations, and Noah walked with God.
> (Genesis 6:9)

As children in Sunday school, we all heard the dramatic story of Noah building the ark prior to the flood and of the animals coming to him two by two. Later, God states that "every living substance that I have made, will I destroy from the face of the earth" (Genesis 6:7). Also, in Genesis 7:19 the Bible states, "And the waters prevailed exceedingly upon the earth, and all the high hills that were under the heavens were covered." In addition, verses 21-23 announce: "And all flesh died that moved upon the earth, both of fowl and of cattle, and of beast, and of every creeping thing that creepeth upon the earth, and every man . . . all in whose nostrils was the breath of life, of all that was in the dry land died . . . And every living substance was destroyed which was upon the face of the ground." Similarly, in Hebrews 11:7, "He (God) condemned the world." In detailing these events, the Bible uses words that mean total, complete, and all-encompassing twenty-five to thirty times. The Hebrew word *mabūl* (deluge), used here for the flood, is used nowhere else in the Bible.

Clearly, this children's Bible story is accurate when it depicts the whole world as flooded.

In addition, Noah is listed in Matthew 24, Luke 17, 1 Peter, and 2 Peter as a genuine person and not a fable. Noah is famous not just for the flood, but for another reason. According to Genesis 9:29, Noah is the third oldest person in human history. Only Jared, Noah's great-great grandfather, who died at age nine hundred sixty-two, and Methuselah, Noah's grandfather, who lived nine hundred sixty-nine years, lived longer. To say that Noah came from a long-lived family is an understatement at best! Another reason, the most important reason, why Noah is prominent in the Bible is found in Luke 3:36. Noah is an ancestor of Jesus. Noah is famous not because of the flood and ark story, but because he is an ancestor of Jesus.

Genesis 6:8 states that Noah found grace in the eyes of the Lord. This is the first time grace is mentioned in the Bible, and it is about Jesus's ancestor Noah.

In Genesis 6:9 Noah is called a "just man and perfect in his generation." At the end of Genesis 6 is a simple declaration, "Thus did Noah, according to all that God commanded him, so he did." In Ezekiel, we see Noah listed by the prophet as a holy man. Specifically, Ezekiel 14:14 and 14:20 lists Noah, Daniel, and Job as righteous men. And like his great grandfather Enoch, Scripture states Noah walked with God. God simply states in Genesis 7:1, "For thee have I seen righteous before me in this generation." 2 Peter 2:5 declares, "Noah . . . a preacher of righteousness." In his ministry of ark building, this preacher of righteousness only saved eight souls—and one of the souls was his own. Genesis 7:5 emphasizes Noah's obedience when it says "and Noah did according to all that the Lord commanded him."

Methuselah lived five years longer than his son Lamech. A point to ponder - Methuselah's life span was such that he may have either died just before the flood or may have been one of its victims. Methuselah may have been his grandson Noah's spiritual mentor prior to the flood.

Have you ever considered how much faith Noah had? Noah was still childless after five hundred years. Then he had three sons, Shem, Ham, and Japheth, in approximately a three-year period. Compare Genesis 7:6 and Genesis 6:3, then subtract the numbers. When Noah was about four hundred eighty years old, God gave him a command to build an ark. We know that Noah had been working for twenty years on the ark when Shem was born. It seems likely the three sons grew up around the ark, probably contributed to the building of it, and suffered the same derision and mocking their father endured from their neighbors. Noah's one-hundred-year-old sons appear to be childless, for the sons were almost one hundred years old when the flood started (Genesis 5:32 and 7:6). By this time, Noah was six hundred years old (Genesis 7:6 and 8:13).

Hebrews chapter 11 is the Hall of Fame of Faith. We have already noted Enoch is listed and recognized as being an ancestor of Jesus. Enoch's great grandson, Noah, also an ancestor of Jesus, is named next. Hebrews 11:7 tells us three important things about Noah. First, as in the case of Enoch, the verse starts out, "by faith." *Noah did not have a Bible, so he could not be following the Law of the Old Testament since Moses's birth was seventeen generations into the future.* Noah obeyed God when he got gopher wood and started constructing an ark. Surely, Noah was aware how ridiculous his building project appeared to the neighbors, especially in an arid land. The ark was about one half the width of a football field and one and one-half times as long—four hundred fifty feet long, seventy-five feet wide, and forty-five feet high. No doubt this would have been a sight to see. The top deck covered three quarters of an acre and was nearly three times bigger than Solomon's temple!

This would not be a verbal statement that a twenty-first century politician could retract, apologize for, or clarify. No, this statement of faith was as long as one and one-half football fields and as tall as a four-story building. Undoubtedly, neighbors and travelers throughout the region would bring friends and family to view the spectacle of what they may have seen as Noah's folly.

Second is the important phrase "being warned by God of things not seen as yet, moved with fear." What does "things not seen as yet" mean? Read Genesis 2:5-6: "For the Lord God had not caused it to rain upon the earth. And there was not a man to till the ground, but there went up a mist from the earth and watered the whole face of the ground." Noah is obedient to God. "Noah did according unto all that the Lord commanded him." If he is submissive to God to spend one hundred twenty years building an ark, waterproofing it, making the ark four stories high, and providing enough hay, grain and fodder for all the animals, then he is also a man of enough faith to endure the public humiliation that lasts for over a century. Noah's faith is affirmed when the flood starts. Not only does a mist of moisture rise up from the earth, but for the first time in the history of the world, moisture falls from the skies. God says, "I will cause it to rain upon the earth, forty days and forty nights" (Genesis 7:4 NASB).

In Genesis 6:18-19, God announces He will covenant with Noah as He had with Adam. This is the second covenant in the Bible. God instructs Noah to enter the ark along with his family and to bring two animals of each species on board. Seven clean animals and two unclean animals are listed in Genesis 7:2-3, along with fowls of the air by groups of seven. Verses 9 and 15 tell us the animals come to Noah and go into the ark. Loading maybe twenty thousand to forty thousand animals would have taken time. Bible story books always picture elephants, lions, zebras, etc. But, think of loading rabbits, butterflies, hummingbirds, worms, chipmunks, beavers, ladybugs, goats, and raccoons. Apparently God brought the animals providentially to Noah in an orderly manner. (The distinction between seven clean and two unclean animals is probably due to the sacrifices which would follow and to God's providing clean and unclean foods later in Leviticus 11.) Of the five animal groups listed in Genesis 1:21-25, the only group not on the Ark are the marine animals. They can survive just fine in the flood!

Have you ever considered what Noah's godless neighbors thought about provisions and animals being loaded on the ark? Surely as the ship was being completed, some of the neighbors must have wondered, "What if that crazy Noah might just know something that we don't?" Anxiety would have risen further as food was loaded and even further when the eight souls boarded. This became the moment of truth after one hundred twenty years of preparation. Not only had God given Noah one hundred twenty years to build this great ship, but also man had over a century to repent and follow God. The text shows no evidence of any of those outside Noah's family ever deciding to follow the God of Noah. As noted earlier, Noah lived among his neighbors and was a witness. He was just and perfect, walking before God and doing all God commanded him. He was a righteous man.

In 2 Peter 3:4-5, Peter talks about "earth standing out of the water (creation) and in the water (flood)." In 2 Peter 2:5, he pronounces judgment on Noah's neighbors, "bringing in the flood upon the world of the ungodly."

One other not so obvious statement of Noah's faith is that nowhere does the Bible mention that the ark has any steering mechanism, rudder, or sails. Noah and all on board with him are at the mercy of God's guidance, direction, and leadership. This ark is really more similar to a modern barge. The vessel is totally at the mercy of God—totally dependent on God and totally committed to God's direction.

Genesis 7:16 says God shut them in the ark. Noah had not closed the door. He did not waterproof the entrance, since he was already inside. Noah operated on faith and was shut into the ark by God. He did not know where the ark would travel. Noah had no means to stabilize the craft. He had no control over the ark. The ship was constructed of wood and pitch. It was loaded with animals that continually shifted their weight in response to the waves. The food on board was flammable, the boards slathered in pitch were flammable, and furthermore the only light was from the volatile torches and a twelve-month supply of fuel for the torches, which needed to be on board. Furthermore, Noah didn't have a Bible to comfort him during the twelve-month flood.

Did Noah have nightmares about the godless people clinging to logs or the edge of the ark, begging, crying, and pleading in desperation to be saved? Was Noah's own grandfather, Methuselah, one of the people that died at this time? What about his wife's relatives or the families of his daughters-in-law? Was there resentment or discord on the ark from Noah's sons about their fathers-in-law or sisters-in-law being left to die? Have you ever thought of the panic among the dying animals, fighting a hopeless battle to survive? Would not they all have been baying, mooing, or bleating to no avail? It was stressful outside of the ark, as man and beast were fighting for life, and it was stressful inside the ark's confines, listening to the desperate cries of people and living in close proximity of animals with people, all rolling in a turbulent storm with no means to control their destiny. And everything on board was flammable—the wood, the pitch, the fodder, the animals, the fuel, and most of all, the torches.

But Noah was obedient. He had been mocked for one hundred twenty years. His father, Lamech, had died only a few years before. Noah had no children for half of a millennium. Why build a boat if it is "just me and the missus"? He had been working on the ark for twenty years before his first son was born. Yet Noah was obedient. In the confusion and turmoil of the windows of heavens opening (Genesis 8:2), with animals and humans dying, Noah was still obedient.

Noah was obedient and was not in control. Noah had to trust God.

The Bible gives no record of God's coming to Noah during all of this confusion and turmoil that lasts twelve months. After Noah's ark has been afloat for five months, the Bible says the waters recede. In the seventh month, the ark touches ground on Mount Ararat. Gradually the waters recede over the next three months and mountain peaks can be seen.

Noah and Company have seen no land, no towns, no other people, no other animals, no ships for one hundred fifty days. But the Bible records no lack of faith on Noah's part. He is totally dependent on God. He has no cabinet of advisors, no Parliament, no experts, and no staff. No, it is just God and Noah. As the water level falls, Noah sends forth a raven which goes to and fro. Then Noah dispatches a dove, and it comes back to the ark. Noah waits another week and sends the dove out yet again. This time the dove comes to Noah with an olive leaf in her mouth. This olive leaf is significant because olive trees do not grow at high altitudes (1 Chronicles 27:28). Although the ark has landed at a high altitude upon Mount Ararat, the olive leaf shows Noah the flood is almost over, as olive trees only live at low altitudes. He waits one more week and sends the dove out a third time. This time, she does not return.

After the flood subsides and Noah's family disembarks from the ark, the first action of Noah is to build an altar to sacrifice "of every clean beast and of every clean fowl and offered burnt offerings on the altar." Genesis 8:21 tells us "the Lord smelled a 'sweet savor.'" The term *sweet savor* is prevalent in Leviticus chapters 1-3. This is important, for the book of Leviticus is an instruction manual of how the Israelites were to be sanctified by offering proper, correct sacrifices to God. Some scholars feel that the smoke rising from the burning fat and flesh of the animals being offered was a way God could participate in the sacrifices as the smoke and odors drifted upward into the heavens.

As the barge comes to rest on dry land, God establishes one of His major royal covenants. This covenant, or contract, is with Noah and all living things on the earth. God emphasizes to Noah what He originally told Adam: God promises He will never destroy all life on earth again with water.

Furthermore, as a sign of His commitment, God places the rainbow in the sky. The fact that the world has not been destroyed by floods again in over three thousand years is proof of God's truth.

Genesis 8:13 dates this event as the first day of the first month of the New Year. God is starting over with mankind. Genesis 7:14 and 8:14 teaches us that the flood has lasted one year and ten days. As God told the first man, Adam, now God likewise instructs Noah, "be fruitful and multiply" (Genesis 8:17; 9:1 NASB). However, God gives Noah different instructions than he gave to Adam concerning food. In Genesis 1:29, Adam is given only herbs, seed, and fruit from trees for food. After the flood, in Genesis 9:3, God gives Noah and his family permission to eat meat. Nevertheless, man is forbidden to eat the blood of animals.

This change in diet to include meat is one reason Seventh Day Adventists believe man's life expectancy began to decline. The Adventists tend to be vegetarians and live longer than the typical American. In addition, Adventists operate hospitals, such as Loma Linda in California, where research into diet and health are important. Study the following chart:

TO EAT OR NOT TO EAT MEAT?

NAME	AGE	REFERENCE
God	Infinite	Genesis 1:1
Adam	930 Years	Genesis 5:5
Seth	912 Years	Genesis 5:8
Enosh	905 Years	Genesis 5:11
Cainan	910 Years	Genesis 5:14
Mahalalel	895 Years	Genesis 5:17
Jared	962 Years	Genesis 5:20
Enoch	365 Years	Genesis 5:23
Methuselah	969 Years	Genesis 5:27
Lamech	777 Years	Genesis 5:31
Noah	950 Years	Genesis 9:29

ADDED MEAT TO DIET

NAME	AGE	REFERENCE
Shem	600 Years	Genesis 11:10-11
Arphaxad	438 Years	Genesis 11:12-13
Cainan	?	Luke 3:36
Salah	433 Years	Genesis 11:14-15
Eber	464 Years	Genesis 11:16-17
Peleg	239 Years	Genesis 11:18-19
Reu	239 Years	Genesis 11:20-21
Serug	230 Years	Genesis 11:22-23
Nahor	148 Years	Genesis 11:24-25
Terah	205 Years	Genesis 11:32
Abraham	175 Years	Genesis 25:7

Another interesting point: we have seen in the Garden of Eden that Adam and Eve were vegetarians, as mentioned in Genesis 1:29. In Noah's later days, man had God's permission to eat meat.

We see that life spans dropped precipitously after Noah's life. As we are learning in modern times, the diet guidance in Leviticus 11 points to certain benefits of a vegetarian lifestyle. Of these first nine generations of men, all were vegetarians. Jesus's first nine ancestors were vegetarians. Today we have many vegetarians and lacto-vegetarians. Nevertheless, no vegetarian has yet lived to Abraham's measly one hundred seventy-five years of age, much less Eber's four hundred sixty-four years, Shem's six hundred years, or Adam's nine hundred thirty years.

What do these lists from Genesis 5 and Genesis 11 have in common? Precisely this: In Luke 3, every one of these men is mentioned. They are all ancestors of Jesus—every single one of them. From Genesis chapter 5, our Creator is laying out His master plan for mankind and documenting it every step of the way from Adam. In Genesis 5, we have the first hint of a dynasty. By Genesis 11:1, the first twenty generations are listed. Yet, we are still over fifty generations from the baby Jesus! These are not long, boring lists of hard to pronounce names; these are the first beginnings of the genealogy of Jesus. These events are the beginning of a history documenting Jesus's heritage. They are testimonials to His authority as a king, a high priest, and a prophet.

Read Isaiah 11:6-7. This chapter pictures the righteous reign of the branch of Jesse (i.e. Jesus) in eternity. Verses 6 and 7 read, "The wolf also shall dwell with the lamb and the leopard shall lie down with the kid . . . the lion shall eat straw like the ox." Verse 9 elaborates, "They shall not hurt nor destroy in all my holy mountain; for the earth shall be full of the knowledge of the Lord as the waters cover the sea." What can we conclude? Man started out in the Garden as a vegetarian. In the days of Noah, God gave man permission to eat flesh. Man's span of life declined. One day, Rapture will begin to usher in the New Jerusalem, when the Tree of Life from Genesis 3 reappears in the last chapter of Revelation. In the New Jerusalem, the Tree of Life will supply a different fruit each month and the leaves are to be a balm. Likewise, Isaiah 11 tells us that this Branch will reign in eternity. Animals will kill no more, and the Tree of Life will supply food and balm to man forever. Man and animals in the Garden of Eden were vegetarians. In Isaiah, carnivores become plant eaters in the New City. Man, likewise, will be supplied twelve different types of fruit each year. It appears both animal and man will become vegetarians in the New Jerusalem.

In addition, just as Genesis 2:10 tells of a river in the Garden of Eden, Revelation 22:1 describes a crystal river in the New Jerusalem, proceeding from the throne of God.

Also, the Tree of Life, which offered food in the garden and would have permitted man to live forever, now appears in eternity offering food eternally. The beginning of Genesis has a river, vegetarians, and the Tree of Life in the Garden of Eden. At the conclusion of Revelation, the New Jerusalem has a river, vegetarians, and the Tree of Life.

God had a plan to fellowship with man. Man sinned and disrupted the relationship. God, in His omnipotent power, will bring His original plan to fruition. However, this time, only those men who want to be with God eternally will fellowship with and worship Him. Similarly, those of mankind who decline to fellowship with God will also get their wish. They shall get to spend eternity with Satan.

With Noah, God starts over with His plan for mankind to have fellowship with Him. As we have already seen, God tells Adam, "be fruitful and multiply." In Genesis 8 and 9, God tells Noah the precise same thing. Likewise, just as Adam sins and is naked, Noah gets drunk and is naked.

Also, like Adam, Noah is the father of three sons: Shem, Japheth, and Ham. As the flood subsides, each son is around one hundred years old. When Noah becomes drunk on wine, Ham observes this and tells his two brothers, Shem and Japheth. This incident sentences Ham's descendants to be cursed. Shem and Japheth, in contrast, take a garment and walk backwards to cover Noah's nakedness. In contrast to Ham's curse, Shem is blessed and Japheth "shall be enlarged," as the following verse indicates. Furthermore, verses 26 and 27 state that Canaan will be his (Shem's) servant. Study the following chart summarized from Genesis 10:1-29:

GENEALOGY OF NOAH

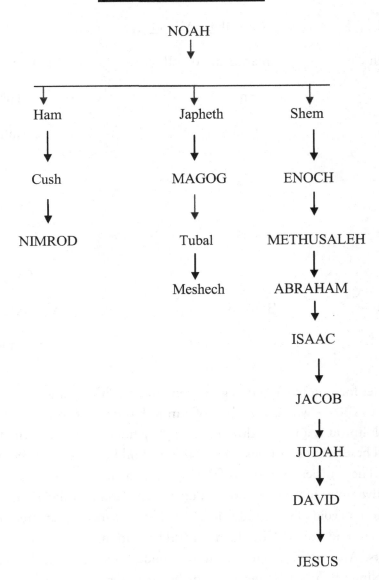

Prominent Bible characters CAPITALIZED

The following graph is a summation of Genesis Chapters 9 and 10.

NOAH'S THREE SONS

SON	PRONOUCEMENT	DESCENDANTS
Japheth	Enlarge and dwell with Shem	Gomer, Magog, Meshech, Tubal, Togarmah
Ham	Servant to Brothers	Cush (father of Nimrod), Put, Mizraim (Egypt), Canaan (who is cursed) father of Jebusites, Amorites, Girgashites, Hittites
Shem	Blessed	Arphaxad, Salah, Eber, Peleg (all ancestors of Jesus)

Consider for a moment Ham's grandson (and Noah's great grandson), Nimrod. Ham begets Cush (Genesis 10:6), who is the father of Nimrod, verse 8. Nimrod's name means "Let us revolt;" therefore, Nimrod is a rebel. Although a mighty hunter, he is also the founder of the kingdom of Babel. These are the citizens who decide to build a tower to Heaven in the land of Shinar (Babylon). These ancient ancestors of the Babylonians are self-centered (Genesis 11:3-4). The word *us* is used five times in these two verses; nowhere is God ever mentioned. Nimrod establishes his own kingdom devoid of God and full of self. This was man's first attempt at a New World Order based on man and not on God. Genesis 10:11 mentions the founding of Nineveh by Nimrod's descendants. Ancient Nineveh is near the modern city of Mosul, Iraq. This background on Nimrod, Nineveh, and Babylon helps us better understand Jonah's resistance to go preach to Nineveh (Jonah 1:2-3). Later, in Micah 5, a prophecy declares a ruler shall come forth out of Bethlehem and conquer the land of Nimrod (verse 6).

Just as the Lord comes down to inspect Babel in Genesis 11:5, likewise in Revelations 17 and 18, an angel brings the pronouncement of judgment on Babylon. Noah's great-grandson, Nimrod, is the founder of the earth's first authoritarian government. The original conflict at Babel in Genesis 11 finally concludes in the same Babel's (i.e. Babylon's) defeat in Revelation 18.

Noah's life is in the Bible, not because of the flood, but because of his obedient life. God blessed Noah by positioning him in the direct royal lineage of God's son, Jesus.

What have we learned about Noah?

1. Of course, he is the central figure in the children's Bible story of the flood.
2. He is an ancestor of Jesus.
3. He was the third oldest person to walk the earth.
4. He was the first ship builder and vine dresser.
5. He is the second Adam.
6. Noah was a man with whom God established a second covenant.
7. Noah walked with God just as his great grandfather, Enoch, had walked.
8. Noah was a just and perfect preacher of righteousness.
9. He preached one hundred twenty years with only seven other souls saved.
10. Because of Noah's faith, justness, perfection, and righteousness, we see why God chose Noah to be in the lineage of Jesus.
11. Noah's greatest accomplishment is not barge building, but as Adam and Enoch were, Noah is also an ancestor of Jesus.

Noah's Relatives

Name	Relationship	APPROXIMATE Dates
Enoch	Great grandfather	?
Methuselah	Grandfather	?
Nimrod	Great-grandson	?
Magog	Grandson	?
Abraham	Great grandson, 9 generations removed	±2000 BC
Isaac	Great grandson, 16 generations removed	±1900 BC
David	Great grandson, 22 generations removed	1000 BC
Jesus	Great grandson, 64 generations removed	AD 30

Chapter 7

Abraham

> Neither shall thy name anymore be called Abram, but thy name shall be Abraham; for a father of many nations have I made thee . . . And I will establish my covenant between me and thee and thy *seed* . . . for an everlasting covenant to be a God unto thee and to thy *seed* after thee. (Genesis 17:5, 7, emphasis added)

The first eleven chapters of Genesis deal with generic Man (Adam) and are set in what is today Iraq. However, starting with the call of Abram in Genesis 12, the following thirty nine chapters are concerned with Abram and his descendants. Usually we think of the three—Abram, Sarai, and nephew Lot—heading out alone, but that's not what Scripture says. Genesis 12:5 tells us Abram has possessions and slaves (see also Genesis 12:16, 20). The first name to appear in Matthew's list is that of Abraham. Upon careful reading, we can see why God elects to covenant with Abraham. We can understand how Abram becomes "Father Abraham."

Abraham could not keep "the law" of the Old Testament. The law, the Torah, didn't exist, as Moses's birth was yet seven generations into the future. Early on, in Genesis 15:6, God's word gives a nugget of truth. This verse reads, "He, Abram, believed in the Lord, and God counted it to him for righteousness." (See also Galatians 3:6.)

Early in Genesis, we see it is *not* about keeping the law, but it is about *believing* in God. Abram believes God. Abram trusts God. Abram has faith in God. Verse 18 of this same chapter declares the Lord made another covenant. This covenant is with Abram—"unto thy seed have I given this land." Abram means "exalted father." When God changes Abram's name to Abraham, his name's meaning changes as well. Abraham means "father of a multitude." One of the Jewish words for home is a synthesis of two other words: little and synagogue. In other words, each Jewish male is to be a little rabbi in his little synagogue, (that is, his home). The family of Abraham learned why God chose to covenant with him. First, Abraham believed God. Second, God knew Abraham would be faithful to lead (command) his children and to teach (instruct) his children to keep the way of the Lord. Furthermore, Abraham taught his children about the holy things (righteousness and justice) and about Godly living (Genesis 18:18-19 NASB).

The faith Abraham expressed in Yahweh (God) is important because possibly Abraham's father, Terah, worshiped the moon. Terah had moved his family from Ur, in what is now southern Iraq, to Haran in southern Turkey. In ancient Babylon, Ur, in the South, and Haran, near northern Iraq, were the two regional cult centers for worshippers of the moon. Were Terah and his descendants worshippers of the moon? We do not know for sure, but it is intriguing that the two most prominent moon cult centers were situated in precisely the two communities where Terah lived, first in Ur, and later in Haran. (The reader is encouraged to study moon worship, Hagar, Mecca, and Islam for further insights.) Because the moon, on occasion, appears larger in the sky than the sun, the ancients became moon worshippers. Some scholars believe Terah's very name is derived from an ancient word for moon. (See Genesis 31:30-35, 53; 35:2-4; Joshua 24:2, 15.) Joshua 24:15 is the famous statement of faith, "As for me and my house, we will serve the Lord." As a result, we may question whether the spiritual battle was between worshippers of Yahweh and moon worshippers. Modern Muslims are not moon worshippers; nevertheless, consider the fact that even today, atop every mosque is a crescent moon.

It is appropriate at this juncture to consider a timeline surrounding the time of Abraham. These are approximate dates and are not universally accepted. Nevertheless, they do give us a vague timeline.

The Times of Abraham

±2500 BC	Pyramids are built
±2165-1990 BC	Abraham goes to Egypt
±1907 BC	Joseph sold into slavery
±1877 BC	Joseph brings Jacob (Israel) to Egypt

When a tourist in modern day Egypt gazes on the pyramids, he is viewing the same sight Abraham saw, because the pyramids were five hundred years old when Abraham first laid eyes on them. Furthermore, God told Abraham his seed would be afflicted for four hundred years in a foreign land (Genesis 15:13). This prophecy was made about three hundred years before Joseph went down to Egypt.

Men's spiritual leadership in the home is seriously important to God, for Genesis 15 expresses Abram's belief in God and God's covenanting with him. Covenants are so important to God that within the Bible, God makes a covenant with only five people: Adam, Noah, Abraham, Moses, and David. Of these five men, four of them are direct ancestors of Jesus.[8] Moses is the lone exception, although the Bible expresses how Moses is related to the Messianic line of Jesus. Because of his faithfulness to God, what does God contract or covenant with Abram? God declares Abram's family will have a Promised Land that reaches from the river Nile to the Euphrates, after a four hundred year detour in Egypt (Genesis 15:13). Abram's belief in God was so powerful that he had adequate faith to believe in God's fulfillment of a promise *four centuries* into the future! Abram's faith in God was affirmed when the descendants of the Hebrew slaves came out of Egypt at the appointed time.

Today we think of these slaves as poor, destitute, and needy. But when these Hebrew slaves crossed the Red Sea, the Biblical text states the Egyptians had been plundered (permanently borrowed) of their silver, gold, and raiment (clothing). As an addendum, Exodus 12:38 includes the phrase "with very much cattle." Not a bad haul for a bunch of slaves, huh? Could this be one reason today why Egypt is not particularly fond of Israel?

God did not wait to bless Abram four hundred years after the covenant. No, God showered material blessings on him while he was living. His wife, Sarai, was so attractive that Pharaoh took her into his house. Once Pharaoh learned who Sarai really was, he told Abram to remove his half-sister (and wife) from Pharaoh's house. In Genesis 20, Abram again claims Sarai as his sister to King Abimelech of Gerar. In a dream, Abimelech learns the truth and like Pharaoh, he too not only restores Sarai to Abram but also provides "gifts" of livestock, servants, and silver (vv. 14-16).

Sarai was an obedient wife. Twice she lied for Abram: once to Pharaoh and then again to Abimelech. Each time she said she was Abram's sister (and she *was* his half-sister) rather than stating she was his wife. Even in her obedience to Abram's half-lies, she is praised as an example of a Godly wife in 1 Peter 3:6. Many have called Hebrews 11 the Faith Hall of Fame for the sixteen biblical characters the author of Hebrews exalts. Only two women, Sarah and Rahab, are listed among the fourteen men.

Abraham and Sarah are the only married couple in the Hall of Fame. Verses 11-12 of this chapter mention Sarah's faith. First Peter 3 and Hebrews 11 show Sarah to be a Godly wife—to be a woman of faith—because "she judged Him faithful who had promised."

Abram is called by God immediately after the pride of man has led Nimrod to build the Tower of Babel and God has confused human language. In Genesis 12, God proclaims He "will make of thee a great nation and I will make thy name great and thou shalt be a blessing. . . . I will bless them that bless thee and curse them that curseth thee."

Abraham's faith and belief in God is quoted in Romans 4:3, Galatians 3:6, 27 and James 2:23. Galatians 3:16-17 declares, "Now to Abraham and his *seed* were the promises made. He saith not, 'And to as seeds of many, but as of one. *And to thy seed which is Christ.*' . . . And this I say, that the covenant that was confirmed before of God in Christ, the law which was 430 years after cannot disannul, that it should make the promise of no effect" (emphasis added). In Genesis 15:6, Moses records "he (Abraham) believed in the Lord." The faith of Abraham had to be a believed faith, because Abraham lived six hundred years before Moses was even born (John 20:31 NASB). It was after the Exodus that God had selected Moses, while in the Sinai Desert, to write the very first five books of the Bible.

In Genesis 15:1-6, God's word comes to Abram in a vision, announcing, "I am thy shield and thy exceeding great reward." Abram appreciates the cattle, silver, and gold, which has made him not just rich, but very rich (Genesis 13:2 NASB). However, Abram talks to God not just as God but as "Lord God," which is a special title for God. In Hebrew it is "Adonai Yahweh." This first word denotes God's majesty, rule, and sovereignty. The second word declares God's perpetual, eternal, infinite existence. Abram declares in the loftiest of terms, "You are Creator, Ruler, Omnipotent, Wonderful, and Almighty." But Abram, though he still believes, struggles with doubt and fear. He is also bold enough to commune with God in verse 2 and ask, "What will thou give me seeing how I go childless and the inheritor of my house is this Eliezer of Damascus?" In other words: *Lord, I appreciate the good things you have given me, a beautiful wife and lots of assets,* but "Behold to me, thou has given me no seed" (singular).

In verse 4 God answers Abram saying, "This shall not be thine heir, [i.e. this Eliezer of Damascus]; but he that shall come forth out of thine own bowels shall be thine heir."

Then God reaffirms to Abram what he has promised in Genesis 11:2, instructing Abram to look up to heaven and count the stars. God states if you can count all the stars, so shall your seed (singular) be. Abram has not developed his faith based on the law written by Moses, but that he "believed in the Lord and that He (God) reckoned it to him as righteousness" (Genesis 15:6; 1 John 5:11-13 NASB).

In Genesis 16, we see Abram and Sarai waiting on the Lord for ten years in Canaan for God to fulfill His promise for an heir to "come forth out of thine own bowels," but no child has come. Abram wonders if he might be the problem. Sarai wonders if she is the problem. Yet God has promised. After all, God has promised from Abram's bowels, but not necessarily by Sarai. God has not said it would not be by Sarai, but neither has He said Sarai will be the mother of this promised child.

By its very definition, *seed* infers the child will be a male. Abram is expecting, trusting, waiting, and believing God to fulfill that promise. Abram cannot take comfort in the Old Testament—it does not exist. No, all Abram and Sarai have to trust in is that God has come to Abram and spoken an oral promise to him.

Abram was obedient at seventy-five years old (Genesis 12:4) and departed Haran for some yet unrevealed destination (v. 1). For a decade, Abram has been obedient. God blessed him with a lovely wife, material wealth, and with victory in battle. As a result, Abram gave offerings to "a Priest of God most high" (Genesis 14:18 NASB). This mysterious king of Salem, Melchizedek, was not only the king but was also the priest. Abram had everything he wanted except the one thing he wanted most—the fulfillment of God's blessing and promise, a son. This must have been a long, arduous decade for Abram. He must have thought: *Did I just think this up? Did I simply imagine it? Did I want a child so desperately, I just conjured this up? Does Sarai think I'm crazy? Does Sarai believe in me? Is it my fault or is it Sarai's fault? Did I misunderstand God's message? Was it really a vision from God or just a silly pointless dream? Did God really speak to me? Should I have believed God ten years ago?"*

I am sure supervising his many herds of livestock in the lonely desert wadis of Canaan gave Abram many hours to "keep all these things and pondered them" in his heart as Mary will do centuries later (Luke 2:19).

After a ten-year period of waiting on God to move, to work, and to produce the promised heir, this loving wife brought her Egyptian maid to her husband. Was it love or a lack of faith, or was it impatience? We don't know. But we do know that Sarai thought she was the problem, for in Genesis 16:2, Sarai tells her husband, "the Lord hath restrained me from bearing: I pray thee, go in unto my maid; it may be that I may receive children by her."

Sarai's burden was heavy for she had been faithful, even lying for her husband. She was so heartbroken that she was willing to share her husband with her maid in the most intimate of all human actions. Notice, it was Sarai who initiated the offer, not Abram. No doubt if Abram had demanded the maid Hagar during the past decade, perhaps Sarai would have readily agreed.

In today's American culture, we miss the significance of these family dynamics. Tents were made from woven goat hair. Goat hair is unique and most useful in the Middle East. It will expand when it gets wet and shrinks in diameter as it dries out. The dried goat hair tent not only offers shelter from the beating sun, but it also permits ventilation inside the tent to keep the interior from becoming oppressive with heat.

For centuries in the Middle East, due to the laborious effort required to build a tent and with the limited supply of goat hair, when a mother-in-law or a new wife came to live in the family compound, one outside end wall of the family's existing rectangular tent became the interior wall of an enlarged tent. The mother, the mother-in-law, or the second wife lived in the same extended tent—not across the street in the same neighborhood or even the same town. No, in Abram's case, the new "wife" probably lived less than six inches away from Sarai's home, separated only by an interior goat hair wall that was dry and permitted easy ventilation and noise to pass back and forth between the two "homes."

Abram was seventy-five when he received the vision from God to leave Haran (Luke 2:19). Abram and Sarai were then unsuccessful in having a child for ten years in Canaan (Genesis 16:3 NASB). We see that Abram was eighty-five years old when Sarai offered Hagar to her husband. Some ancient traditions believe Hagar was a daughter of Pharaoh and given to Abraham as a peace offering after Pharaoh had taken Sarai into his house. Hagar may have been fifty years younger than Sarai. (Fairly soon, Hagar became pregnant, for Genesis 16:16 states Abram is eighty-six when Hagar's son, Ishmael, is born.)

Daily, even under the flowing robes, Sarai noticed Hagar's midsection get pronounced. She could see it becoming more labored for Hagar to gather firewood or prepare a meal. Sarai saw Hagar's face becoming fuller or her hands filling with fluid and her sandals becoming tighter on her feet. Upon the birth of Ishmael in this close knit (literally) extended family, discord broke out. Finally, Sarai has enough. The discord between a barren Israelite woman and her pregnant Egyptian handmaiden became intolerable. Sarai told Abram she was sending her maid out of the family compound.

Genesis 16:6 states that Sarai, one of two women in the Faith Hall of Fame, dealt harshly with Hagar. So harsh was Sarai that Hagar, who despised Sarai, fled from the camp. Possibly this pregnant Egyptian maid was going home to Egypt to her family for support. Genesis 16:7 is significant. For the first time in the Bible, "the Angel of the Lord" appears to Hagar by a spring in the wilderness of Shur. (Shur was an area along the Mediterranean coast between Israel and Egypt.) In verses 9-12, the Angel of the Lord declares that the pregnant Hagar should return to her mistress and submit to Sarai. This angel also promises that her seed (i.e. descendants) cannot be numbered. Just as promised earlier, we saw the term "her seed" used about Eve. Now the angel of the Lord declares to Hagar, "thy seed will be multiplied exceedingly." As was promised to Abram, now it is promised to Hagar. Hagar's half-Egyptian, half-Israelite son will be named Ishmael, "God hears." In Genesis 21:13, God announces Abraham's son by Hagar, Ishmael, will be the father of nations. Though Ishmael is a child of Abram, no inheritance of any land is mentioned, nor does God declare He will be the God of Ishmael and his descendants. In Genesis 16: 2, God declares that Ishmael will be a wild man. His hand will be against every man but he will dwell in the midst of his brothers. And who will be his brothers? The Jews, the eventual descendants of Ishmael's half-brother, Isaac. Hagar obeyed and returned to Abram's camp where Ishmael was born.

For thirteen years we hear no word of God's appearing to Abram, Sarai, or Hagar. Ishmael grew up to be the only child of his father. Genesis 17 reiterates God's affirming His covenant with Abram and stating, "I will multiply thee exceedingly." It had been twenty-four years since God had first made that promise to Abram. With this encounter though, God changed Abram (exalted father) to Abraham, (father of a multitude) and pronounced that Abraham will be "the father of many nations with kings coming out of thee."

Verse 7 repeats the establishing of a covenant that will be an everlasting covenant "and I will give unto thee and unto thy seed after thee, the land where you are a stranger, all the land of Canaan for an everlasting possession and I will be their God." This covenant applies *only to Abraham's seed* (Isaac in Genesis 17:21) and not to Hagar's seed (Ishmael in Genesis 25:18). Evidence of this Abrahamic covenant is declared in verse 10, "You and thy seed after thee. Every man child among you shall be circumcised." Verse 12 says circumcision is to occur on the eighth day. (A fascinating confirmation of the eighth day for circumcision in the Bible was made by scientist Henrik Dam, who won the 1943 Nobel Prize in medicine for his discovery.)[9]

Abram, now called Abraham, was no longer married to a woman named Sarai, but now her new name was Sarah. Her name means "princess." Abraham, the "father of a multitude," was now married to Sarah, a "princess." At this point, we have the first hint of kingship and royalty. A princess title is irrelevant if you don't have the other trappings of royalty. God, once again, declared to Abraham that you shall have a son. He shall be called Isaac, meaning "he laughs" (Genesis 17:19 NASB).

But in this verse, God defined the mother will be Sarah. Abram, and now Sarah, was promised by God that Abram will be the father of a great nation (Genesis 17:6, 15-16 NASB). Notice it is a singular nation, one nation. It is not many nations. God repeated the blessing in Genesis 13:15, "For all the land which thou seest, to thee will I give it and to thy seed forever." Note, once again, it is not to seeds, but to one seed. This seed, this descendant via Sarah, will be a nation with a land to occupy as an everlasting possession, and "I will be their God" (Genesis 17:8 NASB). In Genesis 17, Abraham laughed at how ridiculous it was that a ninety-nine-year-old man could impregnate an eighty-nine-year-old woman. Because Abraham laughed, God named the expected child "he laughs." Abraham quickly revealed his true character (see Genesis 18:19) of being a God-believer and a spiritual leader in his home. In verse 18 Abraham pled with God for his thirteen-year-old son, Ishmael, "O that Ishmael might live before thee." Abraham was told that Ishmael would be a wild man. Yet this spiritual father implored for his son's spiritual maturity.

After announcing Isaac's birth by Sarah in verse 19, God immediately returned to Abraham's thirteen-year-old son and his petition. In this passage, it is proclaimed by God, "I have heard thee.

I have blessed him, Ishmael, whose name means 'God hears.' He will be fruitful. I will multiply him exceedingly. Twelve princes shall he beget; and I will make him a great nation." Read Genesis 21:13. It is at this time God blessed Ishmael because "he is thy seed." God fulfilled His promise to Abraham (as recorded in Genesis 25:12-18), where Ishmael's twelve sons were listed and the location of their tribes recorded. Ishmael's twelve sons will live from Syria to Egypt to Arabia.

God had now blessed Ishmael. Subsequently, God stated, "My covenant will I establish with Isaac, which Sarah shall bear unto thee at this set time in the next year." Chapter 17 concludes with Abraham being circumcised, as well as Ishmael, on the same day God has first commanded it. Skipping to Genesis 21, Abraham is now once more obedient to God, as Isaac is circumcised precisely on the day God had declared one year earlier.

Not surprisingly, the now fourteen-year-old feud between Sarah and Hagar erupted once again. One handmaiden-mother has a teenage son; the wife-mother has a newborn. Remember, between the two homes there was probably less than six inches of goat hair. Sarah once again demanded Abraham dispense with Hagar and her son. Abraham was heartbroken. God revealed to Abraham to listen to Sarah "for in Isaac shall thy seed be called" (v. 12).

Hagar and Ishmael were sent away from the camp of Abraham. Genesis 21:14-21 tells us that Hagar and her son wandered in the wilderness of Beersheba in the southern part of Israel. They ran out of water. Hagar placed her teenage son under a shrub to die and walked away from him, since it was too painful to watch his death. The Angel of the Lord appeared to her again, as he did the first time when she fled from Sarah into the wilderness of Shur. When she placed Ishmael under the shrub, God heard his cries. God affirmed He will make of Ishmael a great nation. Furthermore, God opened her eyes; she now saw a well of water (Genesis 21:19 NASB). Hagar took an Egyptian woman (like herself) for Ishmael's wife. Ishmael's descendants will be one-fourth Israelite and three-fourths Egyptian. Before we leave Ishmael's life, a few points are worth mentioning.

1. Ishmael will be a wild man (Genesis 16:12).
2. His hand will be against every man (Genesis 16:12).
3. He will dwell in the presence of his brethren (Genesis 16:12).
4. His mother discovered water somewhere south of Beersheba (Genesis 21:19).
5. God promised to make of him a great nation (Genesis 17:20; 21:18).
6. Ishmael fathered twelve sons (Genesis 25:12 -16).
7. These twelve sons settled among their brethren (number 3 above) in the area bounded by Assyria (modern day Turkey), Shur (near Gaza Strip today), and Havilah (present day Arabia).
8. His descendants will be one-fourth Israelite and three-fourths Egyptian (Genesis 25:18).

Muslims believe when Hagar placed Ishmael under the shrub to die, she was far, far south of Beersheba. For Muslims, this location became the most holy city in all of Islam, Mecca. What made Mecca special was Muslims believe this is where Hagar discovered the lifesaving water she carried back to Ishmael. Today, this water source is known as the Well of ZamZam and is located inside the

Grand Mosque of Mecca, only one hundred seventy feet from the Kaa'ba, Islam's most sacred site. The Kaa'ba is an almost cube structure of stone and marble draped over the top and all four sides with black and gold silk curtains. Muslims believe this sacred building was erected by Abraham and Ishmael. It is roughly aligned with the winter and summer solstice. Furthermore, it is positioned to receive maximum exposure to the rising of the star Canopus, a major star in the southern skies. Mohammed's grandfather, Aba-al-Muttalib, was custodian of the building during his life.

A journey to Mecca is one of the five tenets of the Muslim faith. The apex of the pilgrimage to Mecca is to march counter-clockwise around the Kaa'ba during Ramadan. The enormity of the Grand Mosque of Mecca is not readily apparent from viewing television images of the structure. Inside the Mosque is the courtyard where the Kaa'ba and the well of ZamZam are located. Muslims treasure the sanctity of the Grand Mosque of Mecca. Muslims believe *the Jews kicked my ancestors Hagar and Ishmael out of their camp, not once, but twice (Genesis 16:7 and 21:19), but Allah found a spring, not once, but twice, to protect Ishmael* (author's words). A few chapters ahead is the story of Isaac who had two sons, Esau and Jacob. Esau became the father of Edom. Esau despised his birthright and grieved his parents by marrying daughters of Ishmael. Genesis 25:25 tells us Esau became the father of the Edomites. Verse 34 tells us "Esau despised his birthright." In chapter 26:35, Esau was "a grief of mind to Isaac and Rebekah." As we get to Genesis 28:6, Isaac instructed Jacob to not take "a wife of the daughters of Canaan." In contrast, in verses 8 and 9, "Esau seeing the daughters of Canaan, pleased not Isaac, his father. . . Then went Esau unto Ishmael and took . . . wives."

The land of ancient Edom is on the southeast shore of the Dead Sea in present day southern Jordan. Esau was fully Israelite. He married an Ishmaelite woman. Ishmaelites, as we have seen, were one-fourth Israelite and three-fourths Egyptian. The Edomites were likely five-eighths Israelite and three-eighths Egyptian, with many of today's Jordanians probably the descendants of the Edomites.

So far, Lot has not been mentioned. Lot was Abraham's nephew who accompanied his uncle from Haran. It's time to take a moment to study Lot. We know Lot settled in Sodom. As he fled Sodom with his wife and two daughters, his wife looked back and turned into a pillar of salt. Lot was sent out of Sodom not because of who he was, but because "God remembered Abraham." His daughters got Lot drunk in a cave in the mountains; Lot committed incest, impregnating his two daughters, resulting in two sons/grandsons.

The first son/grandson was named Moab. He became father of the Moabites. The Moabites' area was the east shore of the Dead Sea. The younger daughter named her son Ben-Ammi. He became father of the Ammonites. The Ammonites occupied the northeast coast of the Dead Sea. Their name lives on today in the name of Jordan's capital, Amman.

In later life Abraham took a second wife or concubine. The fact she is called a concubine in 1 Chronicles 1:32 might mean Sarah was still alive when it was first recorded.

Concerning Keturah's sons, Genesis 25:6 tells us that Abraham sent them away from his son, Isaac. However, they received gifts before they were sent away. Nevertheless, Genesis 25:1-3 lists Keturah's sons, who established many nations. The most prominent son was Midian. Moses's father-in-law, Jethro, was a holy man from Midian (Exodus 3:1 NASB). Midianites lived to the east and southeast of Palestine. Sometimes they traded with the Israelites and Egypt. An example of such was when Joseph was sold into slavery by his brothers; it was to an Ishmaelite caravan of Midianite traders traveling to Egypt. The most prominent grandsons were Sheba and Dedan. The Queen of Sheba who later came to visit Solomon likely came from southern Arabia. Meanwhile, Dedan settled in northern Arabia.

After Hagar and Keturah were sent away with their sons, Abraham was left with only his one wife, Sarah, his "princess," and one son, Isaac, "He laughs."

If you were one of the sons sent away from a father who was very wealthy, with no real inheritance, only gifts or even just bread and water, would you be angry? As an abandoned son, how would you feel? Would your anger be further kindled by the name of the favored child: "He laughs"? In Genesis 25:5, the Bible states: "Abraham gave all he had unto Isaac." Later in the same chapter, it states that after the death of Abraham, God blessed his son, Isaac.

Can you telescope down through the millenniums until today? Does the detail of Genesis shed any light on the current world geopolitics of today? Muhammad was supposed to have studied the Bible. Most of the Bible was over one thousand years old when the Koran was written, and the entire Bible was at least five hundred years old. If you were the descendant of Midian traders or Ishmaelites or Egyptians living in the sands and barrenness of the Arabian Peninsula, might you too have a touch of resentment, anger, rage, jealousy, envy, or greed? If you were to somehow channel all of those emotions into one book, do you think you would find an audience among your fellow traders, neighbors, and peers? Why not share your feelings in writings with the descendants in the northern land with the half-breeds who received no inheritance in Edom? And while you are at it, go a little further north and share your emotions with the citizens of Moab and Ben-Ammi who got nothing as well. They knew they were despised by Israelite society as the children of incest between a man and his two daughters. So we are left with the following situation: a group of people, seething with resentments, boiling over with anger for two thousand years, living in an area bounded by Turkey, Egypt, and Saudi Arabia. If you were to make a chart, it might look like this:

The First Winnowing

Parent	Concluded Genealogies	Reason
Hagar	Ishmaelites	½ Israelites, ½ Egyptians
Esau	Edomites	Rebellious, intermarry with Ishmaelites to spite his parents
Lot	Moabites	Son of incest
Lot	Ammonites	Son of incest
Keturah	Midianites	Sons of concubine
Keturah	Dedanites	Sons of concubine

Notice in the chart above, tribes, nations, kingdoms who are not "pure" are condemned as being mixed race, descendants of rebellion or concubines. However, before we get too condescending, recall Joseph's two sons were birthed to the daughter of an Egyptian priest. Also, remember Lot is called "righteous" in 2 Peter 2:7-8. Furthermore, Judah's incestuous relationship with his daughter-in-law Tamar is also part of the Messianic heritage. Obviously, modern Muslims, Arabs, Persians, and other Middle Easterners are acutely aware of "the chosen race" in the Bible and have a feeling of their own ancestors being condemned as second class people. Nevertheless, the children who were not of the promised seed ease into the shadows of the narrative.

God promised to bless Abraham with wealth and power. Furthermore, he now had a wife and the seed of promise, his only son, Isaac by the princess Sarah. Is the old, stale, boring genealogy relevant to today? Does it provide answers for today's world? Absolutely! It is plain to see why citizens of Egypt, Syria, Jordan, Iraq, and Saudi Arabia, being portrayed as descendants of half-breeds or sons of incest or concubines, would resent the concept of a chosen race, blessed by God, living in a land "flowing with milk and honey."

Most Bible students today tend to lump 1 Kings and 2 Kings and 1 Chronicles and 2 Chronicles into one group and declare, "Oh, those books are about the kings of Israel, Judah, Samaria, etc." Study the following chart for a few moments.

The Second Winnowing

Bible Book	Chapter	Theme
1 Kings	Chapters 1-11	United Kingdom of Israel
	Chapters 12-22	Divided Kingdoms of Samaria and Judah
2 Kings	Chapters 1-17	Divided Kingdoms of Samaria and Judah: (northern kingdom defeated, carried off into captivity)
	Chapters 18-25	Southern Kingdom of Judah
1 Chronicles	Chapters 1-9	Genealogy of Judah (Adam - David)
	Chapters 10-29	History of King David in Judah
2 Chronicles	Chapters 1-9	History of King Solomon in Judah
	Chapters 10-36	History of King Solomon's descendants as kings of Judah

First Kings is about all the twelve tribes who later divide into ten northern tribes (Samaria) and two southern tribes (Judah). Second Kings begins recording reigns of kings in both nations. After two hundred years, Samaria is conquered. Second Kings concludes by following just the nation of Judah. *First and 2 Chronicles are an account of only the kings of Judah.*

The above chart outlines the winnowing from all twelve tribes of the Israelites in the Promised Land to the one tribe of Judah as kings.

An excellent example of this is found beginning in 1 Chronicles 2:1-2 where all twelve sons of Israel are listed. By verse 3, the focus is on just the tribe of Judah and continues for one hundred verses until 1 Chronicles 4:23. Emphasis is just on the descendants of Judah to the total exclusion of the other eleven brothers.

This book seeks to dig a little more thoroughly into the genealogies mentioned in Matthew and Luke to find out more about Jesus than just His being a poor carpenter's son from Nazareth. Did Mary and Joseph teach their young son stories from the Old Testament? Did these parents talk around the dinner table or in the carpenter shop about grandparents or great-great-great-great-great grandparents? For God to select Mary and Joseph out of all the potential parents from millions of Jewish homes, I believe Mary and Joseph were faithful to follow the Jewish *Shema* which means in Hebrew, "Hear!" (Deuteronomy 6:4-7). They taught their firstborn about God, about Noah, Ruth, David, Solomon, and others—all being ancestors of the young lad, Jesus.

The question remains: who even attempts to present a dynasty of seventy-three, seventy-five, or seventy-seven generations over thousands of years of family history that has remained unrivaled and intact for two thousand five hundred plus years? Only the Bible shows a family heritage of over seventy generations from God to Jesus.

In concluding this chapter, what did we learn about Abraham?

1. God called a man out of northern Iraq to follow Him, along with his wife, Sarah, and nephew, Lot.
2. This man, Abraham, believed God.
3. God promised to give him land for a new nation and he will have many descendants. Because of his obedience, in James 2:23, Abraham is called "a friend of God."
4. Sarah and Abraham get impatient, and Abraham fathered a son by the Egyptian maid, Hagar, and named her son, Ishmael.
5. Abraham and Sarah were blessed with a son, who they name Isaac, when they were one hundred and ninety years old respectively.
6. Lot, via incest, has two sons/grandsons, Moab and Ben-Ammi.
7. In being faithful to Abraham, God blessed Ishmael with twelve sons and made him a father of many nations.

Abraham's Relatives

<u>Name</u>	<u>Relationship</u>	<u>APPROXIMATE Dates</u>
Sarah	Wife	± 1900 BC
Isaac	Son	± 1900 BC
Jacob	Grandson	± 1800 BC
Judah	Great-grandson	±1700 BC
Levi	Great-grandson	±1700 BC
Ruth	Daughter-in-law, 8 generations removed	±1200 BC
David	Great-grandson, 11 generations removed	1000 BC
Zerubbabel	Great-grandson, 33 generations removed	500 BC
Jesus	Great-grandson, 53 generations removed	AD 30

Chapter 8

Isaac

> And I will make thy *seed* to multiply as the stars of heaven and will give unto thy *seed* all these lands and in thy *seed* shall all the nations of the earth be blessed. (Genesis 26:4, emphasis added)

Most of us are guilty of thinking of this man, Isaac, as nothing more than a bridge between the patriarch Abraham and the patriarch Jacob. At first glance, he appeared in no dramatic Bible stories such as the flood, David and Goliath, or Daniel and the lion's den, but Isaac was a man of God. We have already seen that he was a child of promise to Sarah and Abraham. Isaac was a miracle of birth in that his parents "were as good as dead" (Hebrews 11:11-12 NASB). For the Jews, it was a miracle birth for Isaac to be born.

Does this situation not seem similar to the story in the New Testament of the birth of Jesus? True, the reason for the absence of pregnancy was different, but the results were the same: in the Old Testament account, a son of promise and in the New Testament, also a son of promise. The miracle in Genesis is God's defeat of old age with elderly conception. The even greater miracle in Luke is the Immaculate Conception. Isaac can be considered a miracle baby for the Jews, just as Jesus is considered the miracle baby for Christians.

Genesis 22:5 is the favorite faith verse of many people. Abraham, with the two young men and Isaac approached Mt. Moriah. Abraham instructed his two servants to remain at the base of the mount with the donkeys while "the lad and I will go yonder and worship and come again unto you." Abraham does not yet know how, but in this passage, he fully anticipates that somehow Isaac will be resurrected and return with Abraham to the young men tending the donkeys. Hebrews 11:17-19 tells us Abraham was fully "accounting" on God, to raise him up, even from the dead. In some manner, Isaac will be resurrected in the Old Testament, just as Jesus is resurrected in the New Testament.

God provided a lamb in a thicket for Abraham to sacrifice. This event and place were memorialized by Abraham, naming the site "Jehovah-Jireh," which means "the Lord will provide." Centuries later, this same Mt. Moriah is where Solomon will construct the first temple under instruction from God.

In Genesis 22:17-18, God affirms His covenant with Abraham, telling him how all nations shall be blessed through his seed. Genesis 24 gives us an account of Abraham's servant performing an oath by placing his hand under Abraham's thigh (i.e., near his testicles, the source of the seed) promising to go back to Abraham's homeland to search for a wife for Isaac. (Later, Jacob will likewise ask Joseph to place his hand under Jacob's thigh and promise not to bury Jacob in Egypt (Genesis 47:29-30 NASB). Because of Joseph's oath, Jacob's body is not buried in Egypt, but in the cave of Machpelah, where Abraham, Sarah, Isaac, Rebekah, and Leah were buried (Genesis 49:31)). Likewise, Joseph also requested not to be buried in Egypt. His bones were carried back to Israel during the Exodus and buried at Shechem four hundred thirty years after his death (Exodus 13:19; Joshua 24:32 NASB).

Abraham's servant was specifically instructed not to seek a wife from among the local Canaanite women. In obedience, the servant loaded ten camels in southern Israel at Beersheba. The caravan traveled in a northeastern arc into the area along the border of Syria and Turkey. After the servant's journey of several weeks, he arrived at a community well in the city of Haran. This site is about five hundred miles from Beersheba. Shortly after his arrival, a beautiful young woman by the name of Rebekah came to the well to draw water. She gave the stranger a drink and offered to furnish his camels with water as well. Upon completion of the watering of both man and beast, the stranger gave the attractive maiden a nose ring and two bracelets of gold. The total gold given Rebekah by the stranger weighed almost five ounces. In today's value, the gold is worth approximately $5,000 to $8,000. Rebekah then offered food and lodging in her home. Afterwards she revealed her family tree (which confirmed she was Abraham's niece). Being related to Abraham made Rebekah acceptable to the servant's instructions from Abraham. Rebekah simply walked to get water; now she had returned home with $8,000 in gold. Is it any wonder that she ran home? And it is not surprising that Rebekah's brother, Laban, also ran out to meet the stranger after he saw the nose ring and bracelets.

Once in the house, the servant told the family how God had greatly blessed Abraham with flocks, herds, donkeys, servants, silver, and gold. The servant explained his mission was to find a wife for Isaac. Rebekah received still more silver, gold, and raiment, and her mother and brother were given a dowry. As the caravan departed from Syria (or Turkey), on its way back to Beersheba, Rebekah's family blessed "her seed" (Genesis 24:60).

As the caravan arrived near Beersheba, Isaac was meditating in the field. This was when he first saw his future bride (Genesis 24:63; Psalm 1:2). Genesis 24 concludes with Isaac loving Rebekah and being comforted after his mother's death by her presence. Sarah had birthed Isaac when she was ninety years old (Genesis 17:17 NASB). Then Sarah died at age one hundred twenty-seven (Genesis 23:1 NASB). Therefore, Isaac was thirty-seven years old when he married, but Isaac and Rebekah were unable to have children for twenty years (Genesis 25:20, 26 NASB). Just as Isaac's parents were unable to give birth, it is now Isaac pleading with God for his wife. When Isaac was fifty-seven years old, Rebekah became pregnant with twins. Rebekah inquired of the Lord about her pregnancy, and God told her that two nations are being birthed within her.

The twins were named Esau and Jacob. Esau became the father of the Edomites who dwelled in the land of "red rocks" east of the Dead Sea in what is the southern portion of modern day Jordan. An easy way to remember Esau is that his name means "red," as he had ample red hair (Genesis 25:25 NASB). He sold his birthright for a venison stew which was "red" pottage (Genesis 25:28, 30 NASB). The land where he settled as the father of the Edomites was the land of "red rocks."

God affirmed to Isaac and his seed the blessing which God originally covenanted with Abraham. Isaac was obedient to God and stayed in southern Israel during a severe famine rather than to go down to Egypt. God blessed Isaac and his crops grew a hundred fold. He continued to prosper until he became very wealthy. Isaac constantly worshiped God, despite his repeated struggles with the Philistines. Later, God confirmed, on a second occasion, His multiplying of Isaac's seed. Although Isaac worshiped God, he had his faults. He favored one twin, Esau, while Rebekah favored the other, Jacob (Genesis 25:30 NASB). In Numbers 20, after God had changed Jacob's name to Israel, we can see the result of this family feud when the Edomites and Israelites fight. In those days, the father's blessing was very important. According to custom at that time, the oldest son received a double portion of blessings and birthrights. Since Jacob was a "mama's boy," Rebekah helped him go to great lengths to deceive his aged, nearly blind father. Jacob even told his mother, "I will be seen by my father as a deceiver, and this will bring a curse upon me and not a blessing." Rebekah replied, "Let the curse be upon me. Now do as I say." Jacob went to their herd of goats and brought two kids to his mother to prepare a savory stew for Isaac before he dies.

While Jacob was preparing the two goats, Rebekah found clothes of her older son, Esau, in which to dress Jacob. Because Esau had been born hairy, she also prepared the skins and put the skins upon Jacob's hands and neck to further deceive Isaac. Jacob then lied and told his father, "I am Esau, the firstborn." Although the boys are twins, Esau was born moments earlier, and the birthright was to be his. Isaac questioned his son about how he found the wild game so quickly. Being suspicious, Isaac told his son to come closer in order for Isaac to "feel" him. Isaac declared, "The voice is Jacob's, but the hands are Esau's." Isaac ate the stew and drank the wine. He then asked Jacob to kiss him after he inquired a second time if he was truly Esau. Jacob lied a second time, declaring that he is Esau. Isaac is still wary as he states, "the odor of the clothing smells of the field and is not an aroma of a tent-dweller." Aged, almost blind, Isaac was using all four of his remaining senses to discern to which twin he was talking. He has tasted the stew. He has smelled the clothing. He has heard the voice, and he has touched the hands. As a father, three of his senses affirmed that it was Esau. The fourth, the sense of hearing, was telling Isaac that it was Jacob's voice. In his fear, advanced age, blindness, and facing death, Isaac eventually bestowed the birthright upon Jacob.

Jacob's inheritance is the dew of heaven, fatness of the Earth, plenteous food, other people shall bow down to him, other people shall serve him, he will be master over his brethren, and "your mother's sons will bow down to you" (Genesis 27:28-29 NASB). The birthright blessing concluded with a benediction similar to the one that Abraham received earlier from God himself: "Everyone that curses thee themselves shall be cursed, and everyone that blesses thee shall be blessed."

Immediately after Isaac gave Jacob the birthright blessing, Esau arrived with a savory stew of his own. Isaac was upset, and understandably, Esau became bitter as well. Esau pled with his father for a blessing. Isaac started the blessing for Esau with very similar words to Jacob's blessing. In Genesis 27:39-40, Isaac declared that Esau will have fatness of the Earth and the dew from heaven. This was precisely how Jacob's blessing began in verse 28. However, in verse 40, the second blessing deviated. Verse 40 informs the reader Esau will live by the sword and will serve Jacob. Esau's descendants, the Edomites, "will revolt and claim their independence."

Eventually, Esau's descendants gain their freedom from Jacob's heirs (2 Kings 8:22 NASB). Truly, Isaac had spoken a great truth, when he declared unto Esau, "and by the sword shalt thou live and shalt serve thy brother" (Genesis 27:40 NASB).

Genesis 27:41 states the obvious: Esau hated his brother. He decided, "After my father dies, I will kill my twin." Esau was an impetuous individual, evidenced by his selling of his birthright in Genesis 25 for a simple bowl of red pottage. Just as Esau's situation was predictable, Jacob's response was also predictable. When Rebekah told Jacob that his brother was planning to murder him, she instructed her son to go to her brother, Laban, in her hometown of Haran. Rebekah told Jacob she will send for him when Esau calmed down.

Isaac blessed Jacob again in Genesis 28 and told him not to marry a woman of Canaan. These were the same instructions which were given to Isaac by Abraham. Jacob obeyed his father by not taking a wife of the Canaanites (Genesis 28:6-7 NASB). Esau, however, specifically married local women against his parents' wishes (Genesis 26:34-35; 28:8-9 NASB). In the New Testament, Hebrews chapter 12 calls Esau a profane person since he despised his birthright and actively sought out local Canaanite women to marry. Isaac further blessed Jacob with fruitfulness and a continuation of the Abrahamic covenant of Genesis 12, by mentioning the seed and inheriting the land. Genesis 28:3-4 spends much more time on the seed than on the inheritance of the land, herds, flocks, cattle, gold, and silver. First, the seed, and second, the land are the only two assets mentioned.

Isaac was old, almost totally blind, and dying. He was aware he would probably never see his son Jacob again. This father was speaking his farewell address, emphasizing in his final instructions to his son what was most important to him, which was "the seed" and "the land." Jacob left Hebron and traveled to his Uncle Laban in Haran.

He stayed there for at least twenty years (Genesis 31:38 NASB). In the next chapter (Genesis 32), Jacob returns home and meets with Esau; there is reconciliation between the twins. Isaac has not died and is reunited with his long absent son, Jacob. And Isaac probably got to talk with, listen to, touch, and feel Jacob's twelve sons.

Genesis 35 concludes with Isaac's death (at one hundred eighty years of age) and his reconciled twins burying him beside his parents, Abraham and Sarah, in the cave at Machpelah (Genesis 49:31 NASB). Isaac is mentioned in the Hall of Fame of Faith in Hebrews 11:20 as one of the sixteen faithful mentioned specifically by name. Isaac was credited with blessing his sons concerning things to come.

The Edomites, as descendants of Esau, will later help Nebuchadnezzar invade Judah. The Bible condemns the Edomites in Jeremiah 49:7-22, as well as, in the little book of Obadiah. One of the ancient capitals of Edom was Petra, the famous tourist attraction in southern Jordan. (Read Obadiah verses 2, 4, 10, and 18.)

We learn in Jeremiah 48:8 that Esau will suffer calamity. Verse 10 tells us Esau's "seed is spoiled" and will be no more. Just as the Bible concludes the genealogy of the murderer Cain in Genesis chapter 4, we also see the termination of the genealogy of Esau and the Edomites in Genesis. Earlier we saw the end of the genealogy of the full-blooded Israelite children who were descendants of Lot and his daughters via incest. The genealogy of the Moabites and the Ammonites concludes in Genesis 19. Still other genealogies of Noah's sons, Ham and Japheth are concluded in Genesis chapter 10. Furthermore, other genealogies, such as that of Joktan, are finished in this same chapter. The descendants of Abraham's brothers, Nahor and Haran, also are concluded in Genesis 22, except for how they relate to Abraham's son Isaac and Abraham's grandson Jacob. In the New Testament, John the Baptist even makes a comparison of Jesus using a winnowing shovel to cast grain up into the air in order to remove the husks from the heavier kernels which fall back down to the threshing floor (Luke 3:17 NASB). (Recall the chart "The First Winnowing.")

We can see this same winnowing process very clearly in 1 Chronicles 1. The first word is "Adam." The prophet Ezra, the author of 1 Chronicles, starts with all mankind. In chapter 2, the focus is narrowed to Jacob (Israel) and his twelve sons. Chapter 3 is a further narrowing of the tribe of Judah to only King David's family. Chapter 6 is the lineage of the priests. In contrast, Chapter 7 combines a brief summary of six sons' genealogy: Issachar, Benjamin, Naphtali, Manasseh, Ephraim, and Asher.

In summary, Chronicles chapter 1 is all of humanity. Chapter 3 is specifically focused on the family of royalty, the kings. Chapter 6 is focused on the family of priests, and chapter 7 combines a brief summary of the remaining six sons' genealogy.

The following chart shows Isaac's extended family and the numerous complex relationships.

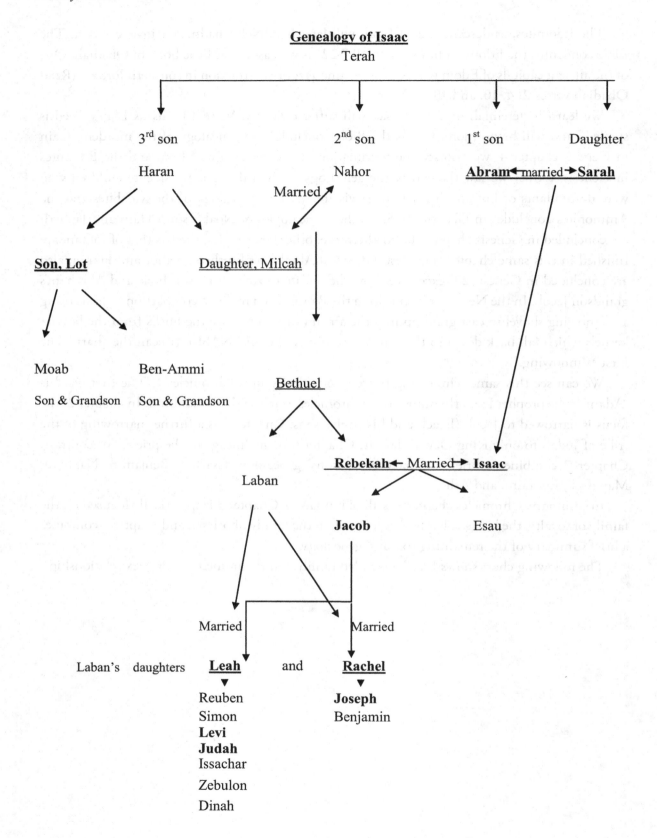

Genealogy of Isaac

Terah

3rd son   2nd son   1st son   Daughter

Haran   Nahor   **Abram** ← married → **Sarah**

Married

Son, Lot   Daughter, Milcah

Moab   Ben-Ammi

Son & Grandson   Son & Grandson

Bethuel

Rebekah ← Married → **Isaac**

Laban

Jacob   Esau

Married   Married

Laban's   daughters   **Leah**   and   **Rachel**

Reuben   **Joseph**

Simon   Benjamin

Levi

Judah

Issachar

Zebulon

Dinah

46

*Nahor marries Milcah, his niece, Lot's sister.

*Nahor's granddaughter, Rebekah, marries Abraham's son, Isaac.

*Abraham's grandson Jacob marries Nahor's great granddaughters, Leah and Rachel. Thus, Jacob's two wives were also his third cousins,

By the conclusion of Genesis 36, the Bible has discontinued the genealogies of the Cainites, the Moabites, Ammonites, Ishmaelites, Edomites, Midianites, the Dedanites, Amalekites, Canaanites, Cushites, Philistines, and approximately fifty other people groups. To update the chart of The First Winnowing, now study the expanded list below.

A SUMMARY OF THE WINNOWING

Parent	People Cast Out of the Text	Reason	End of Biblical Genealogy
Cain	Cainites	Murder	Genesis 4
Hagar	Ishmaelites	½ Israelite, ½ Egyptian	Genesis 25
Esau	Edomites	Intermarry Ishmaelites	Genesis 36
Lot	Moabites	Sons of Incest	Genesis 19
Lot	Ammonites	Son of Incest	Genesis 19
Keturah	Midianites	Son of Concubine	Genesis 25
Keturah	Dedanites	Son of Concubine	Genesis 25
Amalek	Amalekites	Son of Concubine	Genesis 36
Ham	Canaanites	Saw Noah Naked	Genesis 10
Ham	Cushites	Saw Noah Naked	Genesis 10
Japheth	Magog	?	Genesis 10
Nahor (Kemuel)	Aram	?	Genesis 22
Others	± 50 groups	?	Genesis 36

It might be a fair question to ask is anyone left. Does any one person's genealogy continue? The answer is yes. The genealogy of Jacob.

What have we learned about Isaac?

1. Esau, the older twin, was the father of twelve sons and his descendants will live by the sword.
2. He married local Canaanite women.
3. Jacob, the younger twin, stole his brother's birthright.
4. Jacob's name was changed to Israel.
5. Jacob will also father twelve sons, just as Ishmael had.
6. Jacob's (Israel's) twelve sons will be the founders of the Twelve Tribes of Israel. These twelve sons are Isaac's grandsons.

Isaac's Relatives

Name	Relationship	APPROXIMATE Dates
Noah	Great-grandfather, 10 generations removed	?
Abraham	Father	±2000 BC
Sarah	Mother	±2000 BC
Rebekah	Wife	±1900 BC
Esau	One of his twin sons	±1800 BC
Jacob (Israel)	One of his twin sons	±1800 BC
Judah	Grandson	±1750 BC
Levi	Grandson	±1750 BC
Joseph	Grandson	±1750 BC
Jesus	Great-grandson, 52 generations removed	AD 30

Chapter 9

Jacob

> And God said unto him, "Thy name is Jacob; thy name shall not be called any more Jacob, but Israel shall be thy name. . . . And the land which I gave Abraham and Isaac, to thee I will give it and to thy *seed* after thee will I give the land." (Genesis 35:10, 12, emphasis added)

Jacob was fearful of being killed by his impetuous older twin brother. The "deceiver" fled five hundred miles to the north along the border between Syria and Turkey where his uncle, Laban, lived in Haran. On the way to Uncle Laban's house, Jacob stopped at Bethel to rest for the night. As he was sleeping, Jacob had a dream. The dream is remembered in the song from childhood, "we are climbing Jacob's ladder," for in the dream, angels are ascending and descending a ladder between heaven and earth. At the top of the ladder is God, who reminds Jacob of the earlier promise of this very ground where he slept, to Abraham and Isaac. God reaffirms this covenant with Jacob, "and thy seed" (Genesis 28:14). God promises Jacob's seed will be as numerous as dust, and through him all families of the earth will be blessed. God confirms this to Jacob, declaring, "As I was with your grandfather Abraham and your father Isaac, so I will be with you and will keep and protect you wherever you go, and I will bring you again to this land."

This must have been a marvelous relief to Jacob as he fled from his impulsive brother, Esau. Maybe God reminded Jacob of his own father, Isaac, being bound on the altar and his grandfather, Abraham, telling the servants, "The lad and I will go yonder, worship, and return to you." It was also probable that Jacob remembered what God told him, "I will not leave thee and will return with you to this land." Jacob had the assurance that Esau would not kill him. As he was fleeing, Jacob was nevertheless worried, fearful, and nervous. Bethel was only twelve miles or so north of Jerusalem. At Bethel, Jacob was only about sixty miles from home, with over four hundred miles yet to his destination. That night, God came to him in a dream and gave Jacob assurance, peace, and confidence that God will be by his side. The dream was so powerful it awakened Jacob. When morning came, he built a memorial of stones, poured oil on the column of rocks, and named it *Beth-el*, the house of God.

Jacob arrived at Haran and saw flocks being watered. He inquired of the shepherds about his uncle. At that moment, a young lady arrived with her father's sheep. This account is almost identical to Jacob's mother, Rebekah, who brought her father's sheep to be watered and encountered Abraham's faithful servant (Genesis 24:13). This scene is different as the potential groom himself is at the well and not a servant. Jacob introduced himself to his third cousin, Rachel. Rachel then ran home, as her aunt had done decades earlier, and told Laban of the encounter. Once again, Laban ran toward the well.

Jacob stayed at his Uncle Laban's home. Laban had two daughters. The older one, Leah, was "tender-eyed," which some scholars theorize might imply she was cross-eyed. Genesis 29:17 contrasts Leah with her beautiful younger sister Rachel. Rachel was the first sister that Jacob saw and he was smitten. After seven years of labor, Jacob believed he was getting his sought-after younger cousin for a wife, but Laban out-deceived the deceiver. After the feast and the consummation of the marriage that night, Jacob discovered the next morning he is the husband of Leah, the older "tender-eyed" sister. Laban required his nephew to spend a week with Leah. Then after the week, Jacob also received Rachel as his second wife (Genesis 29:27-28).

Jacob then labored for his deceitful uncle another seven years to become the husband of Rachel. Jacob loved Rachel more than Leah, just as Rebekah loved him more than Esau. Jacob first learned about being a family favorite as a twin growing up when his mother preferred him. Of the two sisters, he chose Rachel as his favorite wife.

At Beth-el, God promised Jacob his seed will be as dust upon the earth and as sand upon the ocean. However, there is a problem. Just as Rachel's Aunt Rebekah could not conceive for twenty years before Jacob and Esau were born, Rachel was likewise barren. According to Genesis 29:31, Leah was hated. Yet the Lord blessed tender-eyed Leah, and she eventually bore Jacob six sons and a daughter. Leah had her first four sons while Rachel remained childless. Leah's first son was Reuben, whose name means "see," for Leah thought God had blessed her with a son that would cause Jacob to love her, since Rachel was childless. Then Leah's second son was called Simeon, which means "heard." She thought the Lord heard how she was hated. The birth of Leah's third son, Levi, "attached," was so named because Leah felt three sons will cause her husband to become attached to her. A fourth son was born and named Judah, which caused Leah to praise the Lord, so she named number four son, "praise."

By Genesis 30, Jacob has quit hating Laban and now is angry with Rachel for being barren. Rachel gave her maid Bilhah to Jacob to conceive as her proxy. Bilhah soon has a son, whom Rachel named Dan, meaning "judged." She felt God heard her petition and judged in her favor. Bilhah birthed a second son who Rachel named Naphtali, "wrestling," because she was in a rivalry with her sister.

Leah realized she was no longer bearing children, and decided to follow Rachel's example and offered her maid Zilpah to Jacob. Zilpah bore two sons: Gad, meaning "fortune," and Asher, meaning "happy."

Leah's firstborn, Reuben, was a man who worked in the fields. One day while working, Reuben found an herb known as mandrake, which was considered an aphrodisiac in the Middle East. He delivered the mandrakes to his mother, Leah. Rachel, the pretty, younger, loved sister, was desperate and pled with the unloved, tender-eyed, older sister to give her the aphrodisiac. Leah replied, "First you 'take' my husband, then you want to 'take' my son's mandrakes as well." In desperation, Rachel agreed Jacob would spend the night with Leah as payment for Reuben's mandrakes.

Rachel got the aphrodisiac and Leah got son number five, Issachar, "reward." Leah felt rewarded for giving Zilpah to Jacob. Later, Leah bore a sixth son, Zebulun, "dwelling," because she believed Jacob would dwell with her and their six sons. Then the climax came. After birthing six sons, Leah bore a daughter, Dinah. Then, finally, Rachel had a child, a son of her own, whom she named Joseph. In Hebrew, Joseph means "may He add," since Rachel hoped to have more sons. Jacob now had eleven sons and a daughter and was eager to return to his homeland. Earlier, Laban and Jacob struck a bargain where Jacob received some livestock from Laban. God blessed Jacob, as He had promised at Beth-el. Jacob grew wealthier, and Laban acknowledged that God had blessed him and Jacob because of Jacob's being in Laban's household (Genesis 30:27). This was probably why Laban was reluctant to release Jacob, for he recognized the blessing Jacob had been to his own family.

After being encouraged by his sons, Laban grew angry and resentful of Jacob. Jacob tells Laban, "I've worked for seven years for each of my wives and six more years for my livestock, and you keep altering my wages." For twenty years, Jacob waited for Laban to release him. Laban and Jacob made another covenant and agree to part ways, with Jacob returning to his home. Laban recognized that he would probably never see his two daughters and grandchildren again.

As Jacob, his family, and livestock depart for the homeward journey, Jacob dealt successfully with one of his problems. However, a second, more ominous problem lay before him: meeting his brother Esau after twenty years of being estranged. What will Esau's reaction be? *Does he still want to kill me or has he 'mellowed?' Has his hatred grown even more intense? Will he be jealous of my family, my herds? How is the best way to approach him?* Certainly, all of these thoughts were racing through Jacob's mind.

Jacob's strategy in meeting his brother was to send messengers on ahead of the caravan of people and livestock. The messengers were instructed to speak humbly to Esau. Upon their return, these men report to Jacob: "Your brother is coming to meet you, along with four hundred men." One issue has been answered. Jacob had been greatly blessed over the last two decades, but Esau also had been blessed, for he had at his disposal four hundred men. Upon hearing the report, Jacob was very frightened and worried. He employed a military tactic and divided the caravan into two groups, hoping that at least one of the two companies survives the encounter.

In Genesis 27:20, we see how Jacob deceived his father. Note his reply to Isaac's question:"How did you find wild game so quickly?" Jacob responded, "Because the Lord thy God brought it to me."The Lord was not Jacob's own personal God but his father Isaac's God. After Jacob divided the group into two parties, he prayed to "God of my father Abraham and God of my father Isaac." Notice, Jacob still does not appear to have a personal relationship with the Lord, for he then "reminded" God of the dream from twenty years earlier at Bethel. "You said to me you would protect me when I returned to my homeland and family. Now I fear my brother Esau will kill me and the mothers of my children. You said you would make my 'seed' so numerous they couldn't be counted. If my family is killed, this twenty-year-old promise will be worthless" (Genesis 32:12 NASB).

Jacob sent a gift on ahead of the two groups to help soften Esau's animosity. The present included two hundred twenty goats and two hundred twenty sheep, plus camels, cows, and donkeys. As night fell, Jacob positioned his family and children across the Jabbok River along with his other possessions. The Arab word Jabbok means "wrestled." It was a fitting term for the name of this river flowing through the land of Jordan which empties into the Jordan River itself. Jacob was left alone in the camp, with everyone else across the river. Jacob left home alone and tonight he was returning home alone. But Jacob was not alone, for he spent the night wrestling with a man of God. By the time dawn arrived, Jacob's hip joint was dislocated. Before parting, Jacob insisted that the man of God bless him. The holy man announced his name *Jacob* would be changed to *Israel*. The patriarch's name was changed from "deceiver" to "may God prevail for him." No longer was God just the God of Jacob's grandfather Abraham and his father, Isaac. He had now become the personal God of Jacob as well. The man of God gave Jacob the title "Prince with God" (Genesis 32:28).

As Esau approached with his four hundred men, Jacob placed Zilpah and Bilhah, his two maids and their four sons, at the front of the caravan. Next was Leah with her six sons and daughter, Dinah. At the rear of the entourage was Jacob's favorite, Rachel and her one son, Joseph. It was clear which family Jacob viewed as most expendable and whom he loved the most. Think how Zilpah, Bilhah and their four sons felt being on the front line. How did Leah feel? *"I've birthed Jacob six sons and a daughter, yet he placed Rachel and her one son behind me and my seven children."* Finally Jacob and Esau met. Surprisingly, it was a pleasant, joyous encounter.

As Esau returned home and Jacob (Israel) entered the Promised Land, he approached the location where Joshua will lead the Israelites five hundred years later into the Promised Land. Both sites are just north of the Dead Sea in modern day Israel. He purchased land from Hamor, a Hivite who had a son named Shechem. On this plot of land Jacob erected an altar to God and named the site El-Elohe-Israel, "God, the God of Israel." ("El" in Hebrew is one of the words for God.) Consequently, the name for this altar has the word "El" three times in its title.

Shechem saw Dinah and seduced her. This action caused two of her oldest full-blooded brothers (Simeon and Levi) to kill Hamor, Shechem, and all the neighboring males. The brothers then confiscated the widows, children, and livestock to defile the Hivite city in response to their sister being defiled. Obviously, this fight in the land of the Hivites (who greatly outnumbered Israel's family) caused Israel much stress. In Genesis 35, God told Israel to return to Beth-el where he had had the dream of Jacob's ladder.

The Lord affirmed His blessing of Israel and required allegiance of Israel's family to Himself alone, demanding they put away all foreign gods. (Earlier, Rachel had sat on her father's idol to hide it when her father, Laban, had overtaken Jacob's departing family. Laban was deceitful to Jacob, and Rachel was deceitful to her father. Laban was looking for his personal god, his idol, when his daughter deceived her father by saying she could not rise up as she was experiencing her menstrual cycle.) Laban's search for his personal idol provides further evidence that Abraham's family at Haran were possibly moon worshippers.

The Lord repeated that Israel will be the father of many nations and confirmed the gift of this land to Abraham, Isaac, and now Israel and "to thy *seed* after thee" (emphasis added). With these repeated pronouncements, is it any wonder that when we see the turmoil today in Israel, the Jews hold fast to these oft repeated declarations by God Himself that this is "their" land?

After the building of an altar at Beth-el, Israel's caravan continued its journey southward. Just below what is now Jerusalem, Rachel gave birth to a second son, "Benoni," which means "son of my sorrow." It's not surprising that, after a four-hundred-mile camel ride, this mother died in birthing her son. Six miles to the south of Jerusalem, along the road between Jerusalem and Bethlehem, a mausoleum still exists today that is reputed to be Rachel's tomb. Upon Rachel's death, Israel changed his twelfth son's name to Benjamin, "son of the right hand."

Israel's lineage was now complete with twelve sons and Dinah. A family tree of this family's sons appears as follows:

Four Mothers' Sons

Leah	Bilhah (Rachel's Maid)	Zilpah (Leah's Maid)	Rachel
Reuben	Dan	Gad	Joseph
Simeon	Naphtali	Asher	Benjamin
Levi			
Judah			
Issachar			
Zebulun			

Leah was mother to one-half of all of Israel's sons, while Rachel had only two sons, Joseph and Benjamin. Israel grieved his favorite wife, but a part of her remained with him in his two youngest sons. As he was his mother's youngest and favorite child, he too chose these two youngest boys as his favorite children and provided Joseph with a choice, colorful coat. Genesis 37 describes Joseph as being seventeen years old.

One day, Joseph was tending sheep with four of his older half-brothers. Joseph reported some unsatisfactory event to their father. We do not know what it was, but nevertheless, he recounted it. While Joseph was with his half-brothers, he told them a dream about his older brothers bowing down to him. The dream reminded the older brothers of the incident when Israel's caravan confronted Esau at the Jabbok River. Who did Israel put at the front of the caravan? He placed his two maids and their four sons at the forefront in the greatest danger. This positioning is evident; they were the least valuable to Israel, while Rachel and Joseph bringing up the rear were the most precious to Israel. Second, this younger brother tattled on them. Third, their father gave Joseph a beautiful coat, yet none of the older brothers received such a coat. And now, fourth, Joseph told them a dream he had experienced, where they would all serve him and bow down to him. So, while tending sheep at Dothan, the brothers saw Joseph coming to check on them once again.

The brothers decide to kill him. Leah's firstborn, Reuben, the oldest brother of the twelve, overruled them and said, "Do not kill Joseph, but let's put him in this pit." It was Reuben's plan to later deliver Joseph back to their father after the brothers "taught Joseph a lesson." (The detail in the word of God is fascinating. In verse 24, it tells us that this pit had no water in it.) The brothers then sat down calmly to take a lunch break. While they were eating, a caravan of Ishmaelites carrying spices to Egypt came by. Reuben's full-blooded younger brother, Judah (Leah's fourth son) told his brothers, "Let's sell him to the Ishmaelites and pretend he's been killed." Judah further said, "If we sell him, then his blood will not be upon us, but if he dies in the pit, we will be responsible." Joseph was sold for twenty pieces of silver.

When Reuben returned to the pit and Joseph was gone, he was distraught. The other brothers told Reuben what they have done. They dip Joseph's coat in animal's blood and gave it to Jacob who mourned for a long time over the loss of his son.

The date of Joseph's arrival in Egypt has been a matter of conjecture among scholars for decades. The most commonly accepted date is approximately 1875 BC.

We know well the story of Joseph in Egypt and his ascent from prison to prime minister of Egypt—second only to Pharaoh because of his ability to interpret dreams (Genesis 41:40 NASB). Joseph told the Pharaoh that Egypt will enjoy seven years of plentiful crops followed by seven years of very severe drought and famine. Joseph, as governor, administered Pharaoh's plan of storing the ample food from the bountiful harvests.

As the drought and famine spread throughout the Middle East, the patriarch Israel instructed ten of his remaining eleven sons to leave Beersheba and go to Egypt to purchase grain. Joseph's only full-blooded younger brother, Benjamin, was not to go with the other brothers. Joseph promptly recognized his ten half-brothers. However, the ten half-brothers did not recognize their brother in his appearance as the Egyptian ruler. As Joseph met with them, he remembered his dream of years earlier when he told his older brothers how they would bow down to him (Genesis 37:5-8 NASB).

Joseph created a plot to induce the brothers to bring his younger full-blooded brother, Benjamin, to Egypt. Joseph's father Israel was holding ever so tightly to his only remaining living remembrance of Rachel, her son Benjamin. It is easy to see why Israel held onto Benjamin. Years earlier, he let Joseph go with his older sons, and now "Joseph was no more."

Reuben, the oldest brother, reminded the others that they will be judged for harming their little brother. Now, Simeon, the second-oldest brother, became a surety deposit in an Egyptian prison to ensure the nine remaining brothers will bring Benjamin back to secure Simeon's release. Naturally, Israel objected to losing his last thread to Rachel. He declared, "Joseph is no more, Simeon is in an Egyptian prison, and now you want to take Benjamin as well?"

God had blessed Israel with twelve sons. Now he was down to nine. Surely Israel wondered, "How many more sons will I lose before I die? And if I agree to this, then Joseph and Benjamin, my two very favorites of the twelve, both will be gone." Reuben pledged his two sons to his father, "if I don't deliver Simeon and Benjamin back to you." But Israel refused Reuben's offer. As time passed and their food supplies further diminished, Judah asked his father to send Benjamin with him; Judah promised he will be a surety for his little half-brother.

Judah had been the brother who wanted to sell Joseph into slavery and not kill him (Genesis 37:26 NASB). By making this offer to his father, Judah ran the risk of becoming a slave in Egypt himself. Although Judah was the number four son, this was the first time Judah stepped up to become a leader among the brothers. Later Judah will be chosen by Israel to lead their family to the region of Goshen upon getting Joseph's directions to the land of Egypt (Genesis 46:28 NASB). Judah was willing to be surety to save his full, older brother, Simeon. Furthermore, Judah had interceded in the plot of Joseph. For his half-brother Benjamin, Judah now offered himself as a ransom (Genesis 44:14-34). On multiple occasions, Judah began to exhibit his leadership qualities.

Joseph finally revealed his true identity to his eleven brothers. The Bible does not record that Joseph wept when he was sold into slavery. Neither does it state Joseph wept when being accused by Potiphar's wife. Nor did he weep when the Pharaoh thrust him into prison. Obviously, Joseph was not hardened by life, for when he saw all his brothers, he found a private place to weep. When Joseph revealed himself to his brothers in Genesis 45, he informed them that God has sent him to Egypt to preserve a remnant of their family and to save their lives by a great deliverance. In addition, he told them, "You didn't send me here, but God."

Furthermore, since the brothers were herdsmen (and Egyptians despised herdsmen), Joseph commanded them to get their father, Israel, at Beersheba, their families and all their belongings and travel to the land of Goshen, the most fertile area in all of Egypt (Genesis 45:18; 46:34 NASB). Goshen was the delta where the Nile emptied into the Mediterranean Sea. This choice, fertile delta with ample water was in total contrast to the rest of arid Egypt, which was nestled close by the Nile for sustenance. As herdsmen, it is not surprising the Israelites and their livestock grew in this environment and prospered mightily (Exodus 1:7). Goshen was close to the royal court where Joseph lived, yet it was distant from most of the Egyptians since it was a peninsula protruding out into the Mediterranean.

Israel prepared for his trip to Egypt by offering a sacrifice unto God at Beersheba. Previously, at Beersheba, Israel's grandfather Abraham first offered sacrifices (Genesis 21:33) and later, his father Isaac did as well (Genesis 26:25). After he worshiped God with the sacrifice that night, God affirmed to him in yet another dream that He is with Israel; "I will bring you up out of Egypt as a great nation" (Genesis 46:3 NASB).

After all the cattle and goods are listed, the Bible twice notes that Israel's entire *seed* will journey to Egypt with him. Twenty verses list by name all the seed of Israel moving down into the Goshen region of Egypt. Genesis 46:27 had a census of seventy descendants of Israel traveling down into Egypt. The number seventy also appears in Deuteronomy 10:22 and Exodus 1:5. Some translations have a population of seventy-five. (Acts 7:14 and the Dead Sea Scrolls have the higher number, which may have included Joseph's grandsons.) Of the seventy people moving to Egypt, the most important person is Judah because he is to be the carrier of the *Royal Seed*.

Israel met the Pharaoh but was not intimidated; instead he twice blessed Pharaoh (Genesis 47:7, 10 NASB). Pharaoh gave provisions, wagons, and land to the family of Joseph in appreciation for the contribution Joseph made as governor of Egypt.

Years later, Israel's sons are gathered at their father's deathbed to receive Israel's blessing. The blessings are as follows:

The Blessings

Mother	Son	Blessings	# of Verses
Leah	Reuben*	Unstable, incest	2
Leah	Simeon	Simeon and Levi murder Shechem and the Hivites	1.5
Leah	Levi		1.5
Leah	Judah	Lion, Scepter not depart, Shiloh	5
Leah	Zebulun	Dwell by sea	1
Leah	Issachar	Strong donkey	2
Bilhah	Dan	Serpent, judge	3
Zilpah	Gad	Troop overcomes	1
Zilpah	Asher	Be rich	1
Bilhah	Naphtali	Deer, beautiful words	1
Rachel	Joseph	Fruitful	5
Rachel	Benjamin	Ravenous wolf	1

*Reuben was intimate with Israel's concubine Bilhah, mother of Reuben's half-brothers, Dan and Naphtali (Genesis 35:22)

What did we learn about Israel?

1. Jacob was a twin. He stole his brother's birthright.
2. God changed Jacob's name to Israel. He married two sisters, Leah and Rachel, who were also his cousins.
3. He was the father of twelve sons. His sons' descendants become the twelve tribes of Israel.
4. Israel was wealthy in a foreign land.
5. God made provision for Israel's seed.
6. Israel "lost" his favorite son for several years.

7. Israel issued prophetic blessings to his twelve sons and announced through which sons the lineage of spiritual and royal leadership will come.

8. The sons' descendants became tribes, and later, as slaves in Egypt, wait four hundred thirty years for their blessings to be bestowed upon all of Israel.

Israel's (Jacob's) Relatives

Name	**Relationship**	**APPROXIMATE Dates**
Abraham	Grandfather	±2000 BC
Esau	Brother	±1800 BC
Judah	Son	± 1700 BC
Levi	Son	± 1700 BC
Pharez	Grandson	±1600 BC
Boaz	Great-grandson, 6 generations removed	±1150 BC
Jesus	Great-grandson, 51 generations removed	AD 30

Chapter 10

Judah

> The genealogy is not to be reckoned after the birthright. For Judah prevailed above his brethren and of him came the chief ruler. (1 Chronicles 5:1-2)

The first nine chapters have mostly covered the book of Genesis. A synopsis of the first book of the Bible is as follows:

Genesis 1	God starts with one man.
Genesis 4	Cain's genealogy concludes.
Genesis 6	God is sorry He made man.
Genesis 7	God permits a flood. Only eight people survive.
Genesis 9	God starts over with Noah's three sons.
Genesis 11	God hates pride and confuses language at Babel.
Genesis 12	God commands Abraham to leave Haran in southern Turkey for the Promised Land in Israel.
Genesis 19-36	The genealogy of approximately fifty-to-sixty people groups in the Bible concludes, including the Edomites (Gen. 26, 28), Moabites (Gen. 19), Ammonites (Gen. 19), and Ishmaelites (Gen. 25).
Genesis 37-48	God, through Joseph, provides for Israel's family of seventy people down in Egypt for four hundred thirty years.
Genesis 49	On his deathbed, Israel blesses each of his twelve sons.
Genesis 50	Joseph dies, leaving instructions for his body to be buried in the Promised Land.

In chapters 19-36 of Genesis, due to the sins of murder, incest, homosexuality, adultery, intermarriage with other peoples, and rebellion, the genealogy of almost sixty various people groups are concluded. The text does not say these people were killed. The Bible merely discontinues recording their genealogies. By Genesis 37, God's master plan was once again reduced from many peoples to one man. At this time, the one man's name was Jacob, but God renamed him Israel and made Israel the father of twelve sons. Because the birth order of these twelve sons is relevant to the story, consider the following chart.

Birth Order of Jacob's (Israel's) Sons

Son	**Mother**
Reuben	Leah
Simeon	Leah
Levi	Leah
Judah	Leah
Dan	Bilhah
Naphtali	Bilhah
Gad	Zilpah
Asher	Zilpah
Issachar	Leah
Zebulun	Leah
Joseph	Rachel
Benjamin	Rachel

In Genesis 49, Israel pronounces his blessing on these twelve sons. Israel gives his commentary on his first four sons in their birth order. Next, Israel skips over his four sons birthed to the two concubines, Bilhah and Zilpah, and continues with the two remaining sons of Leah. Israel then comes back to the four sons he just skipped over and blesses them. Finally, Israel concludes with the blessings of Joseph and Benjamin, his two favorite children by his favorite wife, Rachel.

If we skip back a few pages to the chart showing the Blessings of Israel's Sons, notice the blessings are five verses each for Judah and Joseph. Blessings of two and three verses were reserved for Reuben, Issachar, Simeon, Levi, and Dan. All five of these last-mentioned siblings receive condemnations for murder, deviousness, laziness, and sexual perversion. The remaining five sons receive only scant, one-verse blessings. Now, rearrange the charts from birth order to length of blessing and study the pronouncements made for each son.

Israel's Blessing of Each Son

Son	Number of verses	Pronouncement
Judah	5	Lion, scepter, not depart from Shiloh
Joseph	5	Fruitful
Dan	3	Serpent, judge
Reuben	2	Unstable, incest
Issachar	2	Strong donkey, become slaves, lazy
Simeon	1.5	Murder Hivites
Levi	1.5	Murder Hivites
Zebulon	1	Dwell by sea
Gad	1	Troop overcomes
Asher	1	Become rich
Naphtali	1	Deer, beautiful words
Benjamin	1	Ravenous wolf

Verses were not assigned to the text until a few hundred years ago. But the number of verses per each son is an easy, concise way to view the length of blessings or judgments for each of the twelve sons.

The crux of the blessings bestowed upon Joseph and Judah is revealed in 1 Chronicles 5:1-2. Because Joseph was separated from his brothers, he was to receive the double portion of the material blessings. Reuben forfeited the double blessing of the first-born by his actions with Bilhah. In other words, the blessing that should have gone to Reuben, the first-born son of Leah, goes instead to Joseph, the first-born of Rachel.

First Chronicles 5:1 states how the genealogy was to be "reckoned" (made right). Since Leah's first-born, Reuben, forfeited that right, his father promised Joseph "to be fruitful." And it came to pass. In Joshua 17, the tribes of Ephraim and Manasseh (named for Joseph's two sons), received larger portions of the Promised Land than the other tribes.

The firstborn's material birthright belonged to Joseph's two sons, Ephraim and Manasseh, whose mother Asenath was the daughter of an Egyptian priest named Poti-Pherah. Ephraim and Manasseh were one-half Egyptian and one-half Israelite.

The unknown author of Hebrews in chapter 11 sees these sons' blessings as an act of faith. In particular, Israel blessed both the sons of Joseph for the son whose journey to Egypt protected Israel's family of seventy individuals. Joseph's biography runs over ten chapters in the later portion of Genesis, and not one word of sin, judgment, or condemnation is ever uttered about Rachel's firstborn son. In addition, in Deuteronomy 33, the blessings of Joseph's two sons were the longest offered by Moses.

Judah's blessings also materialized. Earlier, Israel had said that Judah will be praised. Leah gave him this name hoping Israel would provide her with "praise" for birthing four sons. Israel stated he will be praised, but for another reason. Judah intervened for Joseph to be sold into slavery rather than killed. Years later Judah told his father, "Send Benjamin with me, and I will be the guarantee of his safe return from the land of Egypt." Israel chose Judah from among the eleven brothers to return to Joseph and get directions to lead all Israel's family to the region of Goshen. Judah's shortfall, however, was he fathered twin sons by his daughter-in-law, who deceived him into this relationship.

Israel quietly tucked two tremendous statements in Genesis 49:9-10. In verse nine, Judah is mentioned as being a lion. In Revelation 5:5, Jesus is called "the lion from the tribe of Judah, the root of David." In contrast, 1 Peter 5:8 depicts Satan as a roaring lion, the king of disobedience. The stage is set for a war between the two lions or two kings—the king of obedient submission and the king of disobedience. The second major prophecy in Genesis 49:10 states, "the scepter shall not depart from Judah." Throughout the ages, lions and the scepter have been signs of royal power, authority, and kingship. Furthermore, Genesis 49:10 contains the phrase "until Shiloh comes." While vague, the personal name "Shiloh" is considered to be one of the numerous names of Jesus, the Messiah.

Centuries later, in settling the Promised Land, the tribe of Judah receives, by lot, the land that surrounded Jerusalem. Much later the northern tribes separated from the southern tribes after the death of Solomon. The remaining southern territory became known as Judah (or Judea) with Jerusalem as its capital. King David will be from the tribe of Judah. Even today, the term Jew is a derivative from the word Judah.

The word Judah can be defined in three ways. First, it was the name of the fourth son of Israel. Second, it became the name of a tribe of Israelites fathered by Judah himself. Third, it became the name of the southern area of the Promised Land. Eventually the term applied to the entire Promised Land.

First Chronicles 5:2 states the chief ruler will come from the family of Judah's descendants. Numbers 24:7 also affirms "a star out of Jacob shall come in a scepter, but not now."

In studying the remaining tribes, we see the blessing of the tribe of Dan was actually a judgment, the longest condemnation of any of the twelve sons. The tribe of Dan probably was the first tribe to fall into apostasy. Furthermore, read Revelation 7. This chapter concerns the one hundred forty-four thousand from the tribes of Israel who are witnesses for Jesus during the Tribulation. Twelve tribes are mentioned in Revelation 7. Joseph's two sons are listed, Ephraim and Manasseh; however, the tribe of Dan is not mentioned at all.

Reuben was the biological first-born and should have received the double portion as the first son, but because Reuben had intimate physical contact with his father's concubine, Bilhah, he lost that privilege (Genesis 35:22 NASB). Reuben was passed over for his expected double inheritance. Not only did Reuben commit a sexual violation, but this action was also a challenge to Israel's family headship and authority.

Sons two and three, Simeon and Levi, avenged their sister Dinah's violation. Through their trickery, these two brothers murdered all of the Hivite males who were recovering from community circumcision (Genesis 34:24-31 NASB). Issachar also had a two-verse condemnation rather than any sort of blessing. At best, Israel viewed his ninth son as a strong donkey who in laziness will become a slave and serve others. Zebulon, Gad, Asher, Naphtali, and Benjamin each only merit brief one-verse blessings. As we saw earlier, the remaining five sons, Dan, Reuben, Issachar, Simeon, and Levi have condemnation and judgment extending for two or three verses.

First Chronicles 5:1-2 gives us very significant information about three of Israel's sons. Reuben lost the birthright of the first-born. Joseph's two sons, Ephraim and Manasseh, received the material blessings. And the kingship, ruler, and lawgiver will come from the tribe of Judah. In Genesis 49, Israel gave deathbed blessings to his twelve sons. The next chapter, chapter 50, concludes the book of Genesis.

Consider another similar situation. The names of the twelve tribes came from the names of Israel's twelve sons. The twelve individual sons' families become the twelve tribes, with tens of thousands of people. Moses is considered the author of the first five books of the Bible known as the Pentateuch. Deuteronomy is the last book of the Pentateuch. In Deuteronomy 33, Moses as leader of all the Israelites blesses the tribes just as Israel blessed his individual sons in Genesis 49, almost five hundred years previously.

In Moses's blessing of the twelve tribes, Simeon is not mentioned at all. Also Joseph is now identified as the tribes of Ephraim and Manasseh. So we see a slightly different configuration in the following chart.

Moses's Blessing of Each Tribe

Tribe	# of verses in blessing
Reuben	1
Judah	1
Levi	4
Benjamin	1
Ephraim	2.5
Manasseh	2.5
Zebulon	1
Issachar	1
Gad	2
Dan	1
Naphtali	1
Asher	1

Once again the material blessings are approved to Joseph via his sons, Ephraim and Manasseh. However, these blessings by Moses offered only one verse for Judah. Notice the length of Levi's blessing by Moses. Levi has a longer blessing than any other single tribe.

Just as Israel died after blessing his twelve sons, after Moses blessed the twelve tribes in Deuteronomy 33, he died in chapter 34, the last chapter of Deuteronomy. Remember Judah's and Joseph's blessing in 1 Chronicles 5. Now, turn to 1 Chronicles 6. This chapter immediately starts into the genealogy of Levi. Notice in verse 3 the names listed as the grandchildren of Levi. Why, it is Moses, Aaron, and Miriam! The tribe receiving the longest blessing in Deuteronomy 33 is the tribe to which Moses belongs—the tribe of Levi.

First Chronicles 5:1-2 and 1 Chronicles 6:1-3 are two extremely important passages! Of the twelve tribes, three were singled out for special service. Israel emphasizes his two sons, Joseph and Judah. In blessing the twelve tribes, Moses emphasized his own tribe, the tribe of Levi. From the tribe of Levi, God will soon appoint Moses's brother, Aaron, the very first high priest (Exodus 29:4-9 NASB).

The Three Prominent Sons

Tribe	Lineage	Special Blessing
Joseph's two sons		
½ Ephraim	½ Egyptian	Material Blessing
½ Manasseh	½ Egyptian	Material Blessing
Judah	Israelite	Scepter, Kingship Blessing
Levi	Israelite	Spiritual Blessing

As mentioned earlier, Ephraim and Manasseh received some of the largest allotments of real estate once the Israelites occupied the Promised Land. Some of their territory was in Israel, but a large portion was also east of the Jordan River in present day Jordan.

Seventy family members had traveled down into Egypt under Joseph's provision for his father Israel's family. Four hundred thirty years later, six hundred thousand males, plus family members and others, will exit Egypt. After the Exodus and the journey into the Sinai Desert, this group of six hundred thousand men "plus children," and "a mixed multitude" have to be organized into some sort of organized families, clans, and groupings (Exodus 12:37-38 NASB).

From the time of Exodus (approximately 1270 BC) until the time the united nation of Israel was divided into a northern (Samaria) and southern (Judah) kingdom was three hundred fifty years. Thereafter the Kingdom of Judah survived nearly an additional three hundred fifty years.

Through this almost seven-hundred-year period of judges, priests, and kings, the two most important tribes were always the tribe of Judah and the tribe of Levi. The prominence of these two tribes is obvious even in the Sinai wilderness shortly after escaping Pharaoh's chariots. Later, the prophet Jeremiah clearly states the leadership roles of the tribes of Judah and Levi among their brothers (Jeremiah 33:17-24 NASB). In Numbers 1, a census of soldiers is taken with a tribal leader named for each tribe. Numbers 1:7 informs us the leader of the tribe of Judah is Nahshon. Elishama is the prince from the tribe of Ephraim. He will become the grandfather of Moses's successor, Joshua.

In Numbers 2, God instructed Moses about the arrangement of the camp while the Israelites are in the Sinai desert. The tabernacle was to always be in the center of the tribes. This configuration with each tribe's population appears as follows:

Configurations and Populations of the Twelve Tribes

North
Camp of Dan – 157,600
1. Dan – 62,700
2. Asher – 41,500
3. Naphtali – 53,400

West
Camp of Ephraim – 108,100
1. Ephraim – 40,500
2. Manasseh – 32,200
3. Benjamin – 35,400

Tabernacle
1. Levites – 22,000
(Numbers 2:33)

East
Camp of Judah – 186,400
1. Judah – 74,600
2. Issachar – 54,400
3. Zebulon – 57,400

South
Camp of Reuben – 151,450
1. Reuben – 46,500
2. Simeon – 59,300
3. Gad – 45,650

The journey from Egypt to the Promised Land was generally eastward. Nahshon, as leader of the tribe of Judah, headed the camp of Judah at the forefront of the caravan, followed by the camp of Reuben. The next contingent was the Levites, who supervised the transportation of the Tent of Tabernacle. Following the Levites were the tribes composing the camp of Ephraim. Concluding the caravan were the tribes who camped to the north of the tabernacle. Notice the Tribe of Judah was the most populous, and the camp of Judah was the largest camp of the four camps. Numbers 10 also is informative, because it describes the processional sequence, when the caravan moved to a new location:

Processional Sequence

Camps		Tribe	Population	Mother	Birth Order
	1.-	Judah	74,600	Leah	4th son
	2.-	Issachar	54,400	Leah	9th son
	3.-	Zebulun	57,400	Leah	10th son
Camp of Judah			186,400		
	4.-	Reuben	46,500	Leah	1st son
	5.-	Simeon	59,300	Leah	2nd son
	6.-	Gad	45,650	Zilpah	7th son
Camp of Reuben			151,450		
	7.-	Levites	22,000	Leah	3rd son
Camp of Levites			22,000		
	8.-	Ephraim	40,500	Rachel	11th son (by Joseph)
	9.-	Manasseh	32,200	Rachel	11th son (by Joseph)
	10.-	Benjamin	35,400	Rachel	12th son
Camp of Ephraim			108,100		
	11.-	Dan	62,700	Bilhah	5th son
	12.-	Asher	41,500	Zilpah	8th son
	13.-	Naphtali	53,400	Bilhah	6th son
Camp of Dan			157,600		

Besides Judah being the largest tribe, several other items are noteworthy. All the tribes in the Camp of Judah were descendants of three of Leah's sons. The Camp of Reuben was headed by two more of Leah's six sons. Zilpah's first-born, Gad, is substituted at the end of this second camp for the tribe of Leah's last son, Levi. The Levites and the Tent of Tabernacle were safely nestled in the middle of this caravan. The third camp was composed of the children of Rachel. The rear guard was all the remaining descendants of the concubines, Bilhah and Zilpah.

These slaves managed to maintain their family tribal identity for over four hundred years, as Numbers 1 indicates. In Numbers 1:18, these Israelites were able to assemble themselves by their ancestry. After more than four hundred years in a foreign land, this people group had kept a distinct identity for each family, each clan, and each tribe. Four hundred years earlier, Israel appointed Judah to lead his family of seventy persons from Beersheba to Goshen in the land of Egypt. Now Moses appointed the most populous tribe, Judah, to lead the tribes out of Egypt. The tribe led by Nahshon was the one we saw with the promise of being the tribe of the "lawgiver," the tribe of future kings. Some translations call Nahshon not only a clan leader, but a "prince of Judah." In Numbers 7:2, Nahshon, along with eleven other tribal leaders, were also called "Princes of Israel."

Moses and Aaron met with these twelve tribal leaders, or princes. In the Sinai wilderness, we see the tribe of Judah assume the leadership role that eventually evolved into the position of regal authority. Not only will the nation of Israel march in this same sequence, but when the time came for making sacrifices and dedication at the altar, the tribes appeared before the tabernacle in this same precise order. Furthermore, it is also worthwhile to observe that on each side of the encampment, the tribes in closest proximity to each other were usually full blood related tribes and not tribes half related by their common bond of fatherhood via Israel. The census taken in Numbers (hence the name of the book) show more than six hundred thousand soldiers over twenty years of age. To these six hundred thousand soldiers, we must add wives, children, the elderly, and the mixed multitudes that voluntarily traveled out of Egypt with the Israelites. Experts have variously estimated this entourage to have a total population of between two and three million. The census and sequence of moving this multitude was important.

The priestly role of the Levites was created to replace the original, spiritual role of the first-born (Numbers 3:11-12 NASB). In Numbers 3, the generations of Levi are shown. Levi had three sons: Gershon, Kohath, and Merari. A census was also taken of these priests and the duties assigned for each sub-clan of Levi are recorded. The Gershonites were to camp on the west side of the tabernacle. The Kohathites were assigned the south side, and the Merarites encamped to the north. On the east side, in close proximity to the Camp of Judah, was where Moses, Aaron, and Aaron's sons were positioned. The grand census of priests totaled twenty-two thousand. Just as Judah was the most populous tribe with seventy-four thousand six hundred adult males, Levi was the smallest tribe with only twenty-two thousand adult males. Each sub-clan of Levi was assigned particular duties which are listed in Numbers 4. First mentioned were the sons of Kohath, who carried the Ark. Then the clans of Gershon and Merari shouldered the rods, poles, and coverings of the tabernacle. The Kohathites transported the special tabernacle furnishings, after wrapping them in the veil, the cloths, and the animal skins. Numbers 4:4 declared the clan of Kohath is responsible "for the most holy things." Outside of the members of the clan of Kohath, no other Israelites ever viewed the sanctuary utensils. It is fairly obvious to see that the east side was the most prominent position among all the tribes and the priests.

Each tribe was instructed to camp under its standard or banner, much like a military flag used in more recent times. With a community of more than three million individuals, the camp was huge. Just imagine the daily need for water, firewood, and disposal of garbage and wastes. Exodus 16 commemorates God's providing manna—describing it as small wafers. How much area would be needed for three million people to collect these small pieces of manna for their daily sustenance? Recall Exodus 12:38 tells us that in addition to the people, there were "very much" flocks, herds, and cattle. What did the animals eat? Did they eat manna? Was still more acreage needed to feed the livestock?

The tribal camps were required to be about three thousand feet, or about six-tenths of a mile from the Tent of Meeting (Joshua 3:4 NASB). The area around the tabernacle was sacred. Numbers 3:38 states anyone even approaching the entrance of the sanctuary can expect to be put to death. Once in the Promised Land, the land will be allotted. The Levites are to receive no land, but they were to be given cities and suburbs amidst all the twelve tribes. The land to provide pasture for Levitical animals is to extend this same three thousand feet out—not from the tabernacle, but from the walls of the cities the Levites receive. A revised map of the three million people encamped appears as follows:

Map of Encampment

Naphtali	Asher	Dan

Ephraim	Merari	Judah
Manasseh		Issachar
	Gershon TABERNACLE Moses / Aaron and	
Benjamin		Zebulun

Kohath

Gad	Simeon	Reuben

Earlier it was noted four tribes were given lengthy, special blessings. In effect, these four tribes were "first among equals." To reiterate, in 1 Chronicles 5, the two tribes of Manasseh and Ephraim are given material blessings as compensation to Joseph's two sons, because of their father's separation from his eleven brothers. Second, the tribe of Judah, for their patriarchs' care of Joseph and being surety for Benjamin, is given the role of kingship and lawgivers. Third, Moses blesses the tribe of Levi with the priestly leadership role. Note the proximity of Moses's and Aaron's camp to the tribe of Judah where Nahshon was prince and leader. If these four tribes were truly "the first among equals," there should be some method to document this "firstness"— and there is.

Concordances reveal the number of times specific words are mentioned in the Bible, so we can measure how often the names of these twelve tribes appear. Here is just such a chart:

Tribes' Name Frequency[10]

Tribe	Mother	Frequency of name in Bible
Judah	Leah	811
Levi	Leah	72
Joseph	Rachel	228
Ephraim	(Rachel's grandson)	172
Manasseh	(Rachel's grandson)	143
Benjamin	Rachel	162
Reuben	Leah	74
Dan	Bilhah	72
Gad	Zilpah	72
Simeon	Leah	50
Naphtali	Bilhah	50
Zebulun	Leah	45
Issachar	Leah	43
Asher	Zilpah	43

The tribe of Judah is mentioned almost as much (eight hundred eleven times) as the other eleven tribes *combined* (nine hundred fifty-three times). Judah is mentioned more than twice as often as his father Jacob (three hundred fifty-eight times). Just as we saw in Genesis where fifty to sixty people groups were dropped from the genealogy of the Bible, now we see two tribes, in particular, rise to far greater prominence than the remaining ten tribes. Judah was the source of lawgivers and kingship on earth, while the tribe of Levi was the source of priestly matters in obedience to Heaven (Jeremiah 33:17-24).

As these tribes grew in population, terms began to be used to describe to which tribe an individual belonged. A member of the tribe of Simeon is identified as a Simeonite in the Bible, while a member of the Reuben clan is known as a Reubenite. The only real exception is that no one shows up as a Judahite. These persons were designated by the term Jew. Now look at the frequency of these terms. The second column of the following chart lists how often the names of Jacob's sons appear in Scripture as individual persons. The third column exhibits how often the name is used to refer, not to a person, but to the tribe fathered by that particular son of Jacob.

Frequency of the Names and theTribes[11]

Son	Name Frequency +	Tribal Frequency =	Total Frequency
Judah	811	243("Jew")	1,054
Levi	72	293	365
Ephraim	172	6	178
Manasseh	143	3	146
Reuben	74	17	91
Simeon	50	14	64
Issachar	43	0	43
Naphtali	50	2	52
Dan	72	4	76
Benjamin	162	17	179
Asher	43	1	44
Gad	72	15	87

It is unmistakable: among the twelve sons of Israel, the text of the Bible points to Judah and Levi as the two most prominent tribes. The combined frequency of these two names, Judah and Levi, occur almost five hundred more times in the Bible than the other ten tribes combined (one thousand four hundred nineteen versus nine hundred sixty). From these two tribes, Judah and Levi, came the kings and the priests of Israel. One final thought: remember, Judah was always camped on the east side of the tabernacle. In addition, the sanctuary was consistently staked into the ground facing eastward. Moses and Aaron, as leaders of the Levites, were always camped at the entrance to the tabernacle, which always opened to the east.

Five hundred years later, Solomon will build a temple on Mount Moriah, and it too will face to the east. A wall will be built around the temple. Furthermore, during the end times, Matthew 24:27 announces Jesus will come from the East. In this wall, around Jerusalem, even today, is an east gate presently stoned shut from earlier times. Revelation 7 informs the reader that sometime in the future, an angel will descend from the east "having the seal of the living God." Verses that follow mention twelve thousand are sealed from each of the twelve tribes of Israel. The first tribe mentioned? It is the tribe of Judah.

The Joseph Narrative is interrupted by Genesis 38 where the entire chapter is devoted to Leah's fourth son, Judah. While Joseph was struggling in Egypt, Judah fathered sons by a Canaanite woman (Genesis 38:2-11).

Judah was aware God had specifically instructed his grandfather Abraham and his father Isaac not to marry local Canaanite women (Genesis 24:3 and 28:1). Nevertheless, this was precisely what Judah did in Genesis 38:2. Judah and the Canaanite women had three half-Israelite sons. The oldest son married Tamar. He soon died, and the middle son then married Tamar. Shortly thereafter, he too, was struck down by God. Judah then directed his daughter-in-law to return to her father's home in obedience to Leviticus 22:11-13, which instructs a widowed daughter of a priest to return to her father's house. Judah told Tamar when his third son grew up, that son could become her husband since Judah's two older sons were dead. We see that Judah was following the custom expressed in Deuteronomy 25:5-9.

After many years, Judah's wife died. He had promised his third son, Shelah, to Tamar— to be Tamar's third husband. With the passing of time, Shelah grew into a young adult. Whether Judah forgot his commitment to Tamar or the number three son simply did not want to marry Tamar (who was several years older than Shelah), we don't know. Perhaps, Shelah realized his two older brothers who were married to this woman had both died, and he simply does not want to die. Several possible reasons exist why this third marriage was never consummated.

Judah, a lonely widower, worked his daily farm chores and tended his livestock. On one occasion, he left Beersheba to shear his sheep at another site. Tamar, Judah's former daughter-in-law, removed her widow's apparel and dressed as a harlot. Tamar was dressed not as a common harlot, but as a Canaanite cult temple harlot (Gen. 38:21-22). Judah had physical relations with the "temple harlot." Months later, when Judah learned his widowed daughter-in-law was pregnant, he resorted to Levitical law.

Following Levitical law, Judah declared Tamar be burned to death (Leviticus 20:14 and 21:9). Tamar was brought to be judged by her former father-in-law. At that moment, Tamar produced the signet, cord, and staff Judah gave her three months earlier as a deposit for her sexual favors. Judah acknowledged these three items as belonging to himself and announced that Tamar is "more righteous than I," because he did not complete his vow of arrangement for his third son, Shelah, to be Tamar's third husband.

A repentant Judah has no further physical encounters with Tamar (Genesis 38:26 NASB). This simple story is important because one of Tamar's twin sons, Pharez, will be the carrier of the Royal Seed. Judah's grandfather, Isaac, sired twin sons. Now Tamar gave birth to twins also, Pharez and Zerah.

<u>Genealogy of the Twins</u>

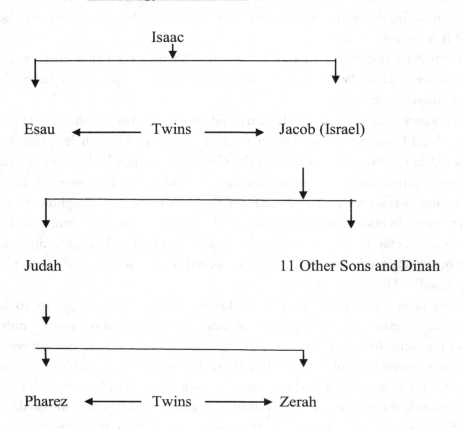

Israel was a twin who had twelve sons. One of these twelve sons, Judah, now fathered twin sons as well.

Revelation 21 is a description of the New Jerusalem. (Read verses 12-13.) The New Jerusalem will have twelve gates, three on each of its four sides. On each gate is written the name of one of the twelve tribes—just like the layout in the Sinai desert. The Bible doesn't say the twelve tribes will surround the New Jerusalem in the same exact way, but if they do, it truly will be consistent with the encampment in the Sinai wilderness three thousand five hundred years ago.

The narrative expanded from one man, Adam, to many. Then it is contracted to Noah and his three sons. Later it shrinks to one man again in the personage of Abraham. The course of the Royal Seed flows through the one man, Isaac, to focus on his son, Jacob, the next carrier of the Royal Seed. After a few chapters, Jacob's name was changed to Israel and expanded into a documentation of his twelve sons and their genealogy and their human foibles. From the charts we have seen, it is plain the narrative will focus on the tribe of Judah and its Jews, with a companion narrative emphasizing Levi and the Levites.

What did we learn about Judah?

1. Judah was Leah's fourth son.
2. Early on, he exhibited leadership qualities, becoming surety for Benjamin and being selected by Israel to lead his family to Goshen.
3. He married a Canaanite woman, a practice specifically forbidden by Abraham.
4. His wife died.
5. He was induced into a one-time physical relationship with a supposed Canaanite temple harlot. Thereafter, he had no further physical relations with Tamar.
6. Twins were born to Judah and Tamar.

Judah's Relatives

Name	Relationship	APPROXIMATE Dates
Abraham	Great grandfather	±1900 BC
Isaac	Grandfather	±1800 BC
Jacob (Israel)	Father	±1700 BC
Levi	Full brother	±1675 BC
Joseph	Half brother	± 1650 BC
David	Great-grandson, 8 generations removed	1000 BC
Jesus	Great-grandson, 50 generations removed	AD 30

Chapter 11

Levi

> And to the sons of Levi, behold, I have given all the tithe in Israel for an inheritance in return for their service which they perform, the service of the tent of meeting. (Numbers 18:21 NASB)

Up until this chapter, every Biblical character we have studied has been a clear, direct ancestor of Jesus. Adam is in the Bible not because he was the first man or lived in the Garden of Eden. Adam is in the Bible as Jesus's first ancestor. Most view Noah's claim to fame is the building of the ark to prepare for the flood. Noah's real claim to fame is being an ancestor of Jesus. Isaac's claim to fame is not because his father, Abraham, is willing to be obedient to God and offer his favorite son in a potentially sacrificial death. Isaac's most prominent claim to eternal fame is being an ancestor of Jesus, and another carrier of the Royal Seed.

With this chapter, we leave the direct royal seed lineage of Jesus's ancestors. Levi is different. As the third son of Leah and Israel (Jacob), he is not in the direct biological lineage of Jesus. Levi's father is in the Messianic lineage of Jesus, as is his younger brother, Judah. Levi is not. Half of the twelve brothers are mentioned more frequently in the Bible than Levi (See the chart Frequency of the Names and the Tribes.) In his father's blessing of the twelve sons in Genesis 49, Levi's most notable action is one of condemnation, not praise. Israel condemned Simeon and Levi for murdering all of the Hivites in retaliation for the rape of their sister Dinah. The book of Leviticus is named for him, but the contents of the book are not about Levi. The theme of the Leviticus text emphasizes the priesthood and technical aspects, as well as the proper procedures for implementing the sacrificial system.

Outside of this single retaliation event, Levi was not particularly notable for any other event in his life. The obvious question becomes: *Why include him in this study of Jesus's heritage?* The answer to this question has two parts. First, we must recall the words of Isaiah. In Isaiah 55:8-9, the prophet declares the words of God himself, "For My thoughts are not your thoughts, neither are your ways My ways, saith the Lord, for as the heavens are higher than the Earth, so are My ways higher than your ways and My thoughts than your thoughts." Second, beyond our human comprehension, God selected Levi's descendants to be the tribe to provide holiness, purity, religious guidance, and direction to the other twelve tribes.

This study includes Levi, not for his accomplishments, but because of who his grandchildren (and great-grandchildren) were. Levi was father to at least three sons and one daughter, according to Exodus 6. This chapter lists Levi's three sons as Gershon, Kohath, and Merari. Their sister's name was Jochebed (Exodus 6:16-20 NASB). The middle son, Kohath, had four sons. Kohath's oldest son was named Amram. Amram, as Levi's grandson, married Levi's daughter, Jochebed. Thus, Amram married his aunt.

After Amram married his Aunt Jochebed, they had three children: Miriam, Aaron, and Moses. By their mother, Miriam, Aaron, and Moses were Levi's grandchildren. However, via their father, Amram, and grandfather Kohath, these three children were the great grandchildren of Levi. All three of these great grandchildren figured prominently in the Jewish nation's special heritage. Miriam rescued the baby Moses floating in the Nile by providing a nurse for the baby to Pharaoh's daughter. Aaron became the nation's first high priest. From his lineage followed successor generations of high priests (at least twenty-three generations, according to 1 Chronicles 6). The youngest child, Moses, grew up in Pharaoh's palace and became the author of the first five books of the Bible. Aaron was the first high priest and Moses was the first scribe. Study the chart The Famous Descendants of Levi which will follow in a few pages.

Jeremiah 33:17 tells us Judah (through David) "shall never lack a man" to sit upon the throne of Israel. In addition, verse 18 discloses that neither shall the priests nor the Levites lack a man to come before God in the Temple. In this same chapter, verse 21 affirms the tribe of Judah to be the source of all the kings and the tribe of Levi will provide ministers before God. Verse 22 refers to the multiplying of the *seed* of Judah and Levi. Read Jeremiah 33:24 and note this verse states that God chose these two tribes, Judah and Levi, to lead the remaining tribes politically and spiritually. Jeremiah documents that the two superior tribes will be Judah and Levi. Up until this chapter, the focus is on studying just the genealogy of Judah. With this chapter, however, the stage is set for the next few chapters which will study the descendants of Levi.

What have we learned about Levi?

1. Levi was the full older brother of Judah. Judah will be in the lineage of the Royal Seed of Jesus. Levi will be an uncle to Judah's son, Pharez, in the Royal Seed lineage.
2. Levi's daughter, Jochebed, married Levi's grandson, Amram. This marriage produced three famous children: Miriam, Aaron, and Moses. These three were both grandchildren *and* great-grandchildren of Levi.
3. Although these three siblings were not in the direct royal lineage of Jesus, they each played a vital religious role in the Jewish nation.
4. Levi was not directly in the Messianic lineage of Jesus; nevertheless, among the three million Jews, he and his grandchildren were very, very closely related to the royal dynasty of Judah by marriage.

5. Jeremiah 33 tells us Judah and Levi were the two most important tribes. The tribe of Judah provided the kings, while the tribe of Levi provided the priests.
6. Much later, these two preferential tribes are joined into the one person of Jesus Christ.

Levi's Relatives

Name	Relationship	APPROXIMATE Dates
Abraham	Great-grandfather	±2000 BC
Isaac	Grandfather	±1900 BC
Judah	Full Brother	± 1700 BC
Tamar	Judah's wife/sister-in-law	±1700 BC
Aaron	Grandson/Great-grandson, High Priest	±1350 BC
Moses	Grandson/Great-grandson, First scribe	±1350 BC
Boaz	Great Nephew, 7 generations removed	±1200 BC
David	Great Nephew, 10 generations removed	1000 BC
Jesus	Great Nephew, 52 generations removed	AD 30

Chapter 12

Moses

"Since then no prophet has risen in Israel like Moses, whom the Lord knew face to face" (Deuteronomy 34:10 NASB).

Moses wrote the first five books of the Bible. These laws of Moses later became the basis of the contentions between Jesus and the Pharisees. God selected Moses for two reasons: first, because of his regal Egyptian education, and second, because of the survival skills he learned living four decades in the desert. At eighty years of age, Moses was now equipped be a leader, ruler, judge, administrative head, and tribal chieftain. Moses will be the man to deal with all the earthly, human issues. Also, God will appoint Moses to be His first scribe.

In contrast, God appointed Moses's brother, Aaron, to be the first high priest. Aaron's work was with the spiritual issues: holiness, purity, obedience, sacrifices, ceremonies, and keeping the law. You might say Moses dealt with the administration of *human affairs*, while Aaron, in a parallel manner, was concerned with *spiritual affairs*. We have seen this pattern before, early in Genesis, as illustrated by Enoch and Noah.

Enoch's life emphasized his spiritual values. Genesis 5:22 said, "Enoch walked with God and was no more, for God took him" to Heaven.

Yet, in Enoch's great-grandson Noah, we see his obedience, not so much in spiritual matters but in faithfully building the ark. This is the pattern of co-laborers—one dependably serving in the Godly, earthly, human role while the companion coworker served just as faithfully in a Godly, heavenly, spiritual role. We will see this pattern repeated and repeated in future chapters. This initial government of the Israelites has Moses serving as the administrative head (executive branch), with Aaron's spiritual focus on the law being the legislative branch. Two months after the Exodus, Moses's father-in-law Jethro encouraged Moses to appoint judges to assist him, creating the judicial branch (Exodus 18:12--22). In a matter of a few months, by God's providence and Jethro's advice, this new nation has a functioning government system with three branches — executive, legislative, and judicial.

First Chronicles 5 provides a basis of the material blessings to Ephraim and Manasseh while the kingly role is assigned to Judah. First Chronicles 6 further enlightens us about the genealogy of Levi. Verses 1-3 show us the grandchildren (or great-grandchildren) of Levi are Aaron, Moses, and Miriam. Typically, whenever we think about baby Moses or the high priest Aaron, or the

Exodus story, it is assumed that out of the three million Israelites, God just happened to pluck Moses or Aaron or Miriam at random from the mass of Israelite humanity.

But 1 Chronicles 6:1-3 clearly shows us these three siblings had a close, direct lineage to the founder of the tribe of Levi. Study the following chart:

The Genealogy of Levi

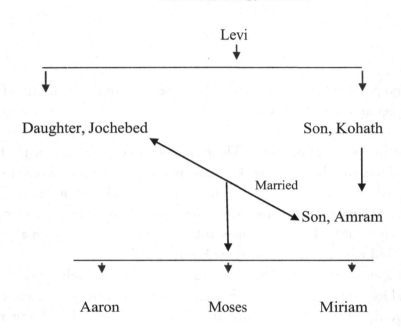

We have seen the Levitical tribe only totaled twenty-two thousand men plus other family members. It is not inconceivable that with the wives, babies, children, and the elderly, the total population of the priestly Levitical tribe could have approached one hundred thousand people. Out of this potential one hundred thousand population in the tribe of Levi, the patriarch's grandchildren (or great-grandchildren) were Aaron, Moses, and Miriam. Were these three Levite children just randomly chosen? No. The three grandchildren of Levi were to be the *leaders of the Exodus*.

The Israelites were residents of Egypt for over four hundred years. During those years in Egypt, circumstances changed for the descendants of Israel. They are no longer welcome guests in Egypt; they have become slaves.

The Nile is one of the earth's longest rivers. Several things about the Nile River make it unique. Unlike most rivers, the Nile flows north. Another peculiar feature of the Nile has to do with commerce. Egypt has a higher altitude in the South than in the North, and merchandise from southern Egypt could be loaded on ships and floated downstream to the ancient port cities on the Mediterranean Sea.

Also, the ships carrying products and goods destined for southern Egypt also had a unique advantage. The sailors would unfurl the sails, and the prevailing winds off the Mediterranean Sea pushed these cargo ships upstream towards southern Egypt. In ancient times, the Nile was vital to commerce, conveniently moving merchandise in both directions, and made the servitude of the Israelites somewhat easier.

To reach the Valley of the Kings in southern Egypt, one must travel sixty to seventy miles across the land. On this trek, one observes not a speck of green—not a tree, not a plant, and not even a sprig of grass. Egypt had the greatest amount of desert per capita of any nation in the world. The Nile made human existence possible in Egypt for thousands of years. The Nile was vital to the well-being of the nation of Egypt, and Egypt became a world super power by utilizing the Nile and developing its ample deposits of gold. With the wealth of a world super power, the Egyptians built the pyramids along the Nile about 2500 BC. By the time of Moses, Aaron, and Miriam, the pyramids were already one thousand years old.

Yet, this very same Nile River is where Satan had wanted to kill baby Hebrew boys. Just as the serpent's seed was at war with Eve's seed in the Garden of Eden, Satan employed Pharaoh in an attempt to kill the future author of the first five books of the Bible. Baby Moses was just one more seed Satan attempted to kill. Pharaoh wanted to drown all the newborn Hebrew boys in the Nile, and of all people, God chose to use Pharaoh's own daughter to prevent it!

Just who was this princess, this daughter of Pharaoh? Pharaoh Thutmose I reigned as a Pharaoh-God from 1525-1508 BC. His only daughter was Hatshepsut, who married her half-brother Thutmose II. Thutmose II reigned about 1508-1504 BC. Upon his death, Hatshepsut became Queen-Pharaoh, usurping the throne and reigning from 1504-1483 BC. Finally, she shared the Pharaoh title with her stepson, Thutmose III, who reigned from 1504-1450 BC. (In reality, Thutmose III's reign did not truly begin until 1483 BC.)

Hatshepsut, this usurper of the throne of Egypt, is easily identified in ancient statues. Hatshepsut's statues always show her with a fake goatee. This beard was held in place by a strap that follows her jaw line to the back of her head. She was the only Pharaoh with such an apparatus. Many Pharaohs were buried in close proximity to each other in the Valley of the Kings along the Nile in Southern Egypt. However, the imposter-Pharaoh Hatshepsut built a tomb for herself which she distanced from the Valley of the Kings and placed over a ridge all by itself. It actually was more of a temple than a tomb. Even in ancient times, this young queen would have been considered a strong woman. Archaeologists are not certain the princess who retrieved Moses from the Nile was Hatshepsut, but Egyptian archaeology and the timeline below make her an excellent candidate.

EGYPTIAN TIMELINE

Pyramids Built	±2500 BC
Abraham Called	±2000 BC
Joseph entered Egypt	±1900 BC
Joseph Died	±1800 BC
Moses Born	±1525 BC
Hatshepsut reigned	1504-1483 BC
Exodus	±1450 BC

To return to our narrative, one day Pharaoh's daughter came to the Nile to bathe. There, among the reeds, she discovers a basket made of bulrushes and covered with pitch. Some Bible translators even call this little boat an ark. The princess opens the basket to find a little, three-month-old, Hebrew boy. Aaron, baby Moses's older brother, is only three years old at the time (Exodus 7:7), so he is of no help in protecting his younger brother. As Jochebed's oldest child, Miriam's assignment is to watch over the basket holding Jochebed's youngest child, Moses, while it floated in the Nile. At age ten or twelve, *Miriam performs the most important task of her entire life*. Upon Pharaoh's daughter discovering the baby, Miriam boldly steps forward as a slave girl to the Pharaoh's daughter and volunteers to find a nurse for the babe among the Hebrew women. Of course, the nurse Miriam found was Jochebed, the baby Moses's very own mother.

The princess named the baby "Moses," which in Hebrew means "drawn out." Because Egyptians believed the Nile is the source of all goodness, Pharaoh's daughter received a wonderful gift from God, a gift "drawn out" of the goodness of the Nile.

Moses grew up to be handsome and received an excellent education (Acts 7:20, 22). Furthermore, Moses was taught for forty years in the world's very best royal education programs, plus he received training in sports, philosophy, and the most advanced engineering systems in the world. After forty years living as an Egyptian, one day Moses visited the Israelites, and he murdered an Egyptian who was hitting a Hebrew. The next day, two Israelites were fighting and Moses tried to intervene. They asked Moses, "Who made thee a ruler and a judge over us?" Moses had thought no one had seen him kill the Egyptian the previous day. He realized he must flee from the royal household of Pharaoh. At forty years old, Moses's royal, Egyptian lifestyle was radically changed forever. Pharaoh began looking for Moses in order to sentence him to death for killing the Egyptian (Exodus 2:15 NASB). Moses fled eastward into the Sinai Peninsula, into the land of Midian and its deserts.

While in the desert by a well, Moses made contact with the daughters of the priest of Midian. The land of Midian was possibly named for one of Abraham's sons by Keturah. She had been Abraham's concubine, whom he had sent away. If this was true, then Midian, the man, had probably been exposed to the God of his father, Abraham. When Moses met the priest of Midian, a common bond may have been their faith in Yahweh. The priest of Midian's name was Reuel,

(Jethro) which means "friend of God." Moses married Reuel's daughter, Zipporah, and they had two sons, Gershon and Eliezer.

Moses became a shepherd for his father-in-law on the backside of the desert. In the second forty years of his life, Moses learned the ways of the desert. Such a fascinating life! Moses learned administration and governance in the royal chambers of Egypt for four decades. In the second four decades of his life, he learned the ways of the desert: How to survive. How to exist. And how to conquer the harsh environment. Could anyone have lived such a contrast in lifestyles?

Ultimately, Moses was prepared and equipped for God's mission for his life. He had forty years of experience in the salons of Egypt and forty years of experience herding livestock in the desert, learning to keep animal and man alive. One day, Moses confronted a burning bush in the desert that was not consumed by the fire. The Lord called to Moses out of the bush. Moses, at eighty years old, responded by simply saying, "Here am I."

God reminded Moses of His covenant with Abraham, Isaac, and Jacob. God then reiterated to Moses His promise that He had made to Abraham six hundred years earlier.

Over the centuries, God also confirmed this same commitment of a Promised Land to Isaac and Jacob. After four hundred thirty years of silence, God spoke from a burning bush to one man.

The Lord appointed Moses to go back to Egypt, where he had been wanted for murder by the Pharaoh for the past forty years. God commissioned Moses from herding flocks quietly in the desert to lead two or three million slaves out of the captivity of Pharaoh. Furthermore, would Pharaoh arrest Moses as a murderer once Moses reappeared before the Pharaoh? Is it any wonder Exodus 3:6 tells us Moses was afraid? He must have thought, *After four hundred thirty years of silence, God now speaks to me while I'm quietly living my own lonely life in the backside of the desert. Why me?* (See Exodus 3:11 NASB.)

The author, Moses, records his own first excuse to God, "Who am I?" God's reply, "Even though you are a fugitive, I want you to collect the elders of Israel in Egypt and go to see Pharaoh. He will not willingly let you go. And Moses, when you lead the three million Israelites out against Pharaoh's wishes, tell the Israelites to ask of their Egyptian masters gifts of jewels, silver, gold, and raiment." Exodus 3:18-22 makes clear the command, "I will call for the Egyptians to favor you Israelites, and not only will you leave Egypt, but you will also plunder (permanently borrow) the Egyptians of their jewels, silver, gold, and raiment."

Moses then records his second response to God—a second excuse, "They won't believe me." To offer proof of His authority, God changed the rod in Moses's hand into a snake. Naturally, he dropped the snake and ran from it. God then told Moses to go pick up the snake by its tail, and it was transformed back into a rod. God repeats the same covenant He made with Abraham, Isaac, and Jacob six hundred and four hundred years earlier. Can you imagine what was racing through Moses's mind? *God has been silent for over four hundred years. I murdered an Egyptian. I haven't spoken to another Israelite in forty years. Pharaoh wants to kill me. I must leave my wife and sons—or do I take them with me? Will the Israelites accept my sons, or will they be considered as half-breeds? Pharaoh won't willingly let us go . . . yet . . . yet . . . yet that bush was burning but not consumed. And yes, God did speak to me out of that bush. And yes, God did turn my rod into a snake and back into a rod again.*

God countered and told Moses the signs he must perform before Pharaoh. In reply, Moses spoke his third excuse, "I am not eloquent, and you have never spoken to me before" (Exodus 4:10 NASB). Since Moses was eighty years old, maybe he got his courage up, for he then added excuse number four, "I am slow of speech and have a heavy tongue." Some scholars have taken this statement to mean that Moses possibly had a speech impediment or was a stutterer. By verse 14, after four excuses, God was angry with Moses and told Moses, "Aaron, the Levite, thy brother, I know he can speak well and he shall be thy spokesman." It is interesting that God identified Aaron to Moses first as "the Levite" and then second as "your brother." With the marriage of Levi's daughter, Jochebed, to Levi's grandson, Amram, it becomes obvious that either as grandchildren or great-grandchildren, that the ancestry of Aaron, Moses, and Miriam is very close to the patriarch Levi. It is possible using the Bible, to trace these two brothers' priestly relatives to include Ezra, Samuel, and other famous priests. This connection to Levi is significant when the census of the tribe of Levites might show a total population of one hundred thousand. God chose Levi from among Israel's twelve sons to be the spiritual leader for the nation of Israel. This one hundred thousand Levite population is to provide spiritual direction and guidance from God to this nation of three million souls. The Levites were only 3 percent of the nation's total population, and these three were the grandchildren of the spiritual patriarch for the entire nation. They were indeed special children! It is little wonder that Levi's daughter, Jochebed, considered her children special. A normal mother's love would cause her to think her children special; the daughter of the spiritual leader appointed by God must have felt an even deeper anxiety for her children, especially when the Pharaoh-god had decreed the murder of all newborn Hebrew males.

The Bible is mostly quiet on Moses's youth and early adulthood to age forty. After years in the desert, Moses, at age eighty, returned to Egypt and reconnected with his siblings. God provided for Moses and Aaron to meet with Pharaoh. In Exodus 6:30, Moses again offers excuse number four in a different format stating, "I am of uncircumcised lips. How then shall Pharaoh harken unto me?"

Have you ever considered the audacity of these slaves even thinking that they might gain an audience with the Pharaoh-god of the world's most powerful nation? The Pharaoh might have reasoned in his own mind, "We built the pyramids one thousand years ago. You are our slaves. Who are you to seek me?"

In Exodus 4:12-16, God replied to Moses, "I have made thee a god to Pharaoh and Aaron thy brother shall be thy prophet. You shall speak to Aaron and Aaron shall speak to Pharaoh." God instructed Moses, "I know Aaron can speak well . . . thou shall speak to Aaron and put words in his mouth. I will be with thy mouth and his mouth and teach you." With God working in Pharaoh's mind to view Moses as a god and Aaron as a prophet, we see the stage being set for the release of the Israelites from bondage. We are familiar with God instructing Aaron to cast his rod down and about its transformation into a serpent. God told Moses to do the exact same thing in the desert (Exodus 4:3 NASB). When Moses picked up the serpent, it became his rod again. In the court of Pharaoh, Aaron's rod also became a serpent. The magicians of Pharaoh all cast down their rods, and they became serpents as well. Aaron's serpent, however, swallowed up the magician's serpents. This is the prologue for the spiritual battle that took place in the next nine meetings between Pharaoh and the men of Elohim. Yahweh will defeat the Egyptian gods of cattle (Apis and Hathor), magic (Thoth), fertility (Min), light (Re) and wind (Amon). After the first two plagues, Yahweh directly attacked nine of the most prominent national pagan gods of Egypt. When Aaron's rod became a serpent and swallowed the magicians' serpents, that event was merely a prelude. The first two plagues raised the pressure on Pharaoh, but the Bible still does not report God distinguishing between His power as Adonai or Yahweh over the helplessness of Pharaoh and his wise men and sorcerers. In eight of the ten plagues, God decisively exhibited His strength and power. In all ten plagues, God triumphed.

After the ten confrontations, what was the score? Egypt lost all its cattle. Three million slaves are preparing to exit Egypt. Strong winds and hail demolished the grain. The other crops were all destroyed. The last remnants of grain in the fields were consumed by swarms of locusts, and all the firstborn humans and beasts died (Exodus 11:15). The earth stank with piles of dead frogs (Exodus 8:14). The land was without water for one week. And, in conclusion, the Egyptians willingly gave their silver, gold, raiment and cattle to the departing slaves. God devastated Egypt, the world's first superpower. Surely this commanded the attention of the Israelites *and* the Egyptians. God demonstrated His power during the first Passover when He protected the Israelites from the death of all first-born man and beasts when He passed over their homes. Immediately thereafter, God instituted the sanctification of the firstborn of man and beast as servants unto God.

In six of the ten plagues, God distinguished between His authority and Pharaoh's pseudo-godly power. Yahweh-Elohim triumphed over Pharaoh in every plague. Not only did He triumph, He also attacked the gods of the Egyptian worshippers of the god of the Nile, the god of cattle, the god of magic, etc. Remember the Egyptians loathed shepherds. As a result, in plague number five, God killed the Egyptian cattle (Exodus 9:6 NASB). The Egyptians considered the Nile as the giver of all goodness. The plagues of the blood, frogs, and flies were related to their dependence on the Nile for their water supply and commerce.

You may wonder why the contest between God and Pharaoh that occurred three thousand five hundred years ago is worth studying today. There are two reasons. One, these events certainly document the spiritual authority of Moses and Aaron and the lineage of Levi. A few months after the Exodus was complete, God instructed Moses to anoint Aaron as high priest. Over twenty five generations of high priests from Aaron's lineage provided spiritual leadership to the nation of Israel for nine hundred years. The ancient historian, Josephus, recorded ninety high priests serving from the time of Aaron to the era of Jesus's life. The second and more important reason is found in Revelation 15:1, which declares, "I saw another sign in heaven. Great and marvelous, seven angels having the seven last plagues, for in them is filled up the wrath of God." Listed in Exodus chapters 7-11 are ten plagues in the spiritual contest between Moses and Aaron versus Pharaoh. In Revelation 16, the dialogue lists the seven plagues at the end of time. Compare the two lists of plagues, one from the second book of the Bible and the other from the last book of God's word.

The Plagues

Ten Plagues of Exodus 7-11		Seven Plagues of Revelation 16
Blood	Sea and rivers	(Bowl #2 & Bowl #3)
Frogs	Frogs	(Bowl # 6)
Lice		
Flies		
Cattle		
Boils	Sores	(Bowl # 1)
Hail	Fire, hail, earthquakes	(Bowl # 4)
Locusts		
Darkness	Darkness, pain	(Bowl # 5)
First-born's Death	"Death" of Babylon	(Bowl # 7)

The march to freedom began in Exodus 12:1-2. Verse 2 announces this is the beginning of the Hebrew calendar that is still in use by Jews to this day. Therefore, the Jewish calendar is dated from the date of the Exodus from Egypt. A new nation is beginning! It was no longer a family, clan or tribe. No, a new nation is marching through the providentially divided waters to freedom and destiny. God's calling of Abraham six hundred years earlier into a covenant is now being fulfilled. In man's eyes, how often do we care about a contract being fulfilled six hundred years into the future? Man may not care or deem it relevant, but in God's eyes "one day is with the Lord as a thousand years and a thousand years as one day" (2 Peter 3:8). To God, the Exodus occurs a *mere* six hundred years after God had made His covenant with Abraham.

At this point, could there be any doubt left in any Egyptian or Israelite's mind as to who was in charge of Earth, life, plagues, or death?

Well, yes, there is doubt. There is doubt in Pharaoh's mind. He ordered over six hundred chariots to pursue the departing three-million-person entourage with its accompanying herds, flocks, and cattle. Studies have been conducted to see how fast a marching group of people and their livestock could travel. When experts analyze livestock, they estimate the animals could only move, at best, five or six miles per hour. More likely, the speed might have been just one to two miles per hour. Consider another observation provided by close reading of the Scripture. Exodus 14 informs us that Pharaoh and his army caught up to the Israelites late in the day at sunset. Notice the Israelites marched into the Red Sea not in the daylight, but "throughout the night."

As the Israelites walked on a dry seabed, the Angel of God, who has been a pillar of cloud before the Israelites, moved behind them to create darkness to the Egyptian army (Exodus 14:16, 21-22 NASB). Simultaneously, the pillar became a pillar of fire to provide light to the Israelites (Exodus 14:20) in order for them to walk at night (Exodus 13:21). These twin pillars of cloud and fire guided the Israelites for the next forty years (Exodus 40:34-38 NASB). As the sun rose, God instructed Moses to stretch out his hand to let the waters be restored to their normal level. Consider these two points: First, the Israelites marched on dry ground, yet at dawn, the Egyptian chariot wheels came off (maybe due to mud?). Second, from sunset to sunrise, three million Israelites and great multitudes of animals cross the sea, whichever sea it may have been. The point is this dry pathway could not have been just a narrow trench or footpath. It had to be very wide to accommodate millions of people and thousands of plodding animals in just one ten-hour night.

In Exodus 12 is a wonderful tidbit. Verses 35-36 describe the fulfillment of Exodus 3:22 when God utterly defeated the Pharaoh's magicians and Egyptian gods. Verse 36 states the departed slaves even found favor in the sight of the Egyptians, as the Egyptians gave them their jewels, silver, and gold. Now we know how the slaves obtained the gold Aaron used to fashion their golden calf. This also explains where Moses found the gold to make the Ark of the Covenant, cherubim, altars, candlesticks, utensils, and other tabernacle equipment. These will be the golden fixtures used in the Tent of Tabernacle, and then later in the Temple for over six hundred years. Exodus 38:24-25 tells us that forty-one thousand ounces of gold and one hundred forty-one thousand ounces of silver will be used for these spiritual purposes. At today's prices, that is over $50 million in gold and almost $4 million in silver. These collected gold and silver amounts are used only in the tabernacle tent and its furnishings. David and Solomon will collect more gold and silver for the Temple's construction.

Scripture notes that it is three months from the time of the Exodus until the Israelites' arrival in Sinai (Exodus 19:1).

The Bible reader needs to keep in mind there has been a lapse of four-hundred-thirty-years between the end of Genesis and the beginning of Exodus. In contrast, once the Exodus occurs, Moses yielded to God and rapidly moved forward with His plan. The Israelites arrived in the Sinai wilderness just three months after the Exodus (Exodus 19:1). In the following months, God gave the Ten Commandments on stone tablets, and an offering was taken. The Ark of the Covenant, bowls, lavers, priestly garments and tools were fashioned under the direction of Bezalel, God's general contractor (Exodus 31:2-4). The tabernacle was erected twelve months after the Exodus (Exodus 40:17). Passover was observed two weeks later (Numbers 9:1-3, 11). About seventeen days after observing Passover, God instructed Moses to conduct a census of soldiers (Numbers 1:1-3). Concurrently, Moses began writing the Book of Numbers. Approximately, three weeks later, the Book of Leviticus was completed (Numbers 10:11). The Israelites march north shortly thereafter to exit the Sinai wilderness.

Busy, Busy Moses

Number of Days after Exodus	Event	Reference
3 days	People complain about thirst	Exodus 15:22-24
45 days	People complain about food	Exodus 16:3
90 days	Arrival in Sinai	Exodus 19:1
93 days	Ten Commandments given	Exodus 19:1, 11
366 days	Tabernacle furnishings created	Exodus 40:17
379 days	Passover is observed	Numbers 9:1-3, 11
396 days	Conduct census of soldiers	Numbers 1:1-3
415 days	Book of Leviticus Completed	Numbers 10:11
415 days	Beginning Book of Numbers	Numbers 10:11

Exodus 19:1 dates this chapter to the third month after the Exodus. This is very early in the forty-year period of wandering. Verse 6 talks about God's desire for a kingdom of priests. Note, *king* and *priest* are used in conjunction with each other. Near the conclusion of the Bible both passages in Revelation 1:6 and 5:10 use the phrase "made us kings and priests to our God." The first evidence of this plan of God is in Exodus 19, and then again we see God's same plan in Revelation 5 (Exodus 19:6; Revelation 5:10). God's ideal design for mankind was the joint rule of kings and priests.

Another informative tidbit of Exodus 12 is discovered in verses 37-38. Verse 37 gives us a census of six hundred thousand men, with the babies, children, women, and elderly added to the six hundred thousand men available for warfare. Verse 38 describes a "mixed multitude" of others accompanied the children of Israel. We do not often hear it mentioned, but Exodus 9:20 and 12:38 makes note of the Egyptians or others who "feared the word of the Lord." When the plague of hail was pronounced, these Egyptians retreated to their homes, taking their livestock inside along with them. In addition, the verse declares "flocks, herds, and very much cattle" also made the Exodus. All the Egyptian cattle were killed in the fifth plague (Exodus 9:6). When the slaves leave, they are taking with them the remaining "very much cattle."

Exodus 16:1 informs the reader the Exodus journey was just six weeks old by this time. Verses 2, 7, 8, 9, and 11 tell us about the three million people complaining to Moses. In verse 3, they complained about having no "pots of flesh." Yet a huge number of livestock traveled with the Israelites in a desert area with little vegetation for nourishment. Did the sheep, goats, and cattle give no milk? Did the livestock "go dry"? As livestock breeders and shepherds, the Israelites did not think of their animals as food but as their investment accounts, their retirement plans, and as an asset. Although surrounded by thousands or millions of head of livestock, the people complained about having no pots of meat. This may also attest to the Seventh Day Adventist point of view that, while God gave Noah's family the permission to eat meat, it was not eaten very often by the Israelites.

A more modern thought: if livestock were the Israelites' "mobile wealth" and retirement plan, when Moses instructed Aaron to sacrifice goats, sheep, and cattle, what God was asking for was their savings accounts and their IRA's. The Israelites saved their emergency funds, their rainy day funds, by investing in their livestock. God required sacrifices of the very cattle they had willingly denied themselves as food. God was asking for their net worth to be freely offered to him as acts of obedience, devotion, love, and trust. God requested the people to trust Him to provide for them. Hopefully, they remembered how God had provided a sacrificial animal to Abraham, in lieu of Isaac, five hundred years earlier.

God heard their grumblings and provided quail as meat to these wanderers. There are several interesting points about those quail God provided. Before the winter months arrive, quail and other birds migrate from Europe down into the Sahel region of West Africa. This flyway may be the largest in the world. It even has a name—the Eastern Mediterranean Flyway. Some ornithologists estimate over three hundred species totaling possibly one billion birds make this semi-annual migration following the Sinai flyway.

This route mimics the Jordan River rift to the south end of the Dead Sea. At that juncture, rather than continuing due south and having to fly one hundred twenty miles over parched desert and then another one hundred fifty miles over the Gulf of Aqaba, the quail fly in a southwesterly direction into the heart of the Sinai Peninsula. Once over the central portion of the Sinai, the course is redirected due south again. In the spring, the quail make the reverse journey from the Sahel of West Central Africa across the Gulf of Suez and the Red Sea. Exodus 13:4 remarks the Exodus occurred during the month of Abib. Abib corresponded to the months of March or April.

By knowing this fact, it is apparent the quail would be migrating northward in the spring and they had just flown over the Red Sea and Gulf of Suez. After their extended flight over a body of water, naturally these birds sought land on which to light and rest.

About twelve months later (Numbers 9:1), the Israelites depart from Sinai, headed more or less north. Once again (Numbers 11:5) we see the people complaining. In the earlier account in Exodus, God promised flesh (quail) for dinner and bread (manna) for breakfast (Exodus 16:12). (Psalm 78:25 calls manna "angel food.") Likewise, in Exodus 16 and Numbers 11, God providentially provided quail. God has the power and authority to provide the quail any way He so chose, but the flyway over the Sinai used by the migrating birds is an interesting possibility.

Quail have long wing spans, which hint at their migratory nature. Most game birds do not exhibit such strong migratory behavior. The diet of this particular species tends to be seeds and insects they find near the ground. They tend to scurry about rather than fly when frightened. Even when forced to fly, a quail will soon come back down to the ground. Read Numbers 11:31-34. The Bible accurately names the quail and describes their behavior. Not only does the Bible give us details about the flyway, but also *when* during the year the quail will appear, *why* they will be tired, *how* high they will fly, and *where* they will be eating. If the Bible is this precise and exact about these birds, is it not even more trustworthy on spiritual matters?

Sadly, not only is the Bible accurate in describing the quail, the Bible is also accurate in describing the Israelites' spiritual condition (Psalms 106:13-17). Consider what God told Moses when he instructed him to come up on Mt. Sinai to receive the Ten Commandments (Exodus 24:12, 31:18 NASB). Notice Moses climbs up alone to Mt. Sinai after he left Joshua down at a lower elevation. After forty-six days, Moses came down the mountain side and brought with him the two tablets of stone. As Moses returned to the people in the camp, he saw the infamous, golden calf that has been molten and fashioned. Aaron has even built an altar before it (Exodus 32:5 NASB). God had already spoken the Ten Commandments to Moses. These are found, with additional commentary, beginning in Exodus 20. But up until this point, all the instructions from God were oral. In ancient Egypt, Pharaoh was considered a god. In all of the archeological digs in Egypt, no *written* law codes have ever been found. This lack of written law in Egypt was in sharp contrast to Moses's receiving the two stone tablets with the Ten Commandments written by none other than God Himself. After the Exodus, in just three months, the Hebrew slaves had gone from rule by a human god and a royal law based on the Pharaoh's changing whims to Moses climbing Mount Sinai into a dark cloud and returning with the Royal Law which never changes, chiseled in stone.

When Moses arrived in the camp, he is carrying the first "concrete" (so to speak) hard evidence of the unchanging Law in his arms. We have all seen painted pictures and replicas of the two tablets of stone depicting the Ten Commandments which Moses brought down from Mt. Sinai. A close reading of Exodus 32:15 shows us an interesting detail. The two tablets had commandments written on *both sides* of the stones. Many scholars believe the tablets were six inches long and less than four inches wide. With writing on both sides, the Ten Commandments could easily be etched into two small stones of this size. In verse 25, Moses's anger, as the Bible describes it, "waxes hot." In response, Moses threw the two tablets down, breaking them. The golden calf is destroyed and the people are made to drink water mixed with the gold dust (verse 20). After three thousand idol worshippers are killed, God still affirms the giving of the Promised Land to Abraham, Isaac, and Jacob's seed (Exodus 33:1).

God demanded Moses come up on Mt. Sinai once again to receive the Ten Commandments. However, rather than God fashioning the stones as He had done on the first occasion, when Moses and Joshua walked up empty handed, God now instructed Moses to hew for himself two stone tablets. Moses is to bring the two tablets up Mount Sinai and God said, "I will write on these tablets the words that were in the first tablets, which thou breakest" (Exodus 34:1). Unlike the first occasion, when Moses's successor, Joshua, accompanied him, God informed Moses that he is to come up alone. Exodus 32:4 states Moses was obedient and trekked up the incline with the two tablets he had chiseled overnight out of rock.

In going alone and carrying his two hewn tablets, undoubtedly Moses has ample time to ponder his spiritual meeting with God. At this encounter, God speaks further about observing three feasts during the year, various offerings, and Sabbath behavior.

Another occasion when Moses's anger got the better of him is recorded after the death of Miriam in Numbers 20. As they frequently did on this journey, the people complain about not having the diet they wanted of onions, garlic, melons, and pots of flesh. In Numbers 20, the typical complaint was "no grapes, seeds, figs, pomegranates, or water." (Also, consider this thought: *How did the million head of livestock survive with almost no water?*) By this time, the tabernacle had been erected. Aaron and Moses entered the tabernacle and bowed down before God with the people's complaint. God appeared in His glory and told Moses to "speak to the rock" before the complainers' eyes and water will come forth not only for three million people but also for all of the animals (Numbers 20:8 NASB). Aaron and Moses appeared before the people. In a harsh statement, Moses called the Israelites "rebels" and rhetorically asked, "Must we fetch you water out of this rock?" Before the congregation can answer, Moses struck the rock with his rod twice and water bursts forth for the people and animals. Immediately God declared judgment on Moses and Aaron for their lack of faith in His might and authority by not just speaking to the rock, but twice striking it. They were guilty of appearing to usurp God's power by being disobedient. Moses had said, "Must we must fetch you water?" God, not Moses, provided the water. The brothers' punishment is that neither will enter the Promised Land. Aaron, the older brother, will die first; afterward, his son, Eleazar, will succeed him as high priest (Numbers 20:28 NASB). Moses will be permitted to look into all of the land promised to Abraham's seed, but he too will not enter, as reported in Deuteronomy 34:4-5. Nevertheless, despite all Moses's faults, Deuteronomy 34:10 declares Moses to be the single greatest prophet of the Bible.

Before becoming too condescending of Moses and Aaron, consider another point: the word *murmur*, or some extension of this root word, occurs forty times in the Bible. Of these forty occasions, over one half of the time it is when Moses and Aaron were dealing with these three million people in the desert who were living in tents, eating only manna, always short of water, and having to provide sustenance to large numbers of livestock. Legally, a new nation is being formed, but as yet without any real estate. Spiritually, Creator God via Moses and Aaron is introducing His chosen seed of Israel to the Ten Commandments, proper feasts, sacrifices, how to relate to fellow humans as well as beasts, dietary laws, and proper conduct. Furthermore, a tabernacle, altar, candlesticks, rugs, the Ark of the Covenant, skins, ropes, couplings, tents, fabrics and other items need to be constructed. Would we murmur any less?

One final thought: We do not hear too much about Moses's two sons by Zipporah, Jethro's daughter. They were not pure Israelites, as Zipporah was a Midianite. But later, as priests, these sons of Moses had important duties in the temple. They will not be leading the people in worship or sacrifices, but they will be in charge of the treasury and the dedicated things. The following chart will verify the important duties of the sons of Moses in the tabernacle.

Genealogy of Moses

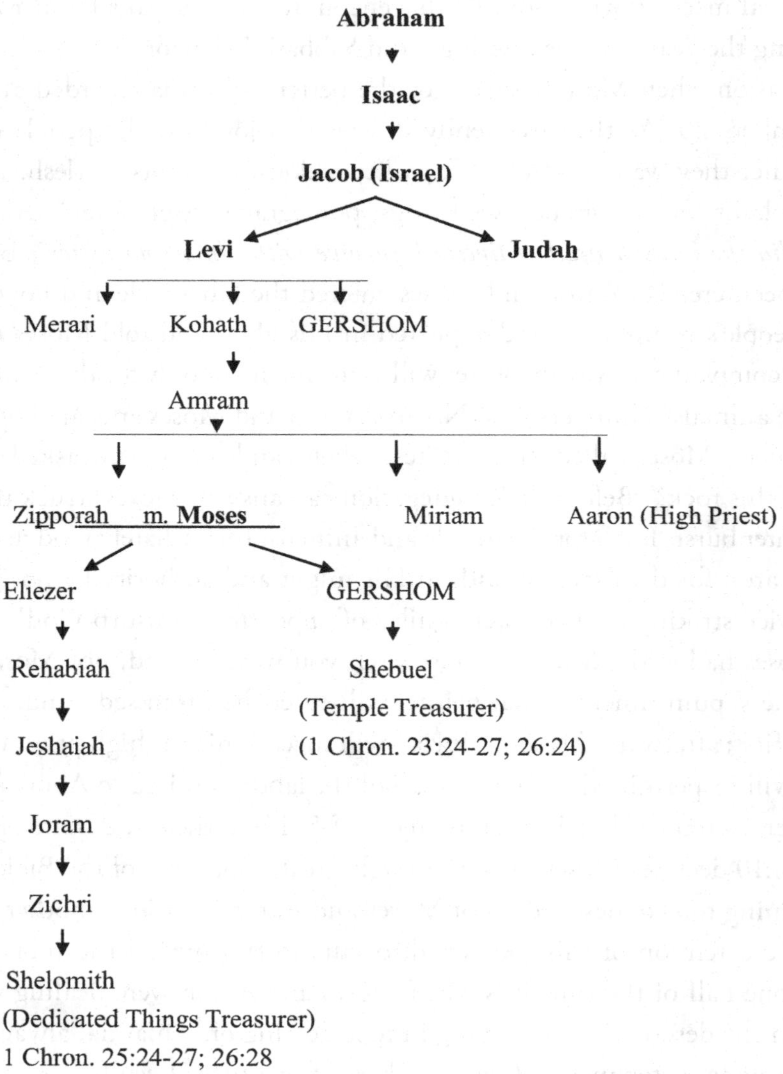

Abraham

↓

Isaac

↓

Jacob (Israel)

Levi   **Judah**

Merari   Kohath   GERSHOM

↓

Amram

↓   ↓   ↓

Zipporah   m. **Moses**   Miriam   Aaron (High Priest)

Eliezer   GERSHOM

↓   ↓

Rehabiah   Shebuel

↓   (Temple Treasurer)

Jeshaiah   (1 Chron. 23:24-27; 26:24)

↓

Joram

↓

Zichri

↓

Shelomith
(Dedicated Things Treasurer)
1 Chron. 25:24-27; 26:28

What have we learned from Moses's life and its divergence from the lineage of the Royal Seed?

1. Moses's mother, Jochebed, was Levi's daughter. Not only was Jochebed Moses's mother, she was also Moses's great aunt. This family was an integral part of the distinguished spiritual tribe designated by God to come through Levi, the spiritual leader of Israel. Moses's father, Amram, was Levi's grandson. The Levites were special. They comprised less than 3 percent of the nation's population, but were the nation's spiritual leadership. Moses's grandfather, Kohath, was "a first among equals."

2. Satan attempted to kill the first scribe of Israel while Moses was just a baby. His mother and sister saved him.

3. God, in His omnipotence, used Pharaoh's daughter, the daughter of the very man trying to kill the babe, to save Moses.

4. Of these two brothers, Moses and Aaron, one became the *first scribe* and administrator of the new nation, while the other became the *first high priest.*

5. Moses lived four decades in regal splendor and four decades as a lowly shepherd in the desert.

6. Moses's first eighty years was spent learning royal governance and then guerilla-like desert training. God has been ideally preparing and equipping Moses for his real assignment. God spent eight decades preparing Moses for his purpose— the last four decades of his life.

7. The challenge of Moses's working environment was almost impossible.

8. The two brothers were in a difficult situation, but were very compatible, utilizing their different strengths.

9. Moses probably had a stutter, and he certainly had a temper. He was also a murderer. Before God selected Aaron as the first high priest, Aaron constructed a golden calf and an altar as idols for the people to worship. Their failures prove God can use anyone who is obedient.

10. As an author, Moses recorded the facts: even his own four excuses, and his own shortcomings. It is plain God began using the two brothers initially to accomplish His eternal plan for a relationship with those who desire to be in the presence of their Creator, the Father God, forever.

Moses's Relatives

Name	Relationship	APPROXIMATE Dates
Noah	Great-grandfather, 14 generations removed	±3500 BC
Abraham	Great-grandfather, 3 generations removed	±2100 BC
Jacob (Israel)	Great grandfather – father of nation	±1800 BC
Levi	Grandfather – Tribal leader	±1700 BC
Jochebed	Mother and great aunt	±1400 BC
Aaron	Brother- First High Priest	±1350 BC
Miriam	Sister – Singer	±1350 BC
Samuel	Cousin, 17 generations removed	±1100 BC
Ezra	Great-nephew, 15 generations removed	500 BC
Jesus	Cousin, 52 generations removed	AD 30

Chapter 13

Aaron

> Make Aaron's garments to consecrate him, that he may minister as priest to me . . . Aaron shall carry the names of the sons of Israel in the breastpiece of judgment over his heart when he enters the holy place for a memorial before the Lord continually. (Exodus 28:3, 29 NASB)

Aaron's selection by God from among Levi's descendants is important. The Levites were to be revered above all other Israelites, and they enjoyed a special and unique status. In Numbers 3, after the fourth census was conducted, the Levites numbered just over twenty-two thousand. The next smallest tribes were Manasseh at thirty-two thousand two hundred and Benjamin at thirty-five thousand four hundred. The remaining ten tribes have populations ranging from forty thousand five hundred to in excess of seventy-four thousand. We see that the tribe of Levi was one-third smaller than even the next smallest tribe.

This unique and specific status of the Levites caused them to focus all their energy on the spiritual needs of the people and the tabernacle. As Numbers 1:51 states, the Levites exclusively were to take down and set up the tabernacle. Among the three clans within the tribe of Levi, each was assigned specific, specialized, duties (Numbers 3-4). First, the duties of the clan of Gershon were concerned with the tent itself, skins, and other coverings and hangings for the doorway, curtains, and cords (Numbers 3:25-26 NASB). Second, the clan of Kohath was responsible for "the most holy things," including the Ark of the Covenant, the tables, the golden candlesticks, gold covered altar, and golden vessels of the sanctuary (Numbers 4:4 NASB). Today's value of these holy things would be over $50 million dollars. The Kohathites were to wrap the holy articles in the veil, then use animal skins as a second covering. Finally, the animal skins were enclosed in blue or scarlet cloth. These wrappings made these precious items safe for travel whenever God directed the nation to move forward (Numbers 4:1-15 NASB). Even among the Kohathites, only selected tribe members actually saw the golden furnishings positioned within the Temple. The other Levites who set up the tabernacle never saw the golden articles used in worship. Third, the family of Merari was in charge of the timbers of the tabernacle, the bars, the pillars, and sockets to uphold the curtains, walls, coverings, and other vessels of the tabernacle (Exodus 26:15-37 NASB). The sanctity of the tabernacle was very evident to both the Levites and the non-Levites.

Recall earlier, if a non-Levite even approached the door of the tabernacle, they were put to death (Numbers 1:51, 3:10 NASB).

Moses' and Aaron's grandfather, Kohath, was "a first among equals." As we just read, of the three sons of Levi and their respective duties, Scripture clearly shows that the more religious and holy duties were assigned to the sons of Kohath over the sons of Gershon and Merari, who were more involved with the physical construction tasks of erecting and dismantling the tabernacle tent whenever it was moved (Numbers 3:36-37 NASB). Kohath's descendants were to be focused on the golden Ark of the Covenant, maintaining the golden candlesticks, golden table of showbread and the various golden bowls, pans, jars, spoons and platters. The sons of Kohath also maintained the bronze altar which was used for the sacrifices offered by fire. Whenever the pillars of clouds or fire moved, that was God's method of instructing the people to move the tabernacle to another location. To prepare for the move, it was the Kohathites who wrapped the golden contents of the tabernacle in the veil, animal skins, and blue, scarlet, or purple cloths for safe travel. This partially explains the mystery of the tabernacle among the worshippers of Yahweh. Even the other Levites from the clans of Gershon and Merari never saw the golden objects used inside the tent to worship Yahweh. Truly, Kohath was a "first among equals."

Even today among Jews, differential treatment is often given to fellow Jews with surnames such as Cohen, Kahn, Kohen, Kantor, Kaplan, Caplan, and Cahn. These names are all considered to be descendants of the original sons of Kohath.

The first census in Numbers 1 assigned a prince to each of the twelve tribes of Israel. For the tribe of Judah, it was Nahshon (there is that name again). Once a prince was dedicated for each tribe, the numbers of available soldiers were counted. Israel had twelve sons. Joseph was dropped out of the listing to be replaced by his two sons, Ephraim and Manasseh (1Chronicles 5: 1-3). When Levi is added to the list, we have thirteen tribes. The Levites, however, were not to fight; they were not counted in the first census of soldiers. This necessitated the second census to determine the number of Levites. The sum of Levites totaled twenty-two thousand (Numbers 3:39 NASB). Later, Numbers 3 tells us of the third census to arrive at the number of first-born sons. The total accounting of the first-born sons was twenty-two thousand two hundred seventy-three (Numbers 3:43 NASB).

These first-born sons were taxed five shekels each in verse 47, and this money was given to Moses for distribution to the Levites in verses 50-51. No longer will the first-born of man and beast be set apart as "special;" God announced in Numbers 3:12, 45 that the Levites were "to be mine." The Bible explains in explicit detail the reason the first-born had been set apart in Exodus 13:2. It was because of the sparing of the first-born lives in Egypt. God took *a census of the Levites and they replaced an approximately equal number of the first-born*. The Levites were to receive no agricultural land, only cities and suburbs in the promised new land. The other twelve tribes were to be herders and shepherds in an agrarian economy. The Levites were to be "city folks," with pasture extending one-half mile beyond the city walls. This half-mile distance from the city walls is about the same distance the tribes were to camp from the tabernacle in the desert. These Levites were to focus on the religious-holy-spiritual needs of the nation. Remember, they were the smallest tribe and were only three percent of the nation's entire population.

Numbers further gives the population totals for each of the three families of Levi's three sons: Gershon, 7,500; Kohath, 8,600; and Merari, 6,200. The men of Kohath numbered only 8,600 out of 625,000 adult males. Percentage-wise, the descendants of Kohath were less than one and one-half percent of the nation's total males. In other words, out of one thousand typical Israelite men, less than fifteen were to be Levites from the sub-clan of Kohath.

Quickly, 1 Chronicles 6:1-3 reduces the broad genealogy of Levi to Kohath's family. Levi's grandchildren (by their mother Jochebed) were Aaron, Moses, and Miriam. Miriam was the oldest, and she had secured a nurse for baby Moses. Aaron was three years older than Moses (Exodus 7:7 NASB). In verse three, we see these three grandchildren from the smallest tribe were not just special because they were children from the tiniest tribe. No, they were the grandchildren and great-grandchildren of the tribe's patriarch, Levi. In addition, through their father Amram, they were also the grandchildren of Kohath, the sub-clan selected to tend to the most holy duties of the tabernacle. It is interesting to note the sequence of the children in verse three. These three siblings were not listed in birth order. Aaron was first, then Moses, and finally Miriam. The listing is not by age or Miriam would be first and Moses last. Neither is it "ladies first." Aaron is listed first because he will become the first high priest. The chapter continues with Aaron's genealogy and the successive high priests until the nation of Judah is carried off to Babylon by King Nebuchadnezzar in 586 BC. This chapter proves that about twenty-five sons of the high priest will also become high priests, fulfilling the same role as their fathers. In 1 Chronicles chapter 3 is something similar, with the twenty kings of Judah listed as successors to their fathers. For over twenty generations, the genealogy is important in both the priestly tribe of Levi (1 Chronicles 6:1-15) and the royal tribe of Judah (1 Chronicles 3:1-16).

Ezra, the returning priest, confirms this genealogy is important, for in the seventh chapter of the book of Ezra, he documents his role and authority by showing his lineage to the first high priest, Aaron. Although Ezra was not a high priest, his brother Jehozadak was. First Chronicles 6:15 mentions the last high priest before Nebuchadnezzar's defeat of Judah. This last high priest's name was Jehozadak. In other words, the prophet Ezra's brother was the high priest at the time of Judah's Babylonian captivity. The genealogy of the high priests is vital to the priestly lineage. Under Levitical law, a man was not allowed to become a priest if he was unable to offer his family's lineage. Ezra 2 and Nehemiah 7 are examples of this. As a former captive, Ezra's genealogy to the first high priest and the last high priest proclaims his authority to address the spiritual needs of the nation. Haggai 1:1, 12 and Zechariah 6:11 exhibits the documentation of the authority and holiness that resided in the high priest.

The following chart verifies the relationship of Aaron to both his priestly and his royal relatives.

Genealogy of Aaron

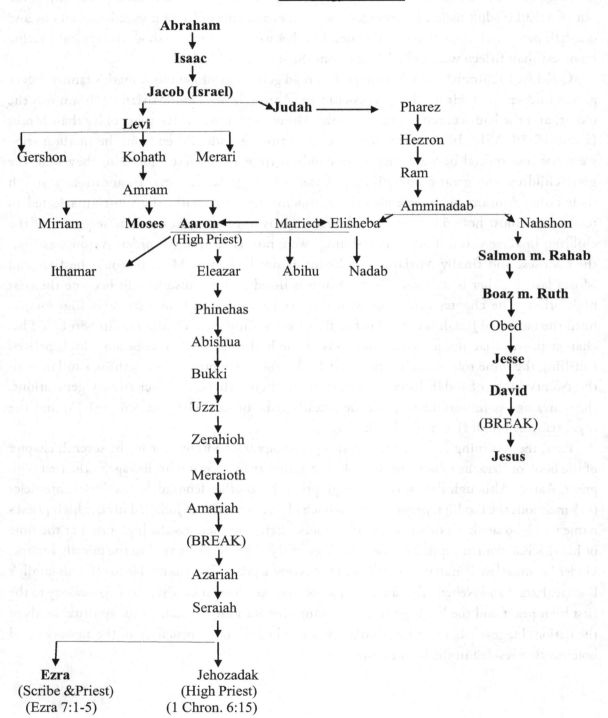

Aaron was the first high priest. The Bible faithfully records the almost thirty high priests that follow Aaron. Earlier, in the desert, when Moses told God he was "slow of speech," God acknowledged this and told Moses He would talk to Moses. In turn, Moses would talk to Aaron, who would speak with the Pharaoh. This same verse also shows God's omnipotence. God declares that Aaron will come out to meet Moses. The edge of the desert was nearly two hundred miles long. How did Aaron know when and where to go into the edge of the desert to meet his brother who disappeared forty years earlier under mysterious circumstances? Yet God directs Aaron to the precise spot where Moses emerged. The answer is that Aaron was obedient to God (Exodus 4:27-28 NASB). Aaron was sensitive to God's prompting. Aaron's wife was Elisheba, the daughter of a man named Amminadab (Exodus 6:23 NASB). We do not know much about him, but in 1 Chronicles 2:3 and 2:10, the Bible shows us Amminadab was from the tribe of Judah, a descendant in fact of Judah himself by Tamar's son, Pharez. Furthermore, he seemed to have religious leanings, for his daughter's name incorporated "El," the Hebrew for "God." Aaron, as Elisheba's husband, was also holy. Aaron was consecrated to the Lord's work in Exodus 28. The bride and groom were each from one of the two most prominent tribes. Aaron was from the tribe of Levi, and Elisheba was from the tribe of Judah. This was very much a high society wedding. Aaron was the grandson of Levi and Elisheba was the great-great-great granddaughter of Judah. In this marriage, the kingly lineage of Judah was represented by Elisheba and the priestly tribe of Levi was represented by Aaron. In a future chapter, we will see yet another princess from the royal family of Judah who would also wed another high priest from the priestly tribe of Levi.

Aaron, a Levite, married Elisheba from the nearby tribe of Judah. (See the chart in chapter 8 showing the encampment of the tribes.) Aaron held the position of high priest for nearly forty years. He and Elisheba had four sons. Although he and Elisheba were holy, the two oldest sons offered "strange fire" at the tabernacle. Because of this, they were killed with fire from God (Leviticus 10:1-2 NASB). Some have supposed the brothers were intoxicated due to the command in verse 9 in a section in which priests are provided guidance on going into the tabernacle.

In Leviticus 16, Moses is told by God to instruct Aaron to enter the Holy of Holies only once a year. Certainly, after the two older sons were killed by fire, Aaron, Elisheba and the two younger sons, Eleazar and Ithamar, paid rapt attention to God's instruction to Moses.

Moses was later instructed to take Aaron and Eleazar up on Mount Hor, to remove the high priest garments from Aaron, and to place the apparel upon Eleazar. Aaron died upon the mountain. After Moses and his nephew came down from the mountain, the Israelites mourned Aaron's death for thirty days. Later, in Deuteronomy 34, Moses also died on a mountain, Mount Nebo, after God showed Moses the Promised Land that the children of Israel were about to enter. This was the real estate that had been promised five to eight hundred years earlier to Abraham, Isaac, Jacob, and their seed. Moses was also mourned for thirty days in Deuteronomy 34:8.

Earlier, we noted the Tree of Life in Adam's Garden of Eden and how it reappeared in the New Jerusalem (Revelation 22:2). Later, when discussing the configuration of the camps and tabernacle while in the desert, we also compared the layout to the twelve gates surrounding the New Jerusalem in Revelation 21.

Before leaving Aaron, it is important to spend a few minutes studying the high priest's attire, specifically as itemized in Exodus 28:15-21. In this passage, God instructed Moses as to the Breastplate of Judgment which Aaron was to wear over his chest and heart. The breastplate was to be a square with four rows of precious and semi-precious stones. Each row was to have three stones. In all, twelve stones were to be set in braided or filigreed gold. Verse 21 denoted the commemoration of the name of each of Israel's twelve sons. Now turn in your Bible to Revelation 21, the New Jerusalem chapter. Especially read verses 19-20. *At least eight of the stones molded into Aaron's breastplate appear as foundation stones in the New Jerusalem.* On the breastplate, the twelve stones were set in gold. In the New Jerusalem, near these twelve foundation stones, the streets are to be paved with gold. In the New Jerusalem, we have the Crystal River, the Tree of Life, the twelve gates, each named for a tribe, surrounding the city, and now the streets of gold with twelve foundation stones similar to several stones on Aaron's breastplate.

Before Aaron established a priestly order, an older order of priests already existed. Hebrews 7:3 describes a priest from the order of Melchizedek and declares Melchizedek was a priest of God Most High (Genesis 14:18).

Furthermore, Hebrews 7:2 also describes Melchizedek as the King of Salem (i.e. Jerusalem). In Melchizedek, we see a dual role for one person. Melchizedek was both priest and king. Hebrews 7:3 offers a glimpse of this priest "without father, without mother, without genealogy, having neither beginning of days nor end of life, but made like unto the son of God abideth a priest continually." The grandfather of Aaron was Levi. Furthermore, Levi was described as coming out of the loins of Abraham. But Abraham offered a tithe to the king of Salem, Melchizedek, hundreds of years before Levi was even born. Hebrews 7:11 tells us "perfection will not be in the Levitical priesthood." The priesthood of Melchizedek will be superior to the priesthood of Aaron.

During Jesus's trials in Matthew 26, the continued corruption in the position of the high priest is unmistakable, as Caiaphas delivers Jesus to Pontius Pilate.

Eventually, the "good news" is found in the New Testament book of Hebrews.

> "Therefore, He had to be made like His brethren in all things that He might become a merciful and faithful High Priest. . . Therefore, holy brethren, partakers of a Heavenly calling, consider Jesus the Apostle and High Priest of our confession" (Hebrews 2:17; 3:1 NASB).

> "Seeing then that we have a great High Priest that has passed through the Heavens, Jesus the Son of God, let us hold fast our profession. For we have not a High Priest which cannot sympathize with our weaknesses but was in all points tempted like we are, yet without sin" (Hebrews 4:14-15).

Hebrews 7:12-14 informed us the priesthood will be changed eventually, but for now, in implementing the Law of Moses, Aaron, Moses's older brother, will be the first high priest. Refer to the chart of Aaron's genealogy at the end of this chapter.

Upon marrying Elisheba, Aaron became the brother-in-law of Nahshon. In turn, Aaron was "Uncle Aaron" to Salmon. Eventually, through the lineage of Salmon, *Aaron was to be the great-great-great . . . great uncle to none other than Jesus himself.* Aaron, the first high priest, through several generations will become a great uncle to none other than Jesus himself, several times removed.

What did we learn about Aaron?

1. Aaron became Israel's first high priest.
2. Because Aaron was eloquent in speech, he was the spokesman for Moses to Pharaoh.
3. Upwards of twenty-five generations of Aaron's descendants served as high priest to the nation of Israel.
4. Upon marrying Elisheba, Aaron became great-uncle to Jesus, over thirty generations removed.

Aaron's Relatives

Name	Relationship	APPROXIMATE Dates
Abraham	Great-grandfather, 4 generations removed	±2100 BC
Isaac	Great-great-great grandfather	±1900 BC
Jacob	Great-grandfather	±1800 BC
Judah	Great-uncle	±1700 BC
Levi	Grandfather (and Great-grandfather)	±1700 BC
Moses	Brother; author of first 5 books of Bible	±1350 BC
Nahshon	Brother-in-law, in direct lineage of Jesus	±1350 BC
Elisheba	Wife; sister of Nahshon	±1300 BC
Samuel	Cousin, 17 generations removed	1000 BC
Ezra	Great-grandson, 14 generations removed	500 BC
Jesus	Great-nephew, 33 generations removed	AD 30

Chapter 14

Nahshon

> Amminadab begat Nahshon, *prince* of the children of Judah. (1 Chronicles 2:10, emphasis added)

Authors of the first fifteen books of the Old Testament were Moses, Joshua, Samuel, Jeremiah, and Ezra. These five authors covered two thousand years and tell the story of an entire people group.

When the material from the five authors is integrated, a cohesive synopsis emerges. One example is Nahshon, who appears in only seven passages in the entire Bible. His name occurs in three Old Testament books and two New Testament books. At first glance, he appears to be less than a minor figure in God's word.

In Numbers 1:7, Moses states Nahshon is the leader of the tribe of Judah. In the next chapter, Moses tells us Nahshon is captain of Judah and leader of the entire caravan when God instructed the nation to move forward in the desert. Numbers 7 calls Nahshon a prince. Nahshon led the tribe of Judah in offerings made as gifts for the dedication of the temple. Numbers 10 is an account of the nation leaving Sinai with Nahshon leading the way under the banner of Judah as directed by God to Moses. Nahshon has a sister; her name is Elisheba. She became the wife of the first high priest, Aaron. Remember still earlier, when we talked about the twelve tribes, Judah and Levi were mentioned more in the Bible than the other ten tribes combined. Nahshon and Elisheba were from the tribe of Judah. Aaron was from the clan of Levi.

From the whole of mankind, the Bible has consistently, slowly, and persistently, sharpened its focus on fewer tribes, fewer people groups, and still fewer clans. In the chapter about Levi, the text strays for the first time outside the lineage of the royalty. With this commentary on Nahshon, the story line returns to the lineage of the Royal Seed. Not only is Nahshon called a prince in Numbers 7:11-12, but the title was repeated in 1 Chronicles 2:10. Recall earlier Sarah had been called a princess. Likewise, is it not altogether fitting to find a *prince* within the royal lineage? Similarly, this prince had important relatives. So who were these important relatives? Rather than tell you, I encourage you to pick up your Bible and read the following passages:

Numbers 7:11-12

Ruth 4:19-22

1 Chronicles 2:1-20

Matthew 1:2-6

Luke 3:31-34

Is this not exciting? Brother Nahshon, it seems, is kin to everyone important.

One more name mentioned above that is not particularly well known: Bezalel. God spoke to Moses concerning Bezalel in Exodus 31:1-11. Bezalel is again mentioned in Exodus 37:1 and 38:22 due to his faithfulness in supervising and building the Ark of the Covenant and attending to the tabernacle, its altars, and its candlesticks, etc. The gold given by the Egyptians was used by Bezalel to cover the Ark, fashion a solid gold top, and make the various vessels to be used in the tabernacle. In addition, the boards, bars, and rings were overlaid with gold (Exodus 26:10-40 NASB).

First Chronicles 2 lists the genealogy of Judah's descendants. Prince Nahshon is first mentioned in verse 10. Ten verses later, Nahshon's probable fourth cousin, Bezalel, is named. Remember the two tribes of Judah and Levi from 1 Chronicles 5:2 and 6:3? Once again view the layout of the camp in the desert:

Layout of the Camp

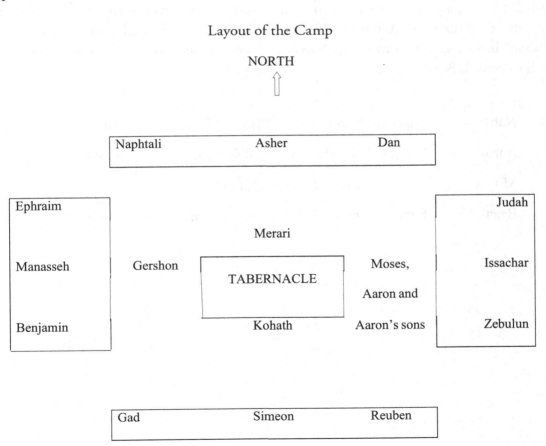

101

Note the proximity of the kingly tribe of Judah to the priestly clan of Levi's leaders, Moses and Aaron. All the clans of the Levites are closely surrounding the tabernacle. It is not surprising that Aaron associated with the people of the nearby tribe of Judah. It makes perfect sense. He would have to walk nearly a mile to visit members of the tribe of Manasseh or Gad. Fraternizing with Judah was less than a half mile away. Furthermore, remember Levi and Judah were full brothers, being the third and fourth sons, respectively, born to Israel and Leah. Nahshon's sister (Elisheba) married Aaron, the first priest. Aaron's brother, Moses, was the first scribe and author of the first books of the Bible. Nahshon's son, Salmon, married Rahab the harlot (Matthew 1:5 NASB). Their son, Boaz, was a man of great wealth, fulfilling the role of Kinsman-Redeemer by marrying the Moabitess, Ruth (Ruth 2:1; 4:10 NASB). Their son was Obed, who fathered a son named Jesse, the father of David.

For three million wandering people in the desert, God had a grand plan. And in God's great plan, virtually everyone important in the implementation was an intimate relative of Nahshon or a very close acquaintance. They would see each other almost daily or even hourly. Have you ever wondered what they talked about at night around the camp fire in the cool night air of the desert? Wouldn't they have talked about their common ancestors — Noah, Abraham, Isaac, and Jacob? Wasn't everything occurring in the desert in preparation to enter the Promised Land? Nearly all the major participants are relatives or related to Nahshon's relatives. Moses was the first scribe recording the Bible. Aaron was Moses's brother and the first high priest, and Aaron was Nahshon's brother-in-law by marrying Nahshon's sister, Elisheba. God had appointed Nahshon's fourth (?) cousin, Bezalel, to construct the tabernacle.

Nahshon — Prince of Judah, leader of Israel's largest tribe, (tribe of Judah)

Aaron — Nahshon's brother-in-law, first High Priest, (tribe of Levi)

Moses — Aaron's brother, first scribe, (tribe of Levi)

Bezalel — Fourth (?) cousin, builder of Tabernacle, (tribe of Judah)

The following chart will help further explain Nahshon's family relationships.

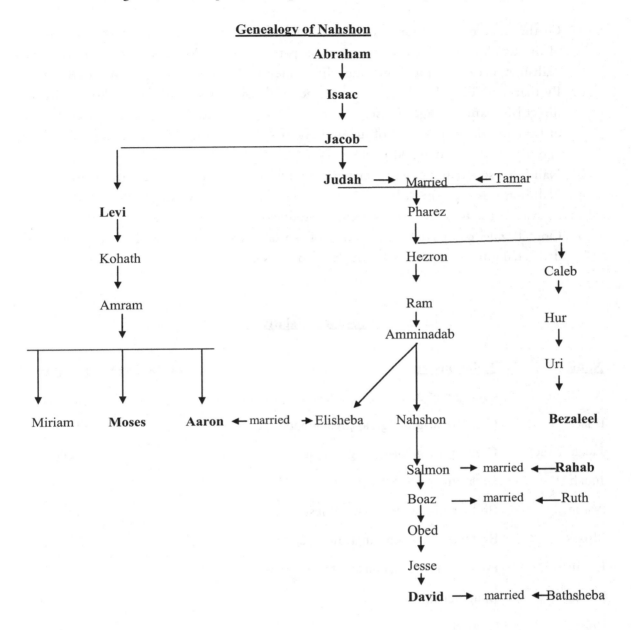

Genealogy of Nahshon

In other words, God's first author of the Bible, God's first high priest, and God's first tabernacle builder—all of them knew Nahshon very well. Most were even related to him. But Nahshon's ultimate relative, as we saw with Noah, will be Jesus.

What did we learn about Nahshon?

1. Of the three million Israelites and "mixed multitude" crossing the Red Sea that night of the Exodus, the single most important person was not Moses nor was it Aaron, but Nahshon, because through his single life came the Royal Seed leading onward to Jesus.
2. By marrying Elisheba, Aaron became the brother-in-law to Nahshon, who was in the direct Messianic lineage of Jesus. We see a second connection between the priestly tribe of Levi and the kingly tribe of Judah. (The first connection was Leah and Jacob's third and fourth sons, Judah and Levi.)
3. Nahshon's son, Salmon, will marry Rahab; his grandson, Boaz, will marry Ruth.
4. Nahshon was a prince, a leader in the tribe of Judah. He was the leader of the entire caravan as the Israelites traversed the Sinai desert.
5. Once Bezalel completed construction of the tabernacle and Moses had consecrated it, dedicated gifts were given by each clan, led by Nahshon.

Nahshon's Relatives

Name	Relationship	APPROXIMATE Dates
Abraham	Great-great-great-great-great-great grandfather	±2100 BC
Isaac	Great-great-great-great-great grandfather	±1850 BC
Jacob (Israel)	Great-great-great-great grandfather	±1800 BC
Judah	Great-great-great grandfather	±1700 BC
Aaron	Brother-in-law, first High Priest	±1350 BC
Moses	Brother-in-law's brother, first Scribe	±1350 BC
Bezalel	Fourth (?) cousin, constructed tabernacle	±1300 BC
Rahab	Daughter-in-law	±1250 BC
Boaz	Grandson	±1200 BC
Ruth	Granddaughter-in-law	±1150 BC
David	Great-great-great grandson	±1050 BC
Solomon	Great-great-great-great grandson	1000 BC
Jesus	Great-grandson, 33 generations removed	AD 30

Chapter 15

Salmon

Nahshon begat Salmon. And Salmon begat Boaz and Boaz begat Obed. (Ruth 4:20-21)

Does this chapter heading seem a little fishy?

The truth is, the Salmon of the Bible was just about as unusual as the salmon fish of the Pacific Northwest waters. Salmon was the son of Nahshon. He is only mentioned in five verses in the Bible. We know virtually nothing about him beyond these few verses. He was not a king or a priest. He was not a famous warrior. He was not famous for much of anything. Most Christians have never even heard his name. Little has been written about him. The obvious question is: why does he deserve a short chapter in this book? The answer is that Salmon married really well. This is not readily apparent to the casual reader. In fact, his marriage would even be considered a disaster by most people, especially with his contemporaries who probably looked down on his choice of a wife. Most likely, his parents did not approve of his bride.

To learn about his bride, we must read the second chapter of Joshua. Before Israel entered the Promised Land, Moses had chosen Joshua and Caleb along with ten other men to spy out their future homeland over *forty days*. Because of the lack of faith among the twelve spies Moses sent out, the only positive responses were the two reports from Joshua (tribe of Ephraim) and Caleb (tribe of Judah). Due to this lack of trust in God's plan, over the next *forty years*, the remaining ten spies and all the other adult Israelites died in the Sinai Desert (Numbers 14:34).

In Joshua 2, Joshua selected two spies to do a similar reconnaissance mission. After forty years in the wilderness, the three million or so Israelites who had left Egypt must have increased to four million, five million, or even six million. Of the millions of potential spies Joshua could have selected, he chose only two. Yet the Bible does not even record their names. Joshua told these two spies specifically to inspect Jericho, since this is the first town the invaders will encounter. The two spies followed instructions and met a harlot named Rahab. She took the spies into her home, which was located on the walls of the city of Jericho. Jericho was one of the first, if not the very first, walled city in the world. The people of Jericho gathered the waterproofing pitch from the nearby Dead Sea to sell to neighboring cities. Because they overcharged their customers, they felt the need to protect themselves by building a wall around their city. Rahab lived upon this wall. The two spies did not enter the city unnoticed. Maybe it was their clothing, or in the small city, most everyone would have known each other. The locals would have noted a stranger (Joshua 2:2 NASB). Any newcomers would be quickly identified. The king is notified that spies from the children of Israel have entered the city. Of course, the residents of Jericho were aware of a nation of six million which was encamped just a few miles to the east across the Jordan River. Even if one lived in a walled city, the sheer number of Israelites demanded some degree of apprehension from the citizens of Jericho.

Furthermore, Rahab recounted to the spies the exploits of the Exodus and battles that Joshua already won over the Amorites. She told the spies, "Our hearts did melt . . . and there is no courage among any man." The harlot Rahab acknowledged, "The Lord hath given you this land." In conclusion, Rahab declared, "The Lord, your God, He is God in heaven above and earth beneath" (Joshua 2:9-12 NASB). After her statement of God's authority, Rahab requested a pledge of protection for herself and her family when the Israelites invade. Rahab hides the two spies upon her roof, which was probably one of the highest points in Jericho since her house was built on the wall. Rahab is confronted by emissaries from the king of Jericho who demand she produce the two men of Israel. Slyly, Rahab tells the king's envoys that the men left her house shortly before the closing of the city gate at night. She says she does not know where the spies are, but they have not been gone very long from her house. The logical conclusion was that the spies are traveling east to cross the Jordan River and re-enter the Israelite camp, so the authorities head eastward. Joshua 2:2 mentions the men came in at night. In verse five, Rahab tells the king's men that the spies left before the city gate was closed for the night. It is unclear if the visit with Rahab was only a few hours or as much as twenty-four hours, but both the entering of the city and the supposed exit from the city occur at night.

In response to her request for a pledge of safety, the spies confirm the Israelites will be kind and truthful to her and her family as compensation for her helping them and risking her own life. Since the city officials are heading east toward the Jordan across the almost flat terrain of the Jordan River Valley, Rahab's instructions in verse 16 are informative. She instructs the spies to travel toward the mountains. The mountains are to the west of Jericho and are dry, barren, and foreboding. They are the same lonely mountains in which Jesus set the parable of the Good Samaritan on the road from Jericho to Jerusalem. Since the authorities were encouraged to go east and Rahab told the spies to go into the mountains which rise to the west of Jericho, some scholars have hypothesized that Rahab's house was on the west wall of Jericho, which would have provided even further protection for the spies to travel. She tells them to hide three days in the mountains. The spies confirm their oath of protection as they prepare to leave Rahab's house. She let them down the wall via a cord from her window. The cord was a silent tool, it was convenient, and it was probably on the best side of town to safely escape towards the mountains. Before leaving her house, the spies tell Rahab to gather all her family into her house. In addition, as a signal to the approaching Israelites, Rahab is instructed to place the same scarlet cord used to let the spies down the wall outside her window. The cord will be a signal to the Israelite soldiers, so they can protect Rahab and her family once the Israelites attack. The spies arrive safely in the mountains and later in Joshua 2 deliver their report to Joshua.

As the Israelites prepare to enter the Promised Land after almost a five-hundred-year absence, *miraculous* things began to happen. At this time of year, the Jordan River should have been overflowing, but God provides dry ground as the waters are dammed by the river bank collapsing upstream (Joshua 3:16-17; Judges 5:4; Psalm 18:7 NASB). The Jordan River is above one of the world's most active earthquake fault lines. Joshua 3 tells us Jericho was near to where the embankment fell into the Jordan River. The passages from Judges 5 and Psalm 18 recount just such a severe shaking of the earth. This event also invokes a comparison between the Exodus and the dry ground upon which the Israelites had left Egypt with the dry ground made available for the Israelites to enter the Promised Land. Possibly, a dramatic earthquake occurred. The Jordan is temporarily blocked twenty miles or so upstream from Jericho. Although we do not know how wide the passageway was in the Red Sea, the fact is that the towns mentioned in Joshua 3:16 are twenty miles upstream from Jericho. It is not unreasonable to assume a twenty-mile wide pathway for six million Israelites and their moving livestock to cross over the dry river bed of the Jordan River.

The Israelites who entered the Promised Land were either under twenty years of age at the time of the Exodus or born in the wilderness. They had not experienced marching across the dry ground of the sea bed; they had only heard about it from their family members. This generation is now experiencing its own dry river bed, possibly caused by a massive earthquake. Another dramatic event occurs at this time. After forty years, the manna ceased falling as the Israelites entered Canaan. The Israelites gathered at Gilgal, a town a few miles north of Jericho (Joshua 5:10 NASB). Joshua 6:1 states Jericho was under lockdown. First, the authorities failed to apprehend the two Israelite spies. Second, a monstrous earthquake has possibly dammed up the Jordan River twenty miles away. Certainly, the residents of Jericho felt the tremor as they huddled in their city. The third danger is the expected onslaught of the Israelites.

Most of us are familiar with the Israelites quietly marching around the city for six days. On the seventh day of marching, the priests blew trumpets and the people shouted (Joshua 6:5, 20 NASB). Scripture states the wall fell flat and the soldiers each marched straight into the city. Consequently, the east wall had to fall towards the east, the north wall towards the north and so on. An intriguing question is: what might have caused the east walls to fall eastward, with the north wall falling to the north, and so forth? For the walls to collapse in opposite directions, the most likely explanation is an earthquake. But Rahab's house on the west wall was not totally destroyed because her family was there. A possible explanation: the west wall was the wall the greatest distance from the Jordan River earthquake fault line. Obviously, Yahweh can do anything, anytime, and any way He so chooses in His omnipotence. But perhaps the collapsing walls were an aftershock from the massive earthquake that occurred a week earlier and which dammed up the Jordan? Furthermore, were the walls of Jericho already weakened from the earthquake of the prior week? Was the earlier earthquake just a preamble (though massive as it might have been) or was it a warning of an even bigger earthquake on the seventh day? Did the trumpets and shouting of millions tramping around on the unstable soil of Jericho precipitate an even larger earthquake or an aftershock?

Joshua instructed the two men who previously contacted Rahab to go protect her and all her family during the time when the walls are being destroyed by the possible earthquake and the city is in hand-to-hand combat. Although Rahab's lying to the authorities and her occupation are not condoned, we find out much about Rahab, not in the Old Testament but later in the New Testament.

Hebrews 11:1 defines *faith* and is the only verse in the Bible that offers us such a definition. In Hebrews 11, the unknown author offers some sixteen named examples of faith—Enoch, Abraham, Sarah, Jacob, Moses, David, Rahab, and others. Verse 31 tells us Rahab "believed," just as we saw earlier that Abraham "believed" four hundred years before Moses was born to Jochebed. It is significant that among sixteen named heroes of faith only two are women. One is Abraham's wife Sarah; the other is the harlot, Rahab. In addition, James commends the harlot Rahab for her efforts (James 2:25 NASB). Near the end of this book, we will learn about James and view Rahab's story again. For now, just remember, James commended Rahab along with Abraham in James 2.

The Bible does not give us the names of the two spies commissioned by Joshua. However, we know that these two spies gave a report to Joshua, according to Joshua 2:24. Joshua was the leader of six million wandering Israelites who had just experienced a major earthquake, endured community discrimination, and who were preparing to do battle. Nevertheless, he still found time to speak to the two spies to make sure there was provision for Rahab. Today, how likely would a governor of a state of six million citizens find time to seek out the well-being of a foreigner, especially if an earthquake has just occurred! What if the governor is also preparing to "battle" a fortified city or mount a defense against an epidemic or a natural disaster such as a hurricane or a blizzard? These two spies have been appointed by Joshua, the master spy. Also as military commander, Joshua verified the spies' oath to Rahab. They were specifically instructed to fulfill their commitment to Rahab.

It seems our "fish tale" has wandered quite a distance from the man, Salmon. However, Ruth 4:20-21 offers us an important clue—a very important clue. These verses tell us that Nahshon was the father of Salmon. It seems likely Salmon was one of the two unnamed spies, for he became the husband of Rahab. Out of six million Israelites, Salmon's random meeting of Rahab was unlikely. If he was one of the two spies, the encounter of Rahab and Salmon becomes much more likely.

As we observed earlier, Matthew's gospel was written to prove to Jews that Jesus is the Messiah. One thing we have seen important to Jews was genealogy, as well as purity of the lineage. The author, Matthew, had two names; his other name was Levi (Mark 2:14 NASB). Certainly, as an educated publican and wealthy Jewish tax collector, he was mindful of his name Levi. Other than his authorship of the book ascribed to his name, we know little about Matthew. However, his tradition and name would make him mindful of his Jewish heritage, manners, and customs; he was aware of his Israelite audience. Nevertheless, he brandished a bold quill when he mentioned women in Jesus's genealogy. In those days, women were little more than chattel. Yet, in following the genealogy of Jesus, Matthew is alone in including five women: Tamar, Ruth, Bathsheba, Rahab, and Mary. These five women are important, because they were all ancestors of Jesus.

What did we learn about Salmon?

1. Be careful whom you marry. Rahab married very well, for she married into Israel's royal family. Salmon also married well—he married a future biblical heroine. Rahab's activities are why Salmon is important as an ancestor of Jesus.

2. Prince Nahshon, as Abraham's descendant, was probably not pleased with his son, Salmon's choice of a foreign harlot to be his bride.

3. We now better understand why Joshua, as the author of the book of Joshua and as a master spy, thought it important to include the second chapter of Joshua and his selection of the two spies. We now also better understand why the story of Rahab is in the Bible.

4. Joshua chapter 2, Ruth chapter 4, and Matthew chapter 1 collaborate one another. Each adds another piece to the puzzle of the ultimate destiny of the Royal Seed.

5. This harlot, Rahab, will become the mother of another famous Bible person, to be studied in the next chapter.

6. It is informative that Joshua tells us the color of the cord. The scarlet cord that Rahab used to let the spies down the wall was not only a signal to the Israelite invaders, telling them where Rahab's family was located, it also signals to us that it was a royal cord, as its color was royal scarlet. At the crucifixion, Jesus was mocked by the Roman soldiers as they placed a royal scarlet robe upon him (Matthew 27:28). Was that scarlet cord a hint that through Rahab the most regal King of Kings would come?

7. God is excellent at choosing and using unlikely people to accomplish His will.

8. Like his father Nahshon, Salmon is biblically documented as a bridge to more famous relatives of Jesus.

9. The narrative of Rahab is not only about God's provision for His chosen people to enter the Land of Milk and Honey, but it is a narrative of yet another ancestor of Jesus.

Salmon's Relatives

Name	Relationship	APPROXIMATE Dates
Nahshon	Father	±1350 BC
Aaron	Uncle, first High Priest	±1350 BC
Rahab	Wife	±1250 BC
Boaz	Son	±1200 BC
Ruth	Daughter-in-law	±1150 BC
David	Great-great-great grandson	±1050 BC
Solomon	Great-great-great-great grandson	1000 BC
Jesus	Grandson, 32 generations removed	AD 30

Chapter 16

Boaz

> And let thy house be like the house of Pharez, whom Tamar bare unto Judah of the *seed* which the Lord shall give thee of this young woman. So Boaz took Ruth and she was his wife . . . and she bare a son. (Ruth 4:12-13, emphasis added)

As we begin this chapter, we must spend a few moments learning about the topography around Bethlehem. Israel is approximately the size of New Jersey. Within this small nation are remarkable contrasts in altitude, land fertility, soil types, plant life, winds, clouds, dews, and precipitation. Since this was an agrarian society, these differences in geographical features alters crops and farming practices as well.

One nation (Israel) occupies a westerly mountain range, the Central Mountain Spine; another nation (Moab) and its residents inhabit the easterly mountain range known as the Trans-Jordan Plateau. Between these two nations is a great chasm five thousand feet below.

Because of the chasm between the two mountain ranges and their close proximity to each other, it is fairly easy to observe what weather is occurring from one mountain range to the other. One factor to consider is that Israel has a rainy season extending from November to March. Some years, the clouds come in over the land at relatively low levels. In years when this occurs, the western slopes of Israel's mountains are well-watered. Crops do well and there is ample pasture for livestock. However, when the winds above the Mediterranean push clouds eastward at higher altitudes, little moisture falls on the mountains of Israel. And after these high clouds cross the hot rift valley, the moisture falls on the mountains of ancient Moab (Jordan). In a typical year, one nation has good crops while the other nation has near drought conditions. Because of the deep gorge between the two peoples, one group can look across the valley and notice if their neighbor is green with abundant vegetation. Likewise, one neighbor can also notice if the other has received the whiteness of snow or the brownness of a dry sun parched landscape.

Deuteronomy 34:1-5 affirms what we have just been studying. Moses traveled up Mt. Nebo which is in the land of Moab. God permitted Moses to look over into the Promised Land. Verses 1-3 describe the land all the way from the Jordan River to the Mediterranean Sea. These verses confirm how a person on one ridge can scan the view from the land of Moab (Jordan) into Judah (Israel), and likewise, how one can look from Judah into Moab as well, seeing the entire region.

Furthermore, the two nations of Israel and Jordan are precariously related by blood. After the destruction of Sodom and Gomorrah, Lot's two daughters got their father drunk and had intimate relations with him. The elder daughter birthed Moab while the younger daughter birthed another boy, Ben-Ammi. Each son founded a nation with their descendants, eventually becoming the Moabites and the Ammonites respectively. The Moabites were fully related to the Israelites by blood and heritage, but they were a product of incest. Today, it is not surprising that Israel and its neighbor immediately to the east, Jordan, do not always have smooth relations. These same tensions existed over three thousand years ago between the Israelites and the Moabites.

Although they were kin in the eyes of Judah (and God), the Moabites had a degree of inferiority due to being descendants of incest. It is not surprising that God raised up a judge, Ehud, to defeat Eglon, King of Moab, as conflicts were frequent and bitter between these two groups.

In some Bible passages, God absolutely forbade the marriage of the Israelites to certain peoples (Ezra 9:1). In addition, in Deuteronomy 23:2-3, the Moabites, along with their cousins, the Ammonites, are specifically mentioned as not being welcome in the tabernacle. Edomites and Egyptians were to be more tolerated than Moabites or Ammonites (Deuteronomy 23:7-8). *Don't skim over this passage for it will be most relevant momentarily.*

Let us now begin our study of the man named Boaz. The story of Boaz is almost exclusively in the book of Ruth. The date of this book is around 1150 BC. The twelve tribes had been allocated their respective regions, battles had been fought against the locals, and tribes had begun to settle into their assigned areas. As we saw earlier, the two tribes who would "be first among equals" were Judah and Levi. The Levites received no land per se, but only towns throughout the nation with some pasturelands just outside the city walls for Levitical livestock. Judah received Jerusalem and the area surrounding Jerusalem and southward.

To truly understand Boaz, it is important to understand the book of Ruth. Beginning in Ruth 1, we read of a famine in the land of Judah. In verse one, Elimelech and his family —wife Naomi and their two sons— leave Judah. Did Elimelech see "greener pastures" in Moab due to the high winter clouds floating over Judah or did he just hear about it? The Bible does not provide the detail, but Elimelech knew Bethlehem-Judah was suffering from famine, and that food is available twenty miles away across the chasm. Verse two also defines this family as Ephrathites of Bethlehem. Some authorities have surmised that the term "Ephrathites" announce that this is a prominent, upper-class family. The famine must have been severe for this probable affluent man to leave his position, real estate, and standing in Bethlehem to journey into a nearby nation that warred with the Israelites in times past. The father died. The two sons married, and they both died. The fourth verse tells us that two marriages and three deaths occurred in the space of a decade. Naomi learned that her homeland was now reaping abundant harvests. In Ruth 1:6, Naomi declared, "The Lord has visited his people and given them bread." The area around Bethlehem is fertile and produces large quantities of food and pasture for livestock when the rainfall is ample. The town's name, Bethlehem, even means "house of bread." So, when Naomi announced the Lord had visited His people and given them bread, she is referring to the people in the land of Judah and the connection of bread to the name of the town of Bethlehem.

The two daughters-in-law, Orpah and Ruth, started the journey with Naomi. After some distance, Naomi blessed them and encouraged the two Moabite widows to return to their parents' homes with the wish that they will remarry someday. After weeping and declaring she was too old to marry and have sons, Naomi asked the two Moabite widows, "Will you wait for me to marry and have new sons, and wait for them to grow up—and will you wait to marry them?" This situation is not unlike the story of Judah and Tamar and the birth of their son, Pharez, which we studied previously (Genesis 38:1-30 NASB).

The women wept. Orpah departed and returned to her people. In verse 15, Naomi remarked to Ruth that Orpah had returned to her people and "her gods." Naomi encouraged Ruth to do likewise. Ruth was drawn to her Godly mother-in-law for she replied, "Thy people shall be my people and thy God, my God." Ruth was leaving behind her family, her country, and her place. Much as we saw Rahab, a harlot, leave behind her occupation, her nation, her city, and "her gods" to accept the faith of the spies of the Israelites, we now see Ruth (Rahab's future daughter-in-law) doing the same thing. Ruth's beautiful prose is intriguing. It is wonderfully composed. It is vibrant, and it is heart rendering. It does sound so appropriate for a bride to say to the groom in a lovely, spiritual wedding ceremony. However, the fact remains that it was the heart of a daughter-in-law speaking to her mother-in-law. It was woman to woman. This verse shows Ruth has accepted Naomi's God now as her own God. Orpah returned to her people and to her god. But Ruth has accepted Naomi's people as her people and more importantly, Naomi's God as her own God. Naomi was a strong woman of faith, although she felt God had dealt harshly with her. She has endured a famine, a new nation, the death of her mate, and the death of both of her sons—and it all occurred in just a decade. We do not know how long Ruth was married to Mahlon, but in observing her mother-in-law under duress, Ruth perceived Naomi had an inner peace and strength that was appealing (Ruth 1:16 NASB). Naomi did not and could not comprehend all of the events in her life. Nevertheless, she was returning to her hometown, Bethlehem, with a daughter-in-law desiring to know more of the God that Naomi worships.

Naomi and Ruth returned to Bethlehem during the beginning of the barley harvest (Ruth 1:22 NASB). Chapter 2 introduces a local, wealthy farmer by the name of Boaz. In the New Testament, Matthew 1:4-5 informs us that Salmon had married Rahab, the harlot. They had a son named Boaz who was this same local, wealthy farmer.

In some way, he was related to Naomi's deceased husband, Elimelech (Ruth 2:1 NASB). Maybe Salmon and Rahab had other sons and daughters. Possibly Boaz and Elimelech were brothers or brothers-in-law, but the Bible is silent on the exact relationship between the two men. As was the custom, Ruth went out to glean the grain not collected by the workers for the landowner. Boaz came from Bethlehem to his fields and inquired about Ruth to his workers. Certainly, Ruth was apprehensive. She had every reason to be. She came to a new land with her mother-in-law, and because they were hungry, Ruth had to go glean from the fields of others. Ruth was desperate, starving, and energetic—maybe even all three, for Boaz's hirelings told him the Moabitess has been in the field "from morning until now and only rested a little" (Ruth 2:7 NASB). Furthermore, Ruth left behind her biological family. Since she was from Moab, living in the land of the Israelites—it would have been realistic for Ruth to be anxious. Boaz spoke with Ruth and told her to follow after his maids in his fields. He reassured her that his young men will not approach her but will protect her. Also, he encouraged Ruth to enjoy the water the men retrieved from a well.

We must notice the wealthy men in the Bible whose first priority is spiritual, and second they are subsequently blessed with material prosperity. Often these Godly men used their material blessings to further promote God's plan. Their wealth was used to build an ark, erect a gold laden temple, or purchase an appropriate crypt for Jesus's body. For example, Genesis 13:2 informs us Abraham is rich. Noah also had to be affluent to provide all the materials needed to construct a four-hundred-fifty-foot-long ark. Genesis 26:13 shows us Isaac became wealthy. Solomon was noted as rich in 1 Kings 3:13. David donated substantial amounts of gold to the building of the temple (1 Chronicles 29:2-4). Jacob was wealthy (Genesis 36:6-7). Two other very rich men in the Messianic line were Jehoshaphat (2 Chronicles 17:5) and Hezekiah (2 Chronicles 32:27). In 2 Corinthians 8:9, Paul even describes Jesus as "rich."

Similarly, Ruth 2:1 told us Boaz is also wealthy, much like his forefathers. Yet his wealth did not appear to interfere with his Godly walk. Evidence of this is exhibited in 2:4 when Boaz greeted his field workers with a greeting of "The Lord be with you." He must have been holy, for his workers responded, "The Lord bless thee." God had blessed this Godly man with material prosperity. Ruth could glean from several fields this man owned. We know he owned other fields because once the barley harvest concluded, Ruth moved on to the wheat fields of Boaz along with his workers (Ruth 2:23 NASB). Furthermore, Boaz told his field workers to leave extra amounts of grain for Ruth to gather as she worked from morning until evening (Ruth 2:17 NASB). Then, at night, she beat out the kernels of grain from the husks she had harvested. Because it was harvest time when they arrived, we can deduce the women had planted no crops, even though Elimelech had retained real estate near Bethlehem. At Elimelech's death, the property had passed to his son, Mahlon. Mahlon had since died, leaving Naomi and Ruth with the property. Although hungry, these two women were not begging from wealthier relatives or seeking assistance. As we have read, they were striving on their own.

Naomi realized her daughter-in-law has been blessed. Earlier, Naomi had felt the hand of the Lord had gone from her (Ruth 1:13 NASB). She has changed her name from Naomi, "pleasant" to Mara, "bitter." After the two moves, three deaths, and poverty, Naomi is aware that Ruth's provisions were not typical. Ruth probably did not realize the blessings coming to her. Possibly, she thought, "The people here certainly are nicer than the Moabites where I used to live."

Naomi instructed Ruth in the ways and customs of Judah. Once Ruth told Naomi it was Boaz who had shown kindness to her, Naomi instructed Ruth to go to Boaz at his threshing floor after he finished working, had eaten, and was asleep. Ruth did as she was commanded by Naomi, and uncovered Boaz's feet and lay down. At midnight, Boaz was startled when he awakened to find someone at his feet. He naturally inquired. Ruth responded by identifying herself as a relative. Boaz again exhibited his faith, for his first words were, "Blessed be thou of the Lord." He noted she was virtuous and has not followed after young men, whether rich or poor. From verse 10, it is a reasonable conclusion to believe this wealthy man was some years older than Ruth. He told her to stay the night, and in the morning, he filled her shawl with a portion of the barley he threshed the night before. She then left before daylight the next morning. This spreading of a garment was actually a pledge of marriage even among royalty (Ezekiel 16:8-13 NASB) and by doing so, Boaz agrees to fulfill his role to Ruth as a possible Kinsman-Redeemer (Deuteronomy 25:5-10 NASB).

Boaz informed Ruth that another man is a closer relative to her than himself. He declared he will go to the city gate where the elders congregate and engage this particular man. Boaz met the relative and told him Naomi has a parcel of land for sale that had belonged to her husband. The relative agreed to buy it. Then Boaz delivered the other terms of the transaction. Not only had Elimelech died, but his son, Mahlon, was also deceased, being survived by Ruth, his widow. With the acquisition of the field, the purchaser's children via Ruth will be considered children of the lineage of Elimelech and Mahlon. Upon hearing this condition, the would-be purchaser declined the entire transaction. As result, the pathway is clear for Boaz to become the Kinsman Redeemer and redeem his relative's inheritance.

The wedding was announced. Residents of Bethlehem-Judah knew they were a preferred tribe. They encouraged this couple to build up the house of Israel as Rachel and Leah had done. Leah, you recall, was the mother of Judah. The people were focused on their genealogy and remembered, of all people, Tamar as a young daughter-in-law, giving birth to Judah's illegitimate son, Pharez, six generations earlier. The comparison was drawn of the older Judah and younger Tamar being a similar situation to Boaz and Ruth. The wedding party encouraged the couple to follow after the heritage of Boaz and to "do worthily in Ephrathah and be famous in Bethlehem" (Ruth 4:11-12 NASB). The women further desired the couple's son will be "famous in Israel." When the baby is born, Naomi became the nurse to the baby. The baby's name is to be Obed. Quickly, the verse follows with, "He is the father of Jesse, the father of David" (Ruth 4:17). *The verses in Ruth 4:18-22 provide critical genealogical data to connect Genesis to King David to Solomon and, ultimately, to Jesus.* These five verses are hugely important.

Let us return to the encounter of Judah with the supposed Canaanite temple harlot Tamar, Judah's daughter-in-law. Unwittingly, the people of Bethlehem have given us an important clue when they mention the illegitimate Pharez from six generations previously. As we saw earlier, an illegitimate male Ammonite or Moabite was not permitted to enter the congregation of the Lord until ten successive generations had passed since the violation of illegitimacy or there had been a change in citizenship from the nations of Ammon or Moab (Deuteronomy 23:2-3 NASB). You are encouraged to pick up your Bible, turn to the book of Ruth, and read these last five verses. Then count the genealogies from Pharez to David—it is ten generations! King David's legacy will be redeemed by the passing of these ten generations since Judah's union with Tamar. With Boaz's father being Salmon and his grandfather being Nahshon, this tells us Boaz's great uncle was Aaron the high priest. Just as his father had married out of the Israelite nation by marrying the former Canaanite harlot, Rahab, Boaz also had a non-traditional mate in Ruth.

Naomi's desire to return to her hometown where God was visiting His people and giving them bread is at the beginning of this chapter. In Hebrew, the name of Bethlehem is interpreted as "house of bread." The chapter concludes with the child of Boaz and Ruth, who will indeed be famous in Israel. He will be the grandfather of Israel's greatest king, David. Furthermore, in Genesis 49, had not Jacob, when blessing Judah, declared, "He would be a lion and the scepter would not depart from him"? Have we not seen Judah along with Levi as the preferential tribes? When the tribes were settling into the Promised Land, where was Naomi from? Was it not Bethlehem-Judah, the "house of bread," located within the territory of the kingly tribe Judah? Naomi had wanted "bread" so she had decided to return to the "house of bread."

Centuries later, where did Mary and Joseph go to be taxed? Was it not to Bethlehem, in the city of David, because Joseph was of the house and lineage of David (Luke 2:4 NASB)? The initial City of David was Bethlehem, where David spent his youth. To further verify his claim to the throne of David, Jesus as the King of Kings will be born in the same town where his forefather, King David was born forty-two generations and one thousand years earlier. (Later, Jerusalem will also be called the City of David because David will rule there for thirty-three years.) Centuries later, a special child, Jesus, will be born in Bethlehem and will declare in John 6:48, "I am the bread of life." So Jesus will be born in the area of Judah, in the hometown of David, the greatest king of Israel. Not only was Jesus the bread of life from the village named "house of bread," he also will be similar to his forefather, Boaz, in the role of a Kinsman Redeemer, not for one person but for all of mankind. Jesus will redeem all the people who believe Him to be the Son of God. Boaz redeemed his relative's bride, Ruth, and much later, Jesus will redeem His bride, the church.

What did we learn about Boaz?

1. Boaz continued in the traditions of his ancestors and was wealthy. He used his wealth to provide food for Naomi and Ruth. He further utilized his assets to redeem the real estate of Naomi and Ruth.

2. Boaz's mother was the harlot Rahab. His great uncle was Aaron, the first high priest and the man whose brother was Moses. Boaz married later in life when he wed the widow from the land of Moab. Through the birth of their son, Obed, Boaz became the great grandfather of King David.

3. The hometown of Naomi and Boaz was Bethlehem in a land that belonged to the tribe of Judah. Earlier, Jacob had blessed his son, Judah, with the kingship of the Israelite nation. Now the tribe of Judah has real estate. One of the prominent towns in Judah will be Bethlehem. Almost one thousand years earlier, Abraham was promised that a great nation would come out of his seed. Now after one thousand years, we begin to see the start of the fulfillment of God's initial covenant with Abraham. Granted, we do not yet have a dynasty or even a king, but we do have in place the immediate ancestors of a king and in the correct town, both conforming to Israel's blessing of his fourth son, Judah.

4. Later, the Jews will reject Jesus as Messiah, partially because the Torah had declared Salmon's wife was a Canaanite harlot and their son, Boaz, had married a Moabitess.

Deuteronomy 23 singled out illegitimates, Ammonites, and Moabites, as being denied the privilege of being a member of the congregation of the Lord for ten generations.

5. Not only was Bethlehem the ancestral home of Israel's greatest king, David, it will be the first home of the King of Kings one thousand years later.

6. Boaz was the great-grandfather of King David, and Boaz was the great-nephew of Aaron.

7. The story of Ruth is in the Bible, not for us to have a phrase to use at weddings but because Ruth became one more ancestor of Jesus, just like those we have studied earlier—Noah, Abraham, Isaac, Jacob, and Rahab.

Boaz's Relatives

Name	Relationship	APPROXIMATE Dates
Adam	Great-grandfather, 27 generations removed	?
Enoch	Great-grandfather, 21 generations removed	?
Noah	Great-grandfather, 18 generations removed	?
Jacob (Israel)	Great-grandfather, 6 generations removed	±1800 BC
Aaron	Great-uncle	±1350 BC
Rahab	Mother	±1250 BC
Ruth	Wife	±1150 BC
David	Great-grandson	±1050 BC
Solomon	Great-great-grandson	1000 BC
Jesus	Great-grandson, 31 generations removed	AD 30

Chapter 17

Samuel

> And the child Samuel ministered unto the Lord before Eli. And the word of the Lord was rare in those days; there was no open vision . . . for the Lord revealed Himself to Samuel in Shiloh, by the word of the Lord. (1 Samuel 3:1, 21)

When we study Samuel's life, we are once again in the lineage of the high priests and not directly in the lineage of the Royal Seed. Therefore, we are in the lineage of Levi and Aaron.

After the Israelites crossed over the dry river bed of the Jordan, they camped at Gilgal, a couple of miles north of Jericho. Circumcision was performed on all the males born in the Sinai wilderness. Also, Passover was observed and the manna ceased. Since all the people had crossed over the Jordan into Canaan, the tabernacle, Ark of the Covenant, and all the holy items were also located in Gilgal at the edge of the land of Canaan. Shortly thereafter, Jericho's walls fell down and Rahab, along with her family, were rescued. At Gilgal, some of the conquered territory was assigned to the tribes of Manasseh, Ephraim, and Judah.

In Joshua 17, the tribes of Ephraim and Manasseh complain that they need more land, since they are among the largest tribes in population. Joshua granted them additional real estate. Remember, Joshua was from the tribe of Ephraim. This fulfilled the prophecy of Jacob's material blessings for the sons of Joseph from four hundred years earlier. As the Israelites were victors in other battles and they occupied still more territory, a more central location was chosen among the twelve tribes to be a gathering place. The conquering Israelites gathered at Shiloh, about twenty miles almost due north of Jerusalem. Later, the remaining tribes received their allocation of land at Shiloh. As the tribes settled into their respective regions, no centralized government existed. However, the tabernacle and Ark of the Covenant were moved to Shiloh. When community wide issues needed to be resolved, the tribes gathered at Shiloh (Joshua 18-22). (This type of independent, yet cooperative, government seems similar to what was experienced by the original thirteen American colonies, where each colony had its own money and laws, but met together at Philadelphia to consider their common "British problem.") It was also at Shiloh that the Levites received their respective forty-eight cities disbursed throughout the tribes of Israel (Joshua 21:1-45). This loose confederation of tribes began to consider Shiloh as their primary city. Furthermore, the tabernacle and Ark were now at Shiloh as well, and this city was most definitely the religious focal point of the confederation. By this time, most Levites had left Shiloh to settle in their appointed cities. However, the high priests and the leaders of the Levites remained in Shiloh along with the Ark and the tabernacle.

During this time, a Levite priest named Elkanah, a descendant of Kohath, served under the high priest, Eli. The Kohathites numbered only one and one-half percent of the population but were the clan with the most holy duties among all the Israelites. Elkanah was of some spiritual note as indicated in 1 Samuel 1:2, which modestly traces Elkanah's genealogy for only four generations. Later, in 1 Chronicles 6 are listed twenty-three generations of Elkanah's priestly family. Elkanah served in the community of Ramah within the region of Ephraim. Unfortunately, Ramah's location has been lost to antiquity, so its exact location is uncertain.

Elkanah was not only a priest of the most holy clan, but also he appeared to be rather prosperous. First Samuel 1:2 mentions his bringing all his family each year to Shiloh to worship and sacrifice before God at the tabernacle. Further evidence of Elkanah's affluence was that he has two wives. However, his favorite wife, Hannah, was barren. The other wife, Peninnah, has multiple sons and daughters. As we saw earlier in the rivalry between Sarah and Hagar, jealousy and competition between the women soon occurred. Such was the case with Hannah and Peninnah. Each year, as Hannah came to the tabernacle in Shiloh, she prayed for the Lord to remove her barrenness. On one occasion, Eli noticed Hannah. She was fervently petitioning God for a son and vowed to give him back to the Lord. In addition, Hannah vowed the commitment of her future son to be a Nazarite (Judges 13:7, 14 NASB). As Eli observed Hannah, he assumes she is drunk—and drunk in the tabernacle no less. Eli then heard Hannah's sorrow and told her to go in peace, and he prayed that God will grant her petition. Later that year, Hannah has a son, whom she names Samuel, meaning "heard by God." Elkanah continued his annual pilgrimages to Shiloh. Hannah, however, stayed home with her child until he was weaned at about two or three years old. Once he was weaned, Hannah took her son, with an offering of three bulls, flour, and wine to Eli. She reminded Eli of their encounter almost four years earlier. Eli blessed Hannah for giving Samuel back to God. One of the sweetest, kindest verses in all of Scripture describes Hannah's care for her son:

> "And his mother would make him a little robe and bring it to him year to year
> when she would come up with her husband to offer the yearly sacrifice" 1 Samuel
> 2:19 (NASB).

Eli asked God to bless the marriage of Elkanah and Hannah with more children. First Samuel 2:21 indicates that Eli's prayers were heard, for later Hannah has three additional sons and two daughters.

Most of us are familiar with the account of God calling Samuel into the service of the Lord at a very young age. Just as the priest wore an ephod (that is, an ornate vest), so will the young Samuel wear an ephod.

First Samuel 3 shows that the Word of the Lord came to Samuel at an early age. Samuel's role of spiritual leadership, even as a child, is reminiscent of Jesus teaching Rabbis in the temple when he was a lad. First Samuel 2:26 affirms:

> "…and the child Samuel grew on and was in favor both with the Lord and also with man."

Now compare this verse with Luke 2:52,

> "…And Jesus increased in wisdom and stature, and in favor with God and man."

Unfortunately, as young Samuel began his ministry, he has to tell Eli that because of his failure as a father, the role of high priest will be taken from Eli's sons.

Sometime later, in battle with the Philistines, the Israelites were defeated, with 4,000 Israelites killed. (More about this fighting will be discussed in the chapter about David.) In defeat, the presumptuous Israelite soldiers remembered the Ark of the Covenant had accompanied their armies into battle at Jericho and they had won a magnificent victory. They decided to take the Ark of the Covenant out of the tabernacle at Shiloh to join the soldiers in a return engagement against the Philistines. At the second encounter, the Philistines won again, killing an additional 30,000 Israelite soldiers and furthermore, capturing the Ark. The Ark was carried into the temple of their god, Dagon. In addition, Eli's two sons were both killed. A runner returned to Eli in Shiloh with the news. Eli, who was 98 years old and almost blind, heard about Israel's defeat in battle, with his two sons being killed and the capture of the Ark. Eli was less concerned about the death of his two sons than about the loss of the Ark. The loss of the Ark of the Covenant was so overwhelming that Eli fell off his seat backwards and broke his neck, resulting in his death. When Eli's daughter-in-law learned of her husband's death and the death of her father-in-law, she went into labor and delivered a son. However, she made no mention of her newborn son for her comments are recorded in 1 Samuel 4:22, where she states, "Glory is departed from Israel, for the Ark of God is taken."

Although the Ark would never again return to Shiloh, the Israelites will later receive the Ark back from the Philistines. Once repossessed, it remained in the home of an Israelite named Abinadab for over 20 years, until it was moved to another Israelite's home, this home belonging to Obed-edom. In the midst of this turmoil, Samuel rose to become not only the next high priest, but also the last judge of Israel. He was also one of Israel's earliest prophets. Samuel will become *judge, priest, and prophet*. Samuel will also be a "king maker" in the sense that God will direct Samuel to anoint Saul to be Israel's first king. Eli's two sons failed as his successors and Samuel's two sons will also fail as priests. As a result, the people desired a king "like all the other nations." Samuel was displeased, but God told Samuel, "They haven't rejected you, but Me."

The tribal system of the previous 300-400 years with God-appointed judges no longer functioned as well as it had earlier. After four centuries of a Godly, benevolent monarchy, the populous now wanted an earthly, human ruler. The people wanted to exchange God and His selection of human judges for a worldly government and a worldly king. In 1 Samuel 8, God tells Samuel to solemnly warn the people against an earthly king.

The prophet made six claims about following a human king, as opposed to the heavenly king. Samuel's six charges were:

1 - A king will take your sons as soldiers, to serve in his wars.
2 - A king will take your daughters as cooks and bakers, to serve his staff.
3 - A king will take a tenth of your seed and vineyards to feed his staff.
4 - A king will take a tenth of your servants and asses to work for him.
5 - A king will take a tenth of your fields and olive groves to give to his servants.
6 - A king will take a tenth of your sheep to feed his workers.

Samuel prophesied that the people would not like having a king, but they refused to listen. God then told Samuel to listen to their voices and make them a king. The people demanded:

- A King who is young rather than old
- A King who is nice looking
- A King who is tall rather than short

First Samuel 9:2 describes Israel's first king, Saul, as young, handsome and tall.

In contrast, in Exodus 18:21, Moses' father-in-law, Jethro, (priest of Midian), offered a radically different job description for Israel's kings and leaders. In Jethro's opinion, the four requirements were:

- Does he fear God?
- Is he capable?
- Is he a man of truth?
- Does he hate greed and covetousness?

What a contrast!

God will later tell Samuel to anoint a second king from the sons of Jesse to replace Saul. God's instructions to Samuel were "look not upon his appearance, or on his height, or on his stature. For a man looks at the outward appearance, but the Lord looks on the heart." Samuel obeys God, and in his last major act, anoints David as Israel's second king.

In chapter 19, it appears that Samuel was the head of a seminary for prophets. Perhaps it was during this time period, while head of this theology school, that Samuel authored the books of Judges, Ruth, and portions of 1 Samuel. It was to this institution David fled when hiding from Saul.

Later, Samuel died and was lamented. In 1 Samuel 28, the deranged King Saul was desperate for advice, because God refused to respond to Saul due to his disobedience. God will no longer respond to Saul in dreams, or via the casting of lots, or through prophets. Saul sought out a witch or a fortune teller for guidance. What is ironic is that King Saul had banished all witches and fortune tellers, based on verse three. Nevertheless, Saul finds a witch from whom he requests that Samuel be brought back from the dead, since God will no longer respond to him. A spirit does reply to Saul. Now, this "spirit" may have been a trick or a satanic deception. If God had so chosen, He certainly could have used His authority and power to enable some commentary from the spirit of the deceased Samuel himself. Whatever the venue, the prophecy is one of imminent death for Saul and his sons in the battle with the Philistines. First Samuel concluded with David assuming the leadership role in Judah upon Saul's and his sons' deaths.

To summarize the past several pages, the following chart will help the reader get a "handle" on the approximate timeline of these events. These dates key off of 1 Kings 6:1. All these dates are approximate, and they are not all in agreement with each other.

APPROXIMATE TIMELINE

±1870 BC	Joseph brings Jacob to Egypt
±1800 BC	End of Book of Genesis. 430 years as slaves in Egypt (Ex.12:41)
±1445 BC	Beginning of Book of Exodus: 40 years of wandering in Sinai desert
±1405 BC	Joshua leads the Israelites in the Battle of Jericho
±1050 BC	Saul anointed King of Israel by Samuel after a 450 year period of the Judges (Acts 13:20)
±1010 BC	David anointed king by Samuel
±967 BC	Solomon anointed king by Zadok & Nathan (1 Kings1:34)
±960 BC	Temple built (1 Kings 6:1, 37-38)

In concluding Samuel's life, it is worth mentioning one of Samuel's future descendants, his grandson, Heman.

As we learned in 1 Chronicles 6:33-38, Heman, from the clan of Kohath, will be the leader of his clan's musicians and singers. Verse 33 contains a gem of information. Heman was the grandson of Samuel and Heman will be Israel's first minister of music. The following "family tree" will document how Samuel and Heman are related to the Messianic lineage of Jesus.

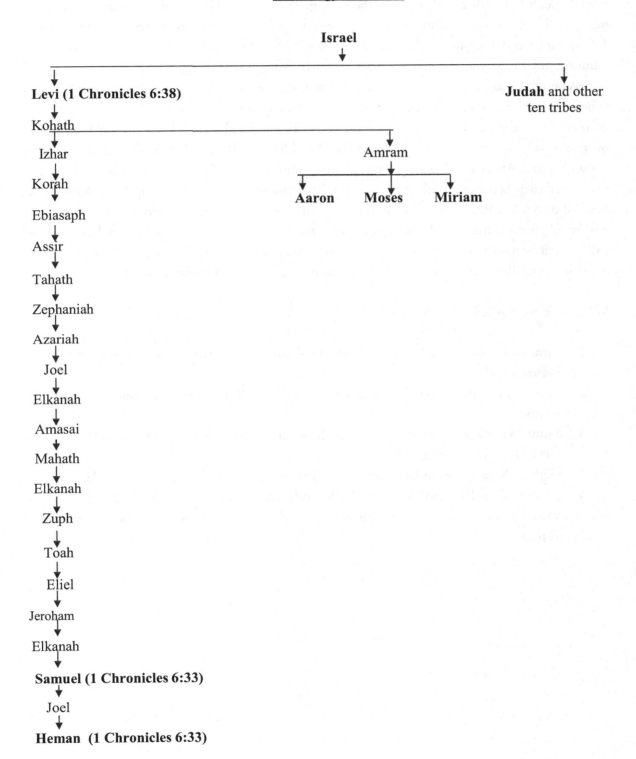

Genealogy of Samuel

Israel

Levi (1 Chronicles 6:38)　　　　　　　　　　　　Judah and other ten tribes

Kohath

Izhar　　　　　　　　　Amram

Korah　　　　　Aaron　　Moses　　Miriam

Ebiasaph

Assir

Tahath

Zephaniah

Azariah

Joel

Elkanah

Amasai

Mahath

Elkanah

Zuph

Toah

Eliel

Jeroham

Elkanah

Samuel (1 Chronicles 6:33)

Joel

Heman (1 Chronicles 6:33)

Biblical genealogies often appear to conflict with earlier books in the Bible, or even differences may exist between passages in the same chapter! As an example, study 1 Chronicles 6:22-28 and 1 Chronicles 6:33-38. For this chart, the passage from verses 33-38 was selected; 1 Chronicles 6:38 exhibited the conclusion of Samuel's genealogy to his grandson, Heman. (The reader of 1 Chronicles 6 is shown a path from the minister of music, Heman, through his grandfather Samuel, and all the way through 22 generations back to Levi's father, Israel.)

As far as we can see, Samuel was not only the last judge of Israel; his great grandfather twenty times removed was Jacob (Israel). Samuel's genealogy in the Bible traces all the way back until it "plugs into" the genealogy of the Royal Seed of Israel. The lineage of 1 Chronicles 6:38 ends once it was connected into the lineage of the Royal Seed of Israel. Obviously, it could continue through Isaac, Abraham, Noah, or even to Adam; but once the Levites and the sons of Kohath connected their heritage into the lineage that will be the Messiah's lineage, the clan of Kohath has reached its destination. They have made their point. Similarly, Ezra's genealogy in Ezra 7 reached backward 16 generations to Aaron to validate Ezra's ministry. Once the genealogy has stretched to Aaron, it becomes evident that it is only four more generations to the lineage of the Royal Seed of Israel. The Bible verifies how both Samuel and Ezra are related to the Messiah, to Jesus Christ.

What have we learned about Samuel?

1. Samuel was Israel's last Judge. He anointed Israel's first two kings. He also served Israel as Priest and Prophet.
2. Samuel probably wrote the book of Judges, as well as Ruth, and some portions of 1 Samuel.
3. Samuel's lineage can be traced twenty three generations, all the way to Jacob (Israel), who was in the direct lineage of Jesus.
4. Heman, Samuel's grandson, will be the first leader of the music in the temple.
5. From reading 1 Chronicles 6:1-3; 33-38 and Ezra 7:1-5, we can see Samuel and Ezra were related to each other, but more importantly these passages show how both were related to Jesus.

Samuel's Relatives

Name	Relationship	APPROXIMATE Dates
Jacob (Israel)	Great-grandfather, 20 generations removed	±1800 BC
Levi	Great-grandfather, 19 generations removed	±1700 BC
Aaron	Cousin, 17 generations removed	±1350 BC
Heman	Grandson, first Levite Priest of Music	1000 BC
Ezra	Cousin, Uncertain generations removed	500 BC
Jesus	Cousin, Uncertain generations removed	AD 30

Chapter 18

David

> Hath not the Scripture said, that Christ cometh of the *seed* of David and out of the town of Bethlehem where David was? (John 7:42; emphasis added)

It is time to return to the direct lineage of the Royal Seed. Previously, we studied three men not particularly well-known, even among Christians—Nahshon, Salmon, and Boaz. Following these three men are two more who are often deemed insignificant– Obed and Jesse. Ruth 4 states the son of Boaz and Ruth was Obed, and Obed's son was Jesse. People often overlook Obed and Jesse. True, the Bible does not have much to say about this father/son duo and our knowledge is limited. Nevertheless, just studying their names and the meaning of their names gives us insight. Boaz and Ruth named their son Obed, meaning "the worshiper." We can conclude that this name "worshiper" inferred worship of Yahweh, because he named his son Jesse, which clearly spoke of God as Yahweh and the child as a "gift of Jehovah." With very little else to go on, we see these two sons were named by their parents with names of spiritual significance.

Four hundred years after Jesse lived and two hundred years after his son David reigned, God raised up the prophet Isaiah. As we will see in a future chapter, Isaiah was likely a member of the royal family. In fact, tradition places Isaiah as a cousin to King Uzziah, although no hard evidence supports this hypothesis. Further evidence of this premise is supported by Isaiah's easy movement among the priests and kings in Jerusalem (Isaiah 37-38). If Isaiah was truly a member of the royal family of Israel, we can appreciate the prophet even more when he begins Isaiah chapter 11 with a term to describe the coming Messiah. Isaiah was not just writing about his own royal family, but a future relative, a coming Messiah who will be born seven hundred years into the future. In his very first words, Isaiah describes the Messiah as "a shoot from the stem of Jesse." After detailing how in eternity the wolf will lay down with the lamb, Isaiah returns to Jesse.

> "Then, it will come about in that day that the nations will resort to the root of Jesse who will stand as a signal for the people" (Isaiah 11:10 NASB).

In Acts 13:22 and Romans 15:12, Paul also refers to "the root," this stem of Jesse. The proof of Jesse's significance is we find both Isaiah and Paul mentioning Jesse. After 450 years of judges, Samuel is to be the last judge of Israel (1 Samuel 7:15; 8:1-5 NASB). God directs Samuel to appoint

Saul as Israel's first king. After he received a new heart, the spirit of God came upon Saul. In 1 Samuel 13, King Saul usurps the authority of Samuel as priest. Samuel condemns Saul for not being obedient to the law of God. In 1 Samuel 14:14, Samuel indicts Saul by announcing, "The Lord will seek a man after his own heart." Because Saul rejected obedience to the Word of God, eventually God will reject Saul. Samuel is grieved over Saul's failure as Israel's first King. As 1 Samuel 16 opens, God challenges Samuel, "How long will you grieve over Saul? Go and anoint a son of Jesse I have selected to be King." After Samuel anointed David as King in the presence of his brothers (1Samuel 16:13), the Spirit of the Lord left Saul. Just as the Spirit of the Lord came upon Saul in 1 Samuel 10:6, now the Spirit of the Lord came upon David.

After King Saul's death, he eventually was succeeded by David, as the second king of United Israel. David was certainly United Israel's greatest king. God described King David as "a man after my own heart" (Acts 13:22). He was the youngest of Jesse's seven or eight sons. Furthermore, he was described as ruddy (reddish) in appearance and handsome. As the youngest of eight (?) brothers, it is not surprising we learn he was a shepherd boy. Often, this task was assigned among farm families to the daughters or youngest son.

David was busy while he was alone with the sheep. He learned to play the harp. He wrote songs. He thought and meditated. But also David had to be diligent. Sheep tending for David was not as peaceful as it had been for Rachel.

An atypical feature of Israel is that some areas along the Jordan River are gorges with water, vegetation and, shade. Above these dense valleys are plateaus on both sides which are windy, dry, arid, and hot. This almost jungle-like environment attracts numerous animals. Because of their reduced size, small animals must forage continuously. This water, shade, and vegetation is especially attractive to them. In turn, an abundant population of smaller animals attracts larger animals. When David was protecting and watering his father's flocks along the riverside, he probably encountered these larger animals and was forced to kill lions and bears. David may have been without human companionship, but he was not idle.

Because of the Lord removing His Spirit, Saul sought a harp player to soothe his own soul. As Saul began to inquire, a servant of the king replied that he knew a harp player who was the son of Jesse, one skilled, brave, wise, and handsome (1 Samuel 16:18 NASB). Jesse must have had some regional importance, for the servant describes this lad as "a son of Jesse." The most significant thing about the verse is how it concludes with the final comment of the servant saying, "The Lord is with him." Although David knew he had been anointed the next king; nevertheless, he faithfully served King Saul. Since David's name meant "beloved," it is not surprising that David was loved by Saul and became his armor bearer. He could also soothe Saul's troubled spirit with his harp.

While David was serving in the king's court, the king went to battle against the Philistines southwest of Jerusalem. In the king's absence, David returned home to tend his father's sheep at Bethlehem, just six miles south of Jerusalem. Only fifteen miles west of Bethlehem, the Philistines and Israelites were in a military standoff. The Philistines lived along the shoreline, while the Israelites lived along the mountain ridgeline. The confrontation was in a fertile valley halfway between the shore and the mountains. Most of us know well the story of David and the nine-and-a-half-feet-tall Philistine giant named Goliath (1 Samuel 17:4). A couple of insights reveal this contest to be an example of God's showing His provision. All of David's brothers were at David's anointing by Samuel to be king. David arrived with food for his three older brothers and David questioned them, "Who is this uncircumcised Philistine that he should defy the armies of the living God?" (1 Samuel 17:26 NASB). Nevertheless, Eliah, David's oldest brother, was angry toward David. He responds to David with a question, "Who have you left to tend those few sheep?" He also charged his little brother David with pride and a sullen attitude. Undoubtedly, part of Eliah's frustration had to do with the Israelites being daily challenged by Goliath for the past forty days.

These confrontations took place where two mountain ridges are not very far apart. The Philistines and Israelites could easily survey each other's daily activities, hence the frustration in Israel and the haughtiness of the Philistines. In this story, we see David's heart for God's matters. He does not call the giant by name, but he calls him an "uncircumcised Philistine." By uncircumcised, this meant that these peoples did not follow God's covenant with Abraham by being circumcised as required in Genesis 17:10. Further, Philistines were worshippers of Dagon (Judges 16:23) and of Baal-Zebub (2 Kings 1:1-2). In contrast with the dead stone idols of the Philistines, David's question includes the phrase, "of the living God." Obviously, this is a *spiritual issue* with David, while it is a *military issue* with all the others.

There was a second reason why the Israelites were afraid of these giants. In addition to their sheer physical size, the Philistines had another major advantage. First Samuel 13:19-20 provides the answer. The Philistines had a closely guarded secret—they knew how to forge iron and had many weapons. The Israelites only acquired or sharpened their metal items at the mercy of these metal-working, monopolistic Philistines. Goliath was heavily suited in a brass helmet, armor, and metal weapons. Experts have calculated all this metal Goliath wore and carried could have weighed almost one hundred fifty pounds. The Philistines had swords and spears. As we saw earlier, Samson was equipped with only his hands or the jawbone of a donkey. David carried only a slingshot. Goliath cursed God by his god, Dagon. We see that even Goliath ended up making this a *spiritual* battle.

David stopped at the small stream to pick up five small stones (1 Samuel 17:40 NASB). Why did David get five stones? Did he think it would take more than one stone to accomplish this task? Probably not. He had defended the sheep against the lion and the bear. The Bible offers us another, more subtle reason why he selected five stones. Goliath had four brothers who were also giants with six fingers on each hand and six toes on each foot. Three of these four brothers are even named in the Bible: Ishbi-Benob, Saph, (also known as Sippai), and Lahmi (2 Samuel 21:16, 18, 20-21; 1 Chronicles 20:4-5 NASB). This same Lahmi will later be killed by David's nephew. The unnamed fifth giant brother appears in 2 Samuel 21:20-21 and in 1 Chronicles 20:6-7. David selected five smooth stones because Goliath had four giant brothers whom David might have to face after he dealt with Goliath.

This was a spiritual battle. The Philistines had spears, helmets, and swords fashioned by their metal-working prowess. They were giants. Earlier, the twelve spies Moses sent into the Promised

Land said the people were giants and "we are in our own sight as grasshoppers" (Numbers 13:33). While the giant Goliath was nine-and-a-half feet tall, the average Israelite adult male was only about five feet tall. (Later, Joshua 13:1-3 tells us the Israelites never completely drove the Philistines out of the Promised Land. Hence, the conflict between the Jews and the Palestinians is still unresolved even today in the twenty-first century, as the land of the Philistines is now occupied by the Palestinians and known as the Gaza Strip.)

Against these odds, David ran to confront Goliath, declaring that he is coming in "the name of the Lord of hosts, armies of the living God, who you defy." (In this era, host was a military term inferring armies.) David also makes this confrontation a "witness that all of the earth may know there is a God in Israel. And this assembly may know that the Lord saves, not with sword and spear for the battle is the Lord's and He will give you into our hands" (1 Samuel 17:47).

Earlier, King Saul announced he would give "great riches" and his daughter to wed to whomever could defeat this giant. It is easy to see that the Spirit of the Lord had left King Saul, for he was focused only on earthly material things. But David's focus was on the living God, those defying God, those defying the armies of God, the uncircumcised, and the Lord's battle. Upon David killing Goliath, Saul fulfilled his vow by giving his youngest daughter, Michal, as a wife to David. Michal loved David; this pleased Saul, but unfortunately for the wrong reason (1 Samuel 18:20-21 NASB). Saul wanted Michal to be a snare to David. As a dowry, Saul requested the death of one hundred Philistines. Certainly David saw Saul's strategy. Now that David had killed Goliath for Saul, the king became jealous of David's popularity. David has already escaped not once but twice from Saul's throwing a spear at him. Saul was still king, but the prophet Samuel had already informed the king, "The Lord has rejected thee as King over Israel." David knew Samuel had anointed him king. Saul recalled that Samuel himself delivered the message of God's rejection of him as king. The king hoped David would be killed in his quest to destroy one hundred Philistines. David came back undefeated with not one hundred, but two hundred dead Philistines. First Samuel 18:12 declares that the Lord was with David and had left Saul. Shortly thereafter, in verse 28, Saul expresses his acknowledgement that the Lord is with David.

Scattered throughout these chapters, the Bible shows Saul was possessed by an evil spirit. We see that Saul was persistent in trying to murder David, first by spear and then by recruiting his servants in the palace. After the servants, Saul enlisted his son, Prince Jonathan (the potential, future king) and his daughter, Michal, David's wife (1 Samuel 19:11-12). Later, Saul recruited his army to seek the band of soldiers coalescing around David. Yet, David was always the real objective, not the rebellious soldiers. David twice spared Saul's life while the King sought to slay him. In 1 Samuel 24:17, Saul acknowledges that David has been good to the king in return for Saul being evil toward David. Furthermore, the King admits David will be his successor. Saul's only request is that his *seed* not be destroyed and David agrees. Just as much has been made about the relationship between Naomi and her daughter-in-law, Ruth, much attention has been given to the friendship that developed between Saul's oldest son, Jonathan, and David. With David's marriage to Saul's younger daughter, Michal, these two young men were no longer just friends but became brothers-in-law.

After Saul and Jonathan died in battle, David became King of Israel. David's reign established the Davidic dynasty, which proceeds through twenty successor kings over a four-hundred-year period. But more important is God's plan for the Royal Seed to flow through David and his descendants. Just as Nahshon was the most important person to survive Pharaoh's six-hundred-chariot pursuit of the Israelites in the parting of the Red Sea, David became Israel's most important and greatest King, not because of his kingship or Davidic dynasty, but because he was the single carrier of the Royal Seed.

The attempts on David's life were numerous and significant. The Royal Seed was continually at risk of being exterminated in the life of David. Over the course of human history, Satan made repeated attempts to snuff out this lineage of over seventy-five generations, with each generation usually having just one man as the carrier of the Royal Seed. David was one of the high watermarks in these seventy-five-plus generations. He was first king in Bethlehem, but later he also ruled as king from Jerusalem. He wrote numerous songs recorded in the Book of Psalms. He brought the Ark of the Covenant into Jerusalem (2 Samuel 6:12-19 NASB). And he gathered the material for Solomon to build the first temple (1 Chronicles 28:11-19; 29:1-2 NASB). In Revelation 22, the last chapter of the Bible, Jesus reaches back one thousand years and thirty generations to declare himself, "the offspring of David." Satan, in his perpetual rebellion against God's plan, struggled mightily to kill David and stop this progression of the Royal Seed. At least ten separate attempts were made to kill David. First were the lions and bears when David was a shepherd. Saul tried twice with a spear. Goliath was another person to challenge him. Saul's demand of the dowry of one hundred Philistines was still another attempt by David's future father-in-law to kill the groom. Yet, David defeated not one hundred, but two hundred Philistines. At least three attempts were made in battles between Saul's army and David's men. On still another occasion, Michal saved her husband's life. And finally, there was the rebellion of his own son, Absalom. Satan made nine or ten attempts (or two hundred) to kill David, but God was the victor every single time. God jealously guarded His Royal Seed and His master plan. Neither Satan nor man would stop the progression of God's plan to protect, shepherd, guard, and advance God's design for His Royal Seed.

After Saul and Jonathan died in battle, David was anointed king in Hebron over just the land of Judah (2 Samuel 2:1-11 NASB). He reigned in Judah for seven-and-a-half years, during which time his first six sons were born. His third oldest son, Absalom, was the grandson of the king of Geshur by Absalom's mother being the Princess of Geshur. (Geshur was just east of the Sea of Galilee, an area commonly known today as the Golan Heights.) Hebron was situated twelve miles south of Bethlehem, and Bethlehem was six miles south of Jerusalem. Hebron, the capital of Judah, was only about eighteen miles from Jerusalem, the capital of all the rest of Israel.

The Lord told David to go to Hebron (2 Samuel 2:1). Hebron is significant for it was the location of the Cave of Machpelah where Abraham, Sarah (Genesis 23:19), Isaac (Genesis 25:9), Rebekah, Leah (Genesis 49:31), and Jacob (Genesis 50:13) were all buried. Caleb, as the spy representing the tribe of Judah, chose Hebron as his reward after he was one of the two spies who gave Moses a positive report. Hebron had a centuries-long heritage close to the heart of

Judah. Conflict soon ensued between the house of Saul trying to retain control in Jerusalem and the reign of David in Judah. After David fled from Saul, King Saul gave his daughter Michal, David's wife, to another man (1Samuel 25:44). In Jerusalem, Abner was loyal to Ish-bosheth, Saul's son who became the succeeding king upon Saul's death. After a brief period of time, the king accused Abner of adultery with Saul's concubine and Abner defected to David's kingdom. David's messengers told Abner that David would not meet with him until Abner retrieved Michal. Michal was David's first wife, but now David has six wives and each has a son. David's demand that Abner bring Michal to him before agreeing to meet with Abner was a strategic one. Having Michal within Judah, in David's Kingdom, would strengthen his claim to her father's larger kingdom.

In the second year of his reign, Ish-bosheth was assassinated by some of his followers. Thereafter, David killed the murderers of Ish-bosheth and David's claim to not just Judah, but to all of Israel became more secure. He became the logical successor to Saul by being married to Saul's daughter, and she has been reunited with David in Hebron. Finally, the elders of Israel came to Hebron to ask David to reign over them. David is now thirty years of age. Second Samuel 5:4-5 summarizes his reign at seven-and-a-half years in Judah and thirty-three years in Jerusalem.

Bethlehem is first called the City of David in Luke 2:4, because Bethlehem was where Jesse (David's father), Boaz, and Ruth (David's great-grandparents) had lived, and it was where David spent his early years. Upon David's "capture" of Jerusalem, Jerusalem also became known as the City of David. Jerusalem became the capital of Jewry and has remained its capital city for these past three thousand years. There were two "City of David" locations—Bethlehem and Jerusalem.

King David had secured his new capital in Jerusalem. His selection of the most significant location in all of Jerusalem will be the site where the permanent temple will be built.

The traveling tabernacle has been mobile for the prior four hundred years. The history of the tabernacle started after Moses came down a second time from Mount Sinai. Moses, along with Aaron, Aaron's two oldest sons, and seventy elders had worshiped on Mount Sinai. There God had instructed Moses in "all of the words of the Lord." At daybreak, Moses constructed an altar on twelve legs to represent the twelve tribes (Exodus 24:4 NASB). God then told Moses to come up and receive the tables of stone. Moses climbed further up Mount Sinai. A cloud covered the summit and the glory of the Lord abode on Mount Sinai for six days (Exodus 24). Immediately afterwards, the Lord told Moses to request an offering of all who would give willingly. Remember, the Egyptians were plundered and had freely given jewels, silver, gold, and raiment to the departing Israelite slaves (Exodus 12:35-36 NASB). Exodus 25 begins with this offering. By Exodus 26, these former slaves had contributed so much gold, silver, and raiment to build the tabernacle that *they are restrained from giving any more gifts*. In verse 8 the Lord speaks to Moses, telling him to instruct the people to "make me a sanctuary that I may dwell among them." God then instructs in precise detail the building of a box, an ark out of wood covered with gold. It is to have a lid of pure gold. The dimensions are approximately 3'9" long and 2'6" wide. Rings are to be attached on the long sides of the Ark, into which poles will be placed to provide for movement of the Ark by certain Kohathite priests. This box became known as the

Ark of the Covenant. Over the centuries, at least two other titles are used for this chest: Ark of the Lord (Joshua 4:11) and Ark of God (1 Chronicles 13:12). It is sanctified as holy to the Lord in Exodus 30:26. God commands them to place these items inside: the law (Exodus 25:16-21), Aaron's rod (Numbers 17:10, Hebrews 9:4), and a bowl of manna (Exodus 16:33, Hebrews 9:4). Above the solid gold lid were two cherubim. Between the cherubim was the area known as the Mercy Seat. This location between the cherubim is where the Lord told Moses, "I will meet thee and commune with thee above this Mercy Seat" (Exodus 25:21-22).

As the entourage traveled for forty years in the desert, the tabernacle and the Ark were at the center of the caravan. However, at the battle for Jericho, Joshua instructed the priest to carry the Ark into battle as the Israelites marched around the city. Thereafter, for the next four hundred years, the Ark of the Covenant was the focal point in the tabernacle. Over these four centuries, the Israelites became presumptuous as God's chosen people and did not bother to follow His commandments and law. In 1 Samuel 4, the people engaged the Philistines in battle and were defeated. The Israelites then decided to bring the Ark from Shiloh to the battle site. The Philistines also won this second battle. After this second encounter, the Philistines carried the Ark of the Covenant back to Ashdod, the city where the temple of Dagon was located.

The Ark was placed in the temple of Dagon. The next morning, the statue of Dagon had fallen down before the Ark. The second morning, the Philistines again went into the temple of Dagon. Once again, the statue of Dagon had fallen on its face before the Ark. Upon this second occurrence, however, the head and both hands of Dagon were broken off. Furthermore, plagues had broken out among the Philistines. With the statue of their god broken and the people afflicted with plagues, after seven months the Philistines decide to return the Ark to the Israelites. The priests of Dagon recommended that a new cart be built and hooked to two milk cows which had never had a yoke placed upon their necks. The Ark of the Covenant was then placed upon the cart and a trespass offering of gold items was placed alongside the Ark on the cart. The unsupervised cows promptly headed toward the land of Judah. Upon arriving in Judah, the Ark was taken off the cart. The cart was burned and the two milk cows offered as a burnt offering sacrifice to God. Some of the Levites looked into the Ark and were killed by the Lord. Because of these deaths, the Ark was then taken to the house of a man named of Abinadab where it remained for two decades.

In one of David's first acts as king of the unified Israel, he desired the Mercy Seat of God dwell no longer in a mobile tent or tabernacle but in a permanent temple of wood and stone. David's goal began to be implemented with the Ark of the Covenant being brought up to Jerusalem. David and thousands of his men were accompanying the Ark on the journey to Jerusalem, playing all kinds of horns, cymbals, harps, and other instruments. Numbers 4:5-6, 15 and 7:9 tell us only the Kohathites were to touch the most holy articles. The Ark was only to be moved by the Kohathites, and the Kohathites were to carry the Ark only by the staves (Exodus 25:14-15). The oxen pulling the cart carrying the Ark of the Covenant stumbled. When one of the men, Uzzah, reached up to steady the Ark, immediately he was struck dead. The merriment stopped after the death of Uzzah.

Second Samuel 6:8 relates that David was displeased with the Lord's killing of Uzzah. However, David quickly realized, "Who am I to question the authority of God?" The very next verse states that David was afraid of the Lord. Upon reflection, David acknowledged the details of God's plan. David ordered the Ark carried into another man's house along the way. For three months, while the Ark was residing in this home, this homeowner, Obed-edom, was blessed.

After acknowledging Obed-edom's blessings, David made a second attempt to get the Ark to Jerusalem. As the trip began, David made sacrifices unto God. This entourage included much merriment, with trumpets and dancing. David danced mightily. His wife Michal, Saul's daughter, saw David jumping up and down, and she despised him in her heart. After the Ark was brought into the tent David had erected to use in lieu of the tabernacle, the people again made offerings, having received bread, meat, and wine to enjoy. Later, Michal verbally attacked David for appearing unkingly. Michal must have still worshiped idols, for she had an idol in her home (1 Samuel 19:13 NASB). She appeared to think only in worldly terms, as her father had, and did not appear to meditate on the deep things of God. Though Uzzah tried to steady the ark and yet died, Michal did not seem to be in fear of (or exhibit reverence for) the holy things of God. David's response was, "I was chosen by God above your father and I will be more excited than this before the Lord." Second Samuel 6:23 tells us that Michal, the daughter of Saul, remained barren until the day of her death.

At the conclusion of its four-hundred-year journey, after residing in a tent in the desert for forty years, after crossing the Jordan River, after the battle of Jericho, after resting in Shiloh, after being carried into battle, after its loss in battle, after being displayed in the temple of Dagon, after being transported by wandering milk cows, and after being stationed in two family homes, the Ark of the Covenant *finally* arrived in Jerusalem. Certainly, David was pleased to have the Ark of the Covenant in the city, although it was only housed in a tent David had erected for it. The Tent of Tabernacle was still in Gibeon (1 Chronicles 21:29 NASB).

Earlier, we learned that Levi had three sons: Gershon, Kohath, and Merari. The sons of Kohath were assigned the most holy duties inside the tabernacle. The transporting, assembling, and taking down of the tabernacle were the obligations of the clans of Gershon, Merari, and other Levites. These job descriptions were appropriate for the Sinai Desert. But after David had established his capital in Jerusalem and consolidated the region into the nation of Israel, the duties of moving the Ark of the Covenant and the Tent of Tabernacle were obsolete (1 Chronicles 23:25-26).

Once David's Tent of Meeting was in an urban and permanent location, new duties were required of the Levites (1 Chronicles 6:31-32; 23:13 NASB). Some of the holy duties of the Kohathites were the same, but no longer did the Kohathites have to pack and unpack the "most holy things" of the tabernacle. In addition, the sons of Gershon and Merari were assigned new tasks. These two clans became porters, overseers, guards, and gatekeepers. Still others from the clans of Gershon and Merari, along with some of the Levites, became musicians and singers in the stationary tent which David erected before the temple was built.

Eventually, Israel had three distinct structures for worship. First was the tabernacle, a tent that was moved in the Sinai Desert. Next, David erected a Tent of Meeting in Jerusalem to house the Ark while the Sinai tent was still in Gibeon (1 Chronicles 16:1 NASB). Finally, Solomon built a permanent temple in Jerusalem constructed with the stone and wood materials that had been gathered by his father, David (1 Chronicles 28:11-19).

King David could not comfortably enjoy his palatial palace with God's Ark of the Covenant located in a tent. David told the prophet Nathan he wanted to build a permanent structure for the Ark of the Covenant, and Nathan gave David approval. That night, in a vision, God told Nathan, "I have not lived in a house for four hundred years but in the Tent of Tabernacle. I took David from being a young shepherd to ruler over my people. I have created a permanent place for my people, Israel. They shall move no more. I have appointed judges to reign until the kingdom is established. Tell David once he is deceased 'I will set up thy *seed* after thee and he shall build a house in my name, and his throne will be forever.'" This first temple will stand approximately four hundred years, until its destruction by Nebuchadnezzar in 586 BC (2 Kings 25:9 NASB).

In 1 Chronicles 28:3, David tells the princes of Israel that "the Lord would not permit me to build a temple, because I had shed blood as a man of war." God chose David's son, Solomon, to erect the permanent temple. Thus, we see another covenant by God much like the Abrahamic covenant God had made one thousand years earlier. True, a great nation has come from Abraham. Yes, the seeds of Abraham are more numerous with each passing day. True, the nation now has its Promised Land. They will never have to leave their permanent possession. Because David saw God fulfilling the one-thousand-year-old Abrahamic covenant, this helped David to believe in the Davidic covenant that God was now making with him. God was declaring to David, through the prophet Nathan, that He will be as faithful to David as He had been to Abraham. (As David was listening to the prophet Nathan, he surely must have been thinking, *"God saved me, a little shepherd boy, from the lion and the bear. I was the youngest of eight sons. With my slingshot, I defeated Goliath, who was wearing one hundred fifty pounds of metal. At least nine or ten attempts have been made to kill me. Nevertheless, God spared my life. The last judge, the prophet Samuel, anointed me. I did not grasp for the throne, but the people came to me. And now God is declaring a covenant with me."*) Although the Lord will not permit David to build the temple due to his shedding of blood in twenty years of wars and conflicts, nevertheless, God will permit him to gather the material for the temple's construction. David replied with a wonderful response:

> And David the King came and sat before the Lord and said "Who am I, O Lord, and what is my house that thou has brought me this far? And yet, this was a small thing in thine eyes, O God...O Lord, there's none like thee, neither is there any God beside Thee" (1 Chronicles 17:16-20).

Just as the Lord invoked this covenant with David, David remembered the covenant he made as a young man with his friend Jonathan, who later became his brother-in-law.

Prince Jonathan was the oldest son of King Saul. Upon his father's death, he should have succeeded his father as king. First Samuel 20 shows a covenant between these two young men, David and Jonathan. Jonathan asks David to promise he will not only show kindness to him while he lives but also after he dies. In verse 15, Jonathan asks David to be considerate of his family forever. Jonathan acknowledges that David will be the future king of Israel. A couple of verses later, the Word tells us "Jonathan loved David as he loved his own soul."

Later in life, David recalled his covenant with the deceased Jonathan, who died in battle along with his father, Saul, and two other brothers (1 Samuel 31:2 NASB). In 2 Samuel 9:1, David inquires if any of Saul's descendants are still alive. A former servant of Saul tells the king that Jonathan had a son who was dropped by his nurse when he was five years old and was lame in both feet (v. 13). His name is Mephibosheth. David searches for the now young adult Mephibosheth, who is summoned to the king's court. David informs Jonathan's son of the covenant that he and his father had made decades earlier. David gives all the land previously owned by Saul to this grandson. Furthermore, the king provides Saul's servant and the servant's son to farm the land for Mephibosheth. This servant, Ziba, will later betray David, and David will kill Ziba and his followers while yet sparing Mephibosheth's life. David pledges to always provide for Mephibosheth at the king's table. Mephibosheth has a son, Micha, who was Saul's great grandson. In 1 Chronicles 8:34, Micha (or Michah) is the father of four sons. This chapter traces the next ten generations of Mephibosheth's descendants, fulfilling David's covenant he had made with Jonathan.

We see the integrity of David's commitment and his purity of heart in sustaining a twenty-year-old covenant with the deceased Jonathan. His integrity reflects God's own honoring of a thousand-year-old covenant with the deceased Abraham.

As 2 Samuel concludes, David takes a census of the soldiers available for warfare. The total number of men is 1.3 million. This census displeases God because He desired David to be a shepherd-king of His flock, Israel, and not a man of war. When Gad, another of God's prophets, confronts the king, David confesses his sin of taking the census of soldiers. In following the Lord's direction, Gad offers David three choices of punishment: seven years of famine, three months of fleeing his enemies, or three days of pestilence. David chooses the shortest time frame and selects the pestilence and seventy thousand people are killed throughout the land. When the death angel reaches Jerusalem, God instructs the angel to refrain. The angel is told to stop when he nears the threshing floor of a man named Araunah, a Jebusite. Gad comes to David and announces God wants the king to go to this particular threshing site. David follows these instructions from the prophet. When Araunah sees the king coming, he falls on his face before the king. David tells the miller he is there to buy the threshing floor as a site for an altar so the plague will be removed. Araunah responds, "Take it. And here are oxen and wood to use for the sacrifice. I will give them to you." David replies, "No, I will surely buy the site at a fair price as I will not make any offering to God that costs me nothing." (Recall a similar account of Prince Abraham when he bought a burial plot for his princess Sarah (Genesis 17:5; 23:8-16 NASB). He was offered a site for free by Ephron, but Abraham objected and told the owner, "I will pay full price." He purchased with silver the cave of Machpelah in Hebron as a burial site.)

David buys the site, the threshing floor and the oxen, and pays with silver. The account in 1 Chronicles 21:25 lists a different price with the full price being paid by gold. (Scholars feel this difference is due to what was being purchased). In 2 Samuel 24:24, the price in silver is for the threshing floor and the oxen. The assets bought with the gold are for a much larger area.

It was not just any man, but the king himself who acquired the threshing floor, the oxen, the wheat, and the surrounding real estate—for a full price. This threshing floor of Araunah and the adjoining real estate was not to be just any ordinary site. David brought the Ark into Jerusalem, but it was situated in a tent. The tabernacle, which Bezalel built under Moses' supervision in the desert, was not in Jerusalem, but still in Gibeon. With the purchase of Araunah's property, God now provided the building site for a temple. (Today we know this site as the Temple Mount.) David purchased the site from Araunah with silver and gold. The Jews have never sold the site. Babylonians, the Ottoman Empire, and Muslims have occupied the site, but it has never been sold. Umayyad Caliph Abd al-Malik erected the Dome of the Rock on this site over one thousand three hundred years ago. But squatters' rights do not apply to this piece of real estate. David bought it, and his heirs have never sold it.

Earlier, the Lord directed Abraham to carry Isaac to Mount Moriah and place him on an altar. Although Abraham dwelled fifty miles away, this was the site God had chosen to test Abraham by instructing him to journey here to sacrifice Isaac.

This precise site was known in Abraham's day as Mount Moriah. Five hundred years later, the area was more developed: the village of Jebus had become the town of Jerusalem. Mount Moriah was now occupied by a business, the threshing floor of Araunah. Even earlier, when Abram (before his name was changed to Abraham) rescued Lot, Abram had been led to bring a tithe to the king of Salem, Melchizedek (Genesis 14:11-19). (Most scholars believe this "Salem" was the older name for JeruSALEM).

Melchizedek was not only the king of Salem but he was also priest of the Most High God. Melchizedek was both *priest and king*. In the very next verse, Melchizedek addresses Abram as "Abram of the Most High God." After blessing Abram, Melchizedek declares God is "possessor of heaven and earth." The *priestly* title implied *ultimate authority* in *heaven*. The *kingly* title implied *supreme authority* on *Earth*. Abram tithed from his spoils of battle to Melchizedek. This action shows Abram's submission to the authority of this king-priest. Most Bible scholars consider Melchizedek to be a pre-New Testament appearance of Jesus. Other evidence of this position is found in Hebrews 7 when the unknown author describes Melchizedek as "king of righteousness" and "king of peace." Furthermore, the author describes this priest-king as being "without father or mother, without a genealogy." To the Levites with their emphasis on tracing genealogy all the way to Aaron, this would have been unthinkable, even blasphemous, but the author of Hebrews does not stop there (Ezra 2:62; 7:1-5 NASB). He further explains that this priest-king has "neither the beginning of days nor end of life, but is similar to the Son of God in his being a continual priest forever." As great as Abraham was, even he showed honor and submission to Melchizedek in tithes and offerings to this king of Salem. Hebrews 6:20 calls Jesus a High Priest of the order of Melchizedek and in 7:11, states that the priesthood of Melchizedek is superior to the priesthood of Aaron. No less than David himself acknowledges the order of Melchizedek in Psalm 110. Of the one hundred fifty psalms, the Davidic Psalm 110 is the most quoted Psalm through the New Testament. It acknowledges the Lord as sovereign king and permanent priest. If Melchizedek was not only Christ-like but also a real person who was King of Salem, it appears that his territory would be very, very close in proximity to the location where Abraham was instructed by God thirteen generations earlier to sacrifice Isaac on Mount Moriah. One of David's final acts as king was to purchase the threshing floor from Araunah, the Jebusite, and its surrounding real estate (2 Samuel 24:19-25 NASB). This same land is where Solomon built the first temple, which was used by the Israelites for over four centuries until its destruction by Nebuchadnezzar.

As David was buying this real estate, as a man after God's own heart, he surely remembered the testimony of his forefather Abraham at this site, and how Abraham had named it *Jehovah-Jireh*, which means "the Lord will provide." Certainly, David recalled how God reaffirmed to Abraham the covenant and the multiplying of his seed (Genesis 22:17-18 NASB).

One hundred years after Nebuchadnezzar razed the first temple, Zerubbabel built the second temple at this same site.

Thus, Salem of Melchizedek's day, Mt. Moriah of Abraham's day, the mountain summit renamed by Abram as Jehovah-Jireh, the threshing floor bought by David from the Jebusite Araunah, the location of the temple built by Solomon, the temple built by Zerubbabel, the temple built by Herod where Jesus as a twelve-year-old lad taught the Rabbinic teachers, the temple where Jesus led his disciples to teach them, and Mount Zion are all part and parcel of this same real estate. All of these events occurred on the *same* plot of ground where the Dome of the Rock, (the Mosque of Omar) stands today. These are *ten different names for the same place.*

Much has been written about David's wife, Bathsheba. His adultery with her and his murder of her husband, Uriah, is well known. The child conceived in this adulterous act died only seven days after birth. The genealogy of David is outlined in 1 Chronicles 3 and 5. It lists David's nineteen sons. These sons have at least eight different mothers. Although David had nineteen sons plus other sons by concubines, David and Bathsheba were blessed with four more sons after the death of their first-born. Assuming their illegitimate son was unnamed, Solomon, their fifth and youngest son, was selected by God to follow David on the throne of Israel. As David was the youngest of eight sons when Samuel anointed him king, Solomon, Bathsheba's youngest of five sons, will succeed his father David as king.

Near the end of his reign, David placed the Ark of the Covenant into a tent in Jerusalem. Earlier, the Ark of the Covenant was housed at Shiloh, about twenty miles due north of Jerusalem, before being captured by the Philistines. (The bronze altar used for sacrificing animals and the other instruments of the tabernacle were still located with the Tent of Meeting in Gibeon, eight miles northwest of Jerusalem.) Later, David purchased real estate in Jerusalem on which to erect a tent to house just the Ark. Later still, David secured the sanctified property of Mount Moriah as the site for the permanent temple. Furthermore, he acquired the construction materials to build a temple (1 Chronicles 22:1-5), but David was not finished just yet. He also had the floor plans, the blueprints of the exact dimensions of the temple and its furnishings, and gave them to Solomon. The temple's dimensions were almost exactly double the size of the tabernacle tent.

It may appear David was overbearing in his treatment of Solomon. But 1 Chronicles 22:5 and 29:1 gives the answer: Solomon was "young and tender, yet the work is great." We know the tabernacle and brazen altar remained in Gibeon during David's life, for Solomon went there to worship. It was also at Gibeon where Solomon was asked by God, in a dream, what he would wish for. Solomon's answer was for "an understanding heart and wisdom" (1 Kings 3:4-9).

At the conclusion of David's life, God's plan slowly unfolded even further. At the end of the king's life, the situation was as follows:

Status of God's Plan

Ark of Covenant - in Jerusalem, in tent David provided
Site of temple – in Jerusalem, real estate had been acquired
Building material for temple – in Jerusalem, inventory had been acquired
Tabernacle Tent – still located in Gibeon
Brazen altar - in Gibeon with the Tabernacle Tent

Finally, as we have seen in most other concluding chapters, mighty King David is an ancestor of Jesus (Psalms 2:6; Matthew 9:27).

> "Christ cometh out of the *seed* of David and out of the town of Bethlehem" (John 7:42; emphasis added).

> "Of this man's [David's] *seed*, God, according to His promise, raised up for Israel a savior, Jesus" (Acts 13:22-23; emphasis added).

> "Jesus was made [born] of the *seed* of David according to the flesh" (Roman 1:3; emphasis added).

> "Weep not, behold the Lion of the tribe of Judah, the *root* of David hath prevailed" (Revelation 5:5; emphasis added).

Perhaps one of the most interesting things about David has to do with genealogy. It is possible that when David was acquiring Araunah's threshing floor, he may have thought of his ancestors, Abraham (thirteen generations earlier) and Isaac (twelve generations earlier). If he did, it would be very consistent with Jesus's thoughts of His own ancestor David. The Israelites had maintained genealogical records for four hundred thirty years while slaves in Egypt. This enabled Moses to appoint Nahshon as Prince of Judah shortly after the Exodus. Over the centuries after David's reign, the Jews *continue keeping their genealogical records for five hundred years after David's death.* Anani is David's last recorded descendant. Anani lived in the time of Malachi, or about 430 BC

(1 Chronicles 3:24 NASB). This exhibits the *Jews' five-hundred-year persistent hope of the restoration of the Davidic dynasty to the throne of Israel and the long-awaited Messiah.*

In the last book of the Bible and in the last chapter of that book, Revelation 22, Jesus, in His last twenty words to mankind, describes His heritage as, "I am the root and offspring of David" (Revelation 22:16).

Though David was an adulterer and murderer, when Jesus invokes the name of Israel's greatest king, He is connecting the lineage of the Royal Seed, not to twelve or thirteen generations prior as David had done to Abraham, but to about thirty generations earlier to King David himself, who lived one thousand years before Jesus.

What have we learned about David?

1. Two hundred years after David's reign, Isaiah prophesied about a future descendant of King David, seven centuries into the future —the Messiah. Isaiah may have been a member of the royal family of Israel. If so, he was writing about his own family. For certain, unlike some of the prophets, Isaiah had access to the royal family. In Isaiah 11:1, we read the Messiah will be "a shoot on the stem of Jesse" and in verse 10, "the root of Jesse." Both of these acknowledge Jesse as David's forerunner and ancestor. Isaiah lays the foundation for both Jesse and David to be ancestors of Jesus.

2. The Philistines knew metallurgy and the Israelites did not.

3. David was prepared not only for Goliath but also for his four giant brothers.

4. Because Israelites never fully obeyed God in securing the Promised Land, the Arab-Jewish conflict continues even today in the twenty-first century. The territory of the ancient Philistines is known today as the Gaza Strip.

5. David established a dynasty of twenty kings who reigned for a period of four hundred years.

6. At least ten attempts were made by Satan to kill David, God's choice to be the next "carrier" of the Royal Seed.

7. Two cities in the Bible are known as "the city of David," Bethlehem and Jerusalem.

8. The Philistines' god, Dagon, "fell flat" before the Ark of the Covenant, breaking the stone idol's head and hands off, while the Philistines suffered a plague. Eventually, the Philistines became the Palestinians, and Dagon was abandoned for Islam.

9. The Levites who looked inside the Ark of the Covenant were struck dead.

10. Jonathan and David were not only very good friends; they became brothers-in-law when David married his first wife, Michal.

11. David honored his covenant from twenty years earlier with Jonathan by restoring the entire land owned by Saul and Jonathan to Jonathan's son, Mephibosheth.

12. David was punished for the adultery with Bathsheba by the death of their one-week-old son. Their fifth son was Solomon, the future king.

13. When David ordered a census of soldiers, he was punished by a pestilence that killed many people.

14. Mount Moriah; Salem; the threshing floor of Araunah; Mount Zion; Jehovah-Jireh; Solomon's, Zerubbabel's, and Herod's temples; and the Temple Mount, are all the same site. For the past one thousand three hundred years, the Mosque of Omar, commonly known as the Dome of the Rock, has occupied this same site. Melchizedek, priest of the Most High God, lived very near this site as well.

15. God specifically stated the Ark of the Covenant was not to travel by any other means than the staves being grasped by the sons of Kohath.

16. When Uzzah just touched the Ark of the Covenant to steady it, he died immediately. Only certain of the sons of Aaron, the Kohathites, were to touch "the most holy things."

17. Michal, Saul's daughter, possibly came close to being chosen by God to birth the next Royal Seed, yet she condemned her husband, King David, and died childless.

18. In the Old Testament, the Ark of the Covenant is last mentioned in Jeremiah 3:16. In the New Testament, in Hebrews chapter 8, Jesus is announced as the High Priest. Hebrews 9 then reintroduces the Ark.

19. Obviously Hollywood has not read Revelation, for although Harrison Ford in "The Raiders of the Lost Ark" may still be searching for the lost Ark, Revelation 11:19 shares an insight with us: "And the Temple of God was opened in Heaven, and there was seen in His Temple, the Ark of His Testament."

20. David gave of his personal wealth, three thousand talents of gold for the temple's construction (1 Chronicles 29:3-4). A talent weighed about seventy-five pounds; three thousand talents equaled two hundred twenty-five thousand pounds. With twelve ounces in a pound, this sum would amount to as much as 2.7 million ounces of gold. At $1,300 per ounce, today's value of the gold would approximate $3.5 billion. If the talents refer to a weight of sixteen ounces per pound, then the value of gold at $1,600 per ounce might be worth as much as $6 billion.

21. In Scripture quoted earlier, John, Luke, and Paul all stressed the seed of David. Jesus called himself an offspring of David. Some translations of the Bible interpret 2 Timothy 2:8 as Jesus being a "descendant of David." Jeremiah used the term "branch of David" for the future Messiah. Matthew 9:27 records two blind men declaring Jesus "the son of David." Mark notes Bartimaeus calls Jesus, "son of David" (Mark 10:47). Isaiah, Jeremiah, Matthew, Mark, Luke, John, Paul, and Jesus himself, all declare Jesus to be the "son of David." This documentation of the lineage of the Royal Seed seems important to Jesus and five writers of the New Testament. One of these authors, Luke, wrote the books of Luke and Acts. Remember, Luke was the only non-Jew to write any of the New Testament. Consequently, a non-Jew wrote over one half of the New Testament. Luke was a frequent companion of Paul, who wrote another one-quarter of the New Testament. The authors of three-fourths of the New Testament emphasized the lineage of the Royal Seed from David to Jesus. Undoubtedly, it was God's plan for the Royal Seed to flow through David and his descendants, and ultimately to Jesus. *Once the royal genealogy*

arrived at Jesus, there are no New Testament genealogies. All the genealogies in the Bible stop with Jesus's birth.

David's Relatives

Name	**Relationship**	**APPROXIMATE Dates**
Adam	Great-grandfather, 31 generations removed	±4000 BC
Noah	Great-grandfather, 22 generations removed	±3500 BC
Abraham	Great-grandfather, 11 generations removed	±2100 BC
Aaron	Great-uncle, 5 generations removed	±1350 BC
Rahab	Great-great-grandmother	±1250 BC
Boaz	Great-grandfather	±1200 BC
Ruth	Great-grandmother	±1150 BC
Absalom	Son	1000 BC
Nathan	Son	1000 BC
Solomon	Son	1000 BC
Rehoboam	Grandson	950 BC
Jehoshaphat	Great-grandson, 3 generations removed	900 BC
Hezekiah	Great-grandson, 11 generations removed	750 BC
Zerubbabel	Great-grandson, 19 generations removed	550 BC
Mary	Great-granddaughter, 39 generations removed	20 BC
Joseph	Great-grandson, 28 generations removed	20 BC
James	Great-grandson, 29 generations removed	AD 30
Jude	Great-grandson, 29 generations removed	AD 30
Jesus	Great-grandson, 29 generations removed	AD 30

Chapter 19

Nathan

> There were yet sons and daughters born to David. And these be the names of those that were born to him in Jerusalem . . . Nathan and Solomon. (2 Samuel 5:13-14 NASB)

First Chronicles 3 lists six different wives as mothers for David's six oldest sons born while David was king in Hebron. Upon the assassination of Saul's dynasty, the leaders of Israel asked David to move his capital from Hebron to Jerusalem and rule over all of Israel. Jerusalem was where the tryst with Bathsheba occurred. Besides Bathsheba, no other wife of David is listed in Scripture as birthing multiple sons to the king. Of David's four (or five) sons by Bathsheba, two of her sons receive particular attention: her son, Nathan, and his immediate younger brother, Solomon.

Before we delve into the life of Solomon, David's most famous son, it is appropriate to study Solomon's older brother, Nathan. Little is known about Nathan, but he must have been a mighty leader of Israel (Zechariah 12:12). It is not clear why David and Bathsheba chose this particular name for their son. Because he was important, the following might be a possibility. The prophet who fearlessly confronted King David about his adultery with Bathsheba was the trusted advisor named Nathan. The meaning of "Nathan" is "He has given." God had indeed "given" sound advice to the king through the elder Nathan's counsel. David acknowledges this counsel in the preamble to his great and wonderful confession known as Psalm 51. Not only was Nathan a Godly prophet, but he also became the biographer of David and Solomon. We can see David's respect and admiration for Nathan the prophet. After the confrontation between David and Nathan, the king and Bathsheba have additional sons. After a period of time and the birth of two sons, yet a third son is born. Possibly out of deference to the prophet, his parents selected the name Nathan. He was Solomon's full older brother. Why is David's son Nathan so important? Up until this point, we can follow thirty-four consecutive generations of Jesus's lineage. Up until now, the lineage of Jesus's parents, Mary and Joseph, has been one and the same—identical. In other words, *with the seventy-five generations of Jesus's earthly ancestors, Mary and Joseph had identical forefathers for thirty-four of the seventy-five generations.*

After thirty-four generations of identical lineage, the initial separation of Joseph's lineage and Mary's lineage occurs. Up until this point, we have seen only a single carrier of the Royal Seed.

Now, we see two of David's sons fathering two distinct and separate lineages. For the first time in thirty-four generations, we now have *two specific carriers* of the Royal Seed.

Mary's lineage is recorded as deviating in Luke 3:31 "which was the son of Nathan, which was the son of David." In Matthew's Gospel, he shared a different lineage. Note Matthew 1:6, "And Jesse begat David the king; and David the king begat Solomon of her that had been the wife of Uriah." Matthew notes five women in Jesus's genealogy in his book: "Tamar, Rahab, Ruth, the wife of Uriah [i.e. Bathsheba], and Mary." Ultimately, in this passage, Matthew does not call Joseph the "father" of Jesus, but the "husband of Mary." Luke's sequence of Mary's lineage mentions no women. Although Mary's lineage in Luke 3 does not call Jesus's mother by name, Matthew, in his documentation of Joseph's lineage, does specify "Mary" by name.

From these two brothers, Nathan and Solomon, will flow the distinct genealogy of both Mary and Joseph. Mary's genealogy comes from Nathan; Solomon is the patriarch of Joseph's lineage. Only God could orchestrate this seventy-seven-generation plan from God to Jesus. From Adam to David had been thirty-four generations of common ancestors for Mary and Joseph, with thirty-four individual men chosen by God to be the single carrier of the Royal Seed. In Matthew 1, over a one-thousand-year period, thirty generations of Joseph's ancestors are listed before Joseph becomes Mary's future husband. In Luke 3, from David's son, Nathan, is a similar millennium genealogy. However, in Mary's ancestors there are over forty generations named. Some scholars believe about halfway into this thousand-year period of twenty generations, the two distinct lineages of Mary and Joseph merge together again. After a five hundred year separation, "the carrier of the Royal Seed" was once again invested in just one man. On this occasion, the single carrier of the Royal Seed was to last only two generations. After these two common generations, the lineages of Mary and Joseph once again divide and follow separate paths for a second five-hundred-year period. Before Jesus's birth, there are ten (Joseph's) or nineteen (Mary's) generations of two separate lineages, each carrying the hope of the Royal Seed—the hope of the Messiah.

After seventy-five-plus generations of Mary's and sixty-five generations of Joseph's heritage, the Old Testament lineage will then be reunited forever—culminating in the birth of the Royal Seed, Jesus, in the little town of Bethlehem.

What did we learn about Nathan?

1. Nathan was a son of David and Bathsheba and an older brother of his more famous brother Solomon.
2. Nathan, although not as well-known as King Solomon, was likely a mighty man in Israel.
3. Nathan's lineage will flow forty generations to Mary, the mother of Jesus.
4. After King David, no other kings will be in Nathan's lineage for forty generations until King Jesus.

Nathan's Relatives

Name	**Relationship**	**APPROXIMATE Dates**
Abraham	Great-grandfather, 12 generations removed	±2100 BC
Isaac	Great-grandfather, 11 generations removed	±1850 BC
Jacob (Israel)	Great-grandfather, 10 generations removed	±1800 BC
Judah	Great-grandfather, 9 generations removed	±1700 BC
Boaz	Great-great-grandfather	±1150 BC
Jesse	Grandfather	±1100 BC
David	Father	±1050 BC
Solomon	Full brother	1000 BC
Absalom	Half brother	1000 BC
Nahum (?)*	Great-grandson, 29 generations removed	620 BC
Zerubbabel	Great-grandson, 19 generations removed	538 BC
Mary	Great-granddaughter, 38 generations removed	20 BC
Jesus	Great-grandson, 39 generations removed	AD 30

*See Chapter 22

Chapter 20

Solomon

> So King Solomon exceeded all the kings of the earth for riches and for wisdom.
> And all the earth sought out Solomon to hear his wisdom, which God put in his
> heart. (1 Kings 10:23-24)

Solomon's name means "peaceful." This was a most satisfactory moniker for Israel's third and final king before Israel divided into the northern and southern kingdoms. His father, David, was a man of war. Because of this, God prohibited David from actually building the temple (1 Chronicles 28:3). During the reign of Solomon, the nation of Israel rose to its zenith in prosperity and influence in the region. Solomon was the fourth (or fifth) son of David and Bathsheba. Their first son, the result of their adultery, only lived a few days. The account of his brief life in 2 Samuel 12 offers no name for this newborn. After King David moved his capital to Jerusalem and wed Bathsheba, she delivered four or five more sons. This uncertainty is because of the birth of that first son. In 1 Chronicles 3:5, four sons are mentioned. Does this include the infant who died, or are their four sons only counted after the marriage of David and Bathsheba? The simple answer is we don't know.

It appears though, whether he was the fourth or fifth son, Solomon was Bathsheba's youngest, just as David was the youngest son of Jesse. In the Bible, the tiniest of details often shines through. Solomon was "ruddy" in complexion according to Song of Solomon 5:10. In describing the future king, 1 Samuel 16:12 describes Solomon's father, David, as having a "ruddy" complexion and "with a beautiful countenance." Likewise, Solomon's handsome countenance registers in Song of Solomon 5:10 and 5:15. Bottom line: the son, Solomon, looked somewhat like his father. David's name interpreted is "beloved." 2 Samuel 12:24-25 gives an account of Solomon's birth and a notice that "the Lord loved him." David's sage, Nathan, brought a name from God for the child, Jedidiah. The relevance in Jedidiah was found in the meaning, "beloved of the Lord." Just as David's name interpreted is "beloved," Prince Solomon's other name, Jedidiah, means "beloved of the Lord." This son was special because Solomon had six older half-brothers born to David by six different wives in Hebron. Once in Jerusalem, David had still other wives, and his number of sons totaled nineteen (1 Chronicles 3:2-9). The king has yet other sons by his concubines. In birth order, Solomon probably ranked number ten, with his immediate, older, full brother Nathan being the ninth oldest.

At number ten son, Solomon was exactly in the middle of the nineteen sons birthed by David's wives. David's very oldest son, Ammon, had been killed by some servants following instructions from number three son, Absalom. The second oldest, known as Chileab in 2 Samuel 3:3 (but as Daniel in 1 Chronicles 3:1) most likely died at a young age, as we hear nothing more about him. Absalom challenged his father's rule and fought to occupy the throne. In the aftermath of one of these battles, Absalom was murdered.

With the death of the three oldest sons, we find the fourth-oldest son is Adonijah. In 1 Kings 1:5, Adonijah also "exalted himself" in seeking the throne after David became feeble in old age. Adonijah secured chariots, his scheming resembling a pretender's power struggle for the throne. He solicited allies from among the military leaders of David's army and from among the priests. However, Adonijah avoided Nathan the prophet, Benaiah, David's personal bodyguard, and Solomon. The faithful prophet Nathan spoke to Bathsheba to intercede with David while Adonijah was preparing to declare himself king. Bathsheba reminded David that earlier, he had declared Solomon would be king after his reign (1 Chronicles 22:5-11 NASB). Solomon was just twelve to fifteen years old when David neared death. This helps us to understand David's calling Solomon "young and tender." It also helps to explain why the prophet Nathan and Bathsheba intervened with the king on her son's behalf. Although the three oldest brothers were now dead, Adonijah was conspiring to usurp the throne, and Solomon still had five older half-brothers. To thwart these potential contenders for the throne, David instructed Nathan, the high priest Zadok, and Benaiah to place Solomon upon David's personal donkey to declare him king. At the temple, Zadok anointed Solomon as Israel's next king.

Most theologians consider 1 Chronicles 28:29 to be David's last will and testament. In these verses, the dying David encourages Solomon to "serve God with a perfect heart and willing mind for God searches all hearts. If you diligently seek God, He will be found. If you forsake Him, He will forsake you. Take heed now, you are to build a sanctuary . . . be strong, and do it" (1 Chronicles 22:5-10; 28:9-10).

At the conclusion of this fatherly advice and admonition, David gives Solomon the "blueprints" of the temple complex. In addition, David gives Solomon adequate gold and silver to complete his task. In today's dollars, the value of the gold and silver might approach a value of $6 billion. Again, David admonishes Solomon, "Be strong and of good courage and do it; fear not, nor be dismayed; fear the Lord . . . He will be with you. He will not fail thee nor forsake thee" (1 Chronicles 28:20). In the final chapter of 1 Chronicles, David tells the listeners, "Solomon, my son, whom God alone has chosen, as yet young and tender and work is great . . . the temple is not for man, but for the Lord God" (1 Chronicles 29:1).

Have you ever considered this teenage boy's situation? His father, King David, was on his deathbed, and he had older brothers being killed in battle contesting for his throne. Although two or three brothers had already been killed, Solomon still had six older brothers with whom he might have to contend. His father had instructed him on details for the most holy structure to ever be built by mankind and entrusted to him several billion dollars of gold and silver. He not only must be vigilant of usurpers within the royal family, he also needed to monitor kingdoms of neighboring nations as well, which would find the land, the gold, and the silver tempting. Furthermore, he needed to be nurtured and mature quickly into the role of the king of a nation, the king of several million people, the king of Israel.

David had erected a tent in Jerusalem to house the Ark of the Covenant. However, the tabernacle still remained in Gibeon. Solomon followed David's counsel in loving the Lord and was obedient in traveling to Gibeon to worship (1 Kings 3:4). While spending the night in Gibeon, the Lord appeared to Solomon in a dream. God asked Solomon, "What shall I give thee?" The King responded to God's inquiry by acknowledging how God had blessed his father, David, with much mercy. Solomon further honored his father by stating David had walked in truth, righteousness, and uprightness with God. It is obvious God has been kind to David by giving him a son equipped with abilities to succeed David as king. Earlier when God proclaimed His covenant with David, King David replied:

> "Who am I, O Lord God, and what is my house that Thou hath brought me this far? And this was yet a small thing in Thy sight, O Lord God, but Thou hath spoken also of Thy servant's house for a great while to come. And in this, the manner of man, O Lord God, and what can David say more unto Thee? For Thou, Lord God, knowest thy servant" (2 Samuel 7:18-26).

Notice David states, "Thou hast spoken also of Thy servant's house for a great while to come." This is certainly true. David's dynasty included nineteen kings, serving for almost three hundred fifty years. Just as David responded in this prior passage to God's blessing, Solomon replies in a similar manner:

> "And now, O Lord my God, Thou hath made Thy servant king instead of David, my father, and I am but a little child; I know not how to go out or to come in, and Thy servant is in the midst of Thy people which Thou hast chosen, a great people. Give therefore Thy servant an understanding heart to judge the people that I may discern between good and bad" (1 Kings 3:7-9).

This response pleased God because Solomon did not ask for riches, the death of his enemies (or his older brothers), or a long life. God declared to Solomon He will give him wisdom and an understanding heart; furthermore, God also promised to give Solomon what he had not asked for—riches and honor. No king before or after Solomon would rise to Solomon's preeminence. Solomon became not only the wisest of kings, but he also became the richest king on earth (1 Kings 10:23 NASB). If Solomon will obey God's commandments, statutes and precepts, then God will strengthen the king and lengthen his life.

The king awakened to learn this encounter with God occurred in a dream. After the dream in Gibeon, Solomon returned to Jerusalem and proceeded to David's improvised tent which housed the Ark of the Covenant. There Solomon offered burnt and peace offerings to Yahweh and proclaimed a feast for his staff. God is true to His word and gives Solomon wisdom, understanding, and kindness. Solomon is considered the father of Jewish wisdom. Scripture records that he spoke three thousand proverbs and composed over one thousand songs (1 Kings 4:32 NASB). Solomon is also accepted as the author of two Psalms: Psalm 72 and Psalm 127. Psalm 127 includes the famous lines "Unless the Lord builds the house, they labor in vain." Ironically, this psalm's focus is on a Godly home and children—penned by the man with a thousand wives and concubines! He was also the author of most of the Book of Proverbs, probably Ecclesiastes and the Song of Solomon. If the verses in these three books are each considered a proverb, then we have over one thousand one hundred proverbs contained in the Bible, or almost 40 percent of all of Solomon's proverbs. Because Solomon's reign was one of peace, the king could focus on building up the nation of Israel financially and militarily with various public projects, and on generally increasing the overall welfare of the Israelite people.

Among all of Solomon's building projects, the construction of the temple on the site of Mount Moriah (or Mount Zion or Jehovah-Jireh) was the king's solitary most important accomplishment. God had covenanted this temple with Abraham almost one thousand years earlier. Now, fifteen generations later, King Solomon will build the permanent temple of God, in God's chosen land, at God's chosen time, in God's chosen city, at God's chosen site, by God's chosen king, and for God's chosen people.

After Joseph's death, the Israelites lived in Egypt for four hundred thirty years (Exodus 12:40). Shortly after the Exodus occurred, God selected one man to supervise and to construct the tabernacle, the Ark of the Covenant, the utensils, altar, spoons, pots, and candlesticks. All these holy articles were constructed in the Sinai Desert by Bezalel, Nahshon's cousin (Exodus 31:1-5). Bezalel's job was to follow God's exact specifications and build these exquisite articles for the Tent of the Tabernacle, not in a city or a town, but in the desert. Bezalel's tabernacle was to be about the size of one-fourth to one-third of a football field. Once the tabernacle was completed, its furnishings endured forty years of travel in the wilderness. Upon entering the Promised Land, these sanctified furnishings withstand an additional four hundred fifty years in the Tent of Tabernacle during the period of the Judges.

The Ark had been removed from the Tent, with no prospect of a permanent home. David eventually brought the Ark into a tent of his creation in Jerusalem. All the sacred utensils were still in Gibeon after earlier being in Gilgal and Shiloh. Now a thousand-year-old promise of God is about to come true. Yes, God remained silent for four hundred thirty years while Abraham's descendants were in Egypt as slaves. Yes, God gave Bezalel instructions for His Tent of Meeting. Yes, God chose to let His people transport the tabernacle forty years in the desert. Yes, upon His people reaching the Promised Land, God even delayed an additional four hundred fifty years during the period of the Judges before establishing a kingdom (Acts 13:20). First Saul, then David, each reigned as king of Israel for about forty years. It is just a matter of simple math: 430 years (Egypt) + 40 years (Sinai desert) + 450 years (Judges) + 40 years (Saul) + 40 years (David) = 1,000 years had elapsed since God's first covenant and promise to Abraham.

God, in His time and in His way, had His plan. Isaiah 55:8 says, "For My thoughts are not your thoughts, neither are your ways My ways, saith the Lord." We humans would never even consider a one-thousand-year building plan, but God did. God planned for a permanent structure, a permanent temple, almost one thousand years into the future. Abraham, Isaac, Jacob, Judah,

Pharez, Nahshon, Salmon, Boaz, and David could only trust and believe God. Solomon was God's man to erect the permanent temple where Yahweh worshippers could meet with their God.

Solomon contracted with Hiram, King of Tyre, to supply timber and other materials, along with additional workers, to help build the temple. Hiram floated the cedar from Lebanon down the Mediterranean to Israel (1 Kings 5:9). In addition to Hiram supplying building materials and manpower, Solomon also inherited extraordinary amounts, huge amounts, of gold and silver from his father David (1 Chronicles 22:1-4). God gave instructions to Moses for the construction of an altar on Mount Sinai; specifically, God ordered no hewn stones were to be used because a hewn stone was be considered polluted (Exodus 20:25). The stones were to be measured and pre-cut at the quarry away from the temple site. The stones comprising the temple were quietly nuzzled together. No hammer, no ax, nor any tool of iron was to be heard at the site (1 Kings 6:7 NASB). After the Exodus, it took one year to erect the tabernacle tent in the desert of the Sinai (Exodus 40:17). To construct this temple, Solomon needed seven years (1 Kings 6:1, 38). Numerous times in the Old Testament, Moses, then David, and finally Solomon, are instructed by God in no uncertain terms to follow "My pattern" (Exodus 25:9, 40; 26:30; Numbers 8:4; 1 Chronicles 28:19 NASB). Furthermore, the importance of diligently following God's plan for erecting the temple is even mentioned twice in the New Testament (Acts 7:44; Hebrews 8:5). The temple's "pattern" was to be almost exactly double the dimensions of the Tent of Tabernacle. In other words, Solomon's temple was to be one-half to two-thirds the size of a football field.

Just as the Tent of the Tabernacle had an outer area, then a holy place, and finally the Holy of Holies, the temple had three sections. As in the Tent, the most sanctified portion was the Holy of Holies which housed the Ark of the Covenant. The interior was completely paneled in cedar (1 Kings 6:16-18). No stone was seen inside the temple. The interior of the temple was lavishly adorned with gold, while silver was used in select places. The roof was cedar and supported by cedar beams (1 Kings 6:9). In the finished temple, gold was so prevalent that in the last seventeen verses of 1 Kings 6, we find the word *gold* used eleven times. First Kings 6:30 advises the reader that even the floor was "overlaid with gold within and without." Scholars disagree about the use of the word *gold* and think a more appropriate term might be floored or inlaid (with cedar boards). Nevertheless, if the floor of the temple was truly covered with gold, this would be a precursor to the New Jerusalem with "the street of the city was pure gold" (Rev. 21:21).

Once the temple is completed, all the various basins, altars, the Ark of the Covenant, and the candlesticks are moved inside. These four-hundred-eighty-year old items are finally permanently, resting at their ultimate destination (1 Kings 6:1 NASB). These four-century-old furnishings residing in the temple were not made from gold accumulated by David or Solomon, but from the gold God commanded the Israelite slaves to ask from the Egyptians just before the Exodus. These temple furnishings were the objects that had been crafted from Egyptian gold by Nahshon's cousin, Bezalel. However, David's and Solomon's accumulated gold and silver were what was used in the construction of the temple itself. The doors and hinges were gold clad. The cedar walls were gold clad. The censers were gold. The tongs were gold. There were gold chains, gold altars, gold candlesticks, gold cherubim, gold seats, gold vats, gold forks, and gold urns. First Kings 6:22

summarizes, "and the whole house was overlaid with gold." We see silver was "accounted for as nothing" (1 Kings 10:21 NASB). Verse 27 further states the king's abundant use of gold resulted in "silver was as stones." In one year, roughly one and one-half million ounces of gold came to the king (2 Chronicles 9:13). This would be valued at about $2 billion today. Once the temple was completed according to God's specifications, the entire facility and its staff are consecrated to God, not by a high priest, but by King Solomon (1 Kings 8:12-61).

Just as the Tabernacle tent had faced eastward in the desert, the permanent temple faced east as well. Scholars think this was to catch the very first rays of daylight in order to get a good start on the day. (Even today, shopkeepers in the Middle East very much want to consummate a transaction with their very first customer who comes in their shop each morning, as a sign of good luck for the day.)

Just as we saw the process in the Book of Genesis, winnowing the people down into fewer and fewer tribes, the temple layout also became more restricted the farther one was permitted to enter into the temple. God was very specific concerning the tabernacle. About fifty chapters in the Bible are devoted to the Tent of Meeting. For example, outside the walls of the tabernacle in the Sinai, Israelites and the Egyptians were all part of the "mixed multitude" which freely intermingled (Exodus 12:38). Anyone other than the selected priests trying to enter the tabernacle site were put to death. Inside the tabernacle walls were the laver and brazen altar. Still, freedom of movement for these fewer priests was permitted. The Tent of Tabernacle grew more holy the farther one walked toward the western wall of the tabernacle. Within the tent was a second area: the holy place, which contained the golden lampstand, the Table of Showbread, and the Altar of Incense. Beyond the veil was the third area, the Holy of Holies, which contained only the sacred Ark of the Covenant (Exodus 26:33-34). *This most Holy place was a cube* (1 Kings 6:20) measuring twenty cubits in each direction. *In the coming New Jerusalem, the entire city will also be a cube* (Rev. 21:16). In Exodus 30:18-21, the priests were instructed to wash their hands and feet in the laver (basin) in the courtyard before entering the holy place. The Holy Place was obviously sacred. No foreigner, no uncircumcised in flesh or heart, could enter the tabernacle. Priests were not to drink wine before entering into the tabernacle as well. In addition, the priests were instructed to wear clothes of linen and containing no wool, and to take off their holy garments in the outer court. Furthermore, priests were admonished to wear nothing which would cause them to sweat (Ezekiel 44:9-22 NASB). God was particular about the people who entered the holy places, who wore the holy fabrics, and who ate the sanctified food, which was for the priest and only selected family members.

Within the tabernacle, the most special area of all was the Holy of Holies. Because this sacred area was very special, the high priest entered the Holy of Holies only once each year. Why? Because the focal point in the Holy of Holies was its single feature—the Ark of the Covenant. As we have already learned, this three-and-three-quarters foot by two –and-a-half foot wooden box, which had been overlaid with gold, contained three items: the Law, Aaron's rod, and the Pot of Manna (Hebrews 9:4). But it was not what was in the box that was important to God. The lid of the Ark was solid gold with two cherubim facing each other. The lid also was not what was important to God. What was of significance to God was the space immediately above the lid between the two cherubim. This space was known as the "Mercy Seat." God declared, "This is where I will meet with you. It is where I will sanctify the tabernacle of the congregation. The tabernacle will be sanctified by My glory. I will dwell among you and you shall know that I am the Lord, your God" (Exodus 29:42-45; Exodus 30:6).

Although the Israelites can now see the splendor and grandeur of this temple that was one thousand years in the making, two problems became distinct in the man who had built and consecrated this temple. Solomon appeared to be more interested in religion outwardly and not inwardly, as his father David had been. To be the outstanding builder of Israel's temple, cities, palaces, ships, silos, and stables, the king required many more assistants. King Solomon had a *thirty-fold increase* in government staff over his father's administration. This required more shekels of revenue flowing to the government with all these governmental efforts needing more staff, workers, and supervisors. David's reign was one of struggle, with military conflicts and limited government. The Bible mentions his cabinet of advisors and lists their respective duties (2 Samuel 8:16-18 NASB). Only eight to ten men are noted within David's inner circle. In contrast, 1 Kings 4:1-19 lists twenty-three attendants and advisors to King Solomon, along with additional officers to supervise the people. The Word tells us five hundred fifty supervisors are needed just to supervise the citizens. Where David had less than twenty assistants, Solomon needs nearly six hundred. David fought just to secure the land. Solomon built the temple, entire cities, and government buildings. Solomon also built storage silos for grain, and military barracks with stables for "quick response teams" in all regions of the land (1 Kings 4:26). Even today, some of these grain silos and stables for the horses can still be seen by tourists, such as in the rock structures at Tel Megiddo. In addition to multiple simultaneous construction projects, the Bible informs us many of Solomon's new buildings were made of expensive stone, thereby further raising costs.

Solomon organized his kingdom into twelve separate districts. Each district had a regional leader and a store city. Solomon further instituted a levy, requiring each district to supply the government in Jerusalem with provisions for one month during the year.

Solomon built his throne out of ivory, overlaid with gold. In addition, his personal bodyguards have three hundred shields of gold. Although the temple was built in seven years, Solomon's palace required thirteen years to complete (1 Kings 7:1 NASB). Solomon was driven to compel forced labor to finance all these expensive government projects. Eighty thousand men worked just in the mountain quarries securing the building stone. The King increasingly taxed the people (1 Kings 5:13-16 NASB). The minorities of Israel had never been fully conquered nor eliminated by Solomon or David. Solomon subjected these minority groups to levies, fines, and taxes.

Fellow Israelites were the standing army and were not subject to the forced labor demands of Solomon's heavy taxation. After only three kings over a one-hundred-twenty-year period, this heavy taxation eventually will be a *primary cause* of Israel's separation into a northern kingdom and a southern kingdom (1 Kings 12:3-4). These two kingdoms will become known as Israel or Samaria in the north and Judah to the south.

Solomon's second problem was his fondness for members of the opposite sex. Although Solomon held high standards early in his reign, with his successes, some evidence of worldliness started to creep in. Early on, Solomon became friends with Pharaoh and later married the Pharaoh's daughter (1 Kings 3:1). This was almost unheard of, due to Egypt's long reign of power and influence over the region. Egypt's early supremacy of the Middle East was partially made possible by the mining of huge quantities of gold within Egypt's borders. This made the pharaohs reluctant for their children to wed anyone outside the nation of Egypt. Pharaoh's acceptance of the Israelite king, Solomon, is noted in the following example. On one occasion, Solomon's future father-in-law came into the area and conquered a Canaanite town, Gezer (which Pharaoh later gave to his daughter as a wedding present). Although Gezer was only about twenty miles northwest of Solomon's capital at Jerusalem, Pharaoh respected Solomon's reign and did not challenge Solomon in Jerusalem, but returned to Egypt.

In a back-handed way, these actions showed respect and honor for Solomon. First, the Pharaoh permitted his daughter to wed Solomon, a man from a nation beyond the borders of Egypt. Second, Pharaoh returned to Egypt without attacking Solomon's capital city of Jerusalem.

While attending to the building projects for the nation, the wisest man who ever lived exposed his frailties. The wise king's standards of stone building materials were very high, necessitating expensive stone, but in other arenas, such as his physical morals, his standards became rather low. King Solomon had seven hundred wives and three hundred concubines. Stop for a moment to consider this: While attending to his building projects and affairs of state, if Solomon daily spent time with a different woman from his harem, the King would see each wife or concubine one day out of every three years. In other words, over a decade, he would average seeing a harem member no more than three days. Obviously, such a harem was very expensive to maintain, one that required substantial governmental support. In addition, a good portion of 1 Kings 10 is devoted to the visit from the Queen of Sheba. Solomon's entanglements with women were not limited to just the one thousand women in his harem.

Finally, it is interesting to observe Solomon's wisdom shine forth. In Proverbs, Solomon uses the phrase "my son" ten times. On five of these occasions, he urges men to avoid "strange women," that is, "foreign women"——and this from a king with one thousand women in his harem (1 Kings 11:3 NASB).

God called His chosen people "a peculiar people" (Exodus 19:5-6). He desired a kingdom of priests, a holy nation. To maintain a holy nation, God wanted *no intermarrying* with foreign nationalities (Ezra 10:2-3 NASB). God's first commandment of the Ten Commandments is "Thou shalt have no other gods before me." God also calls himself a "jealous" God. Early on, the king married the Pharaoh's daughter, and he recognized she should not live in close proximity to the holy things of God in the temple-palace complex. Solomon built her a separate palace away from the temple. With Solomon's harem of one thousand women, the inevitable happened. These foreign wives turned Solomon's heart away from God. 1 Kings 11:3-7 mentions the great builder of Israel, the builder of Yahweh's Temple, followed after the foreign gods of Ashtoreth, Milcom, Chemosh, and Molech. The wise King Solomon later constructed worship centers for these foreign gods who were worshiped by these foreign women. Mostly, these false gods were the national gods of the foreign nations from whence these foreign wives had come. This was a contest not only among different wives with different religions but also among different nations and their influence within Israel.

Well into Solomon's fabulous reign of material prosperity and power, cracks start to appear—a fracturing of his kingdom. The people resent the heavy taxation, forced labor, and resulting heavy-handedness of the multiple layers of bureaucratic governmental supervisors. While typical of many nations of the day, Samuel warns against using forced labor on government projects. Recall when the people wanted a king, Samuel had admonished in 1 Samuel 8:11-14 that a king would conscript "your sons and daughters"? The people further resent the tax revenue being used to construct worship centers for foreign gods.

One day, the aging Solomon encountered a young, energetic soldier named Jeroboam. Solomon soon appointed the young man as a minister of forced labor. A prophet appeared before Jeroboam and told him God was unhappy with Solomon's acceptance of foreign wives, their allegiance to other gods, and the king's building of alternative worship centers. Subsequently, God spoke to Jeroboam through the prophet Ahijah. He informed Jeroboam that if he is obedient and "walk in My ways and do that which is right in My sight, I will be with thee, and will give Israel (i.e. the ten northern tribes) unto thee" (1 Kings 11:38). In verse 39, God states He will not punish the seed of David forever. Nevertheless, because of Jeroboam's success, Solomon soon began to seek out Jeroboam to kill him.

Eluding capture, Jeroboam escaped to Egypt and sought the protection of Shishak, the first pharaoh of Egypt's twenty-second dynasty. Shishak (also known as Sheshonk I) reigned from 945-924 BC. Jeroboam stayed in Egypt until after Solomon's death. Upon Solomon's death, the forty-one-year-old Prince Rehoboam succeeded his father as king of Judah (2 Chronicles 12:13).

Although this new king was in his forties, he was inexperienced and described as "young and tender" in 2 Chronicles 13:7, just as his father Solomon was described in 1 Chronicles 29:1 when Solomon's age was about twelve-to-thirteen-years. King Rehoboam made very poor decisions at the outset of his seventeen-year reign. Although an ancestor of Jesus, wise Solomon's successor was a son with very poor judgment.

What have we learned about Solomon?

1. David's number ten son, Solomon, was David's named successor.
2. Early in his reign, Solomon traveled to Gibeon to worship Yahweh. God appeared in a dream to the young king, who asked for wisdom.
3. God granted Solomon wisdom plus long life and wealth. Eventually, King Solomon was acknowledged as the wisest man who ever lived as well as the wealthiest.
4. Solomon appeared not to be as spiritual as his father, but more interested in earthly, material things. While the temple took seven years to build, the construction of his palace took over thirteen years.
5. The greatest accomplishment of Solomon's reign was the fulfillment of the one-thousand-year old promise to Abraham to erect the first temple of Israel.

6. He ignored the Prophet Samuel's warning and demanded forced labor from his subjects. This became Solomon's first policy failure.

7. Solomon's second major failure was his acceptance of foreign wives and their foreign gods. Not only had Solomon rejected the Prophet Samuel's advice about forced labor, but he also flagrantly violated commandments one, two, and three of the Ten Commandments (Exodus 20:3-5).

8. Solomon was the father of Jewish wisdom and the author of Psalms 72 and 127 and most of the Books of Proverbs, Ecclesiastes and Song of Solomon.

9. Like his father, King David, Solomon was ruddy in complexion, handsome, and loved (at least initially) by his subjects.

10. The king's reign was a period of peace, permitting grandiose building projects.

11. Solomon's government became bloated with a thirty-fold increase in government administrators, necessitating the punitive oppression of the populace by taxation.

Solomon's Relatives

Name	Relationship	APPROXIMATE Dates
Adam	Great-grandfather, 30 generations removed	±4000 BC
Noah	Great-grandfather, 21 generations removed	± 3000 BC
Abraham	Great-grandfather, 12 generations removed	±2000 BC
Jacob (Israel)	Great-grandfather, 10 generations removed	±1800 BC
Aaron	Great-uncle, 4 generations removed	±1250 BC
Rahab	Great-great-great grandmother	±1225 BC
Ruth	Great-great-grandmother	±1150 BC
Jesse	Grandfather	±1050 BC
David	Father	1000 BC
Rehoboam	Son	950 BC
Jehoshaphat	Great-great-grandson	870 BC
Hezekiah	Great-grandson, 10 generations removed	700 BC
Zerubbabel	Great-grandson, 18 generations removed	550 BC
James	Great-grandson, 29 generations removed	AD 30
Jude	Great-grandson, 29 generations removed	AD 30
Jesus	Great-grandson, 29 generations removed	AD 30

Chapter 21

Rehoboam

> And it came to pass when Rehoboam had established the kingdom, and had strengthened himself; he forsook the law of the Lord and all Israel with him. (2 Chronicles 12:1)

Earlier, David's kingdom functioned well with only eight to ten advisors. By the time of Solomon's reign, his administration was bloated with approximately twenty-five cabinet members. Solomon, as the great builder, constructed the magnificent temple, multiple palaces, store cities, ships, and silos. All this activity by the king created a need for still more tax revenues and forced laborers on his projects.

First Kings 11:1 begins, "Now King Solomon loved many foreign women, along with Pharaoh's daughter." This verse concludes by listing the heritage of these "strange" women as being Moabites, Ammonites, Edomites, Sidonians, and Hittites. In order to appease his harem, Solomon built worship centers for Chemosh (god of Moab) and for Molech (god of the Ammonites). First Kings 11:7-8 further states Solomon's grandiose building plans also included other worship centers for all his foreign wives' gods. The first of the Ten Commandments declares: "Thou shalt have no other gods before me. Thou shalt not make unto thee any graven image or any likeness of anything that is in heaven above or that is in the earth beneath . . . Thou shalt not bow down thyself to them; for I am the Lord, thy God, I am a jealous God" (Exodus 20:3-5). This wise man was not ignorant of the Ten Commandments; consequently, it is unmistakable that Solomon was in open rebellion against God's laws.

In addition to the general population's unhappiness, the more observant Jew was also becoming increasingly discontent. The devout were restless for two reasons.

The primary reason was Solomon's flagrant violation of the Law of Moses. The first commandment concludes with God's promise that when other gods are served, He will "visit . . . the iniquity of the fathers upon the children to the third and fourth generation." The Jewish population had self-interest: they simply do not want to be the recipients of God's judgment.

The second reason the people were restless, however, affected everyone: increased taxation. The holy people were being taxed to provide revenue for Solomon's construction of worship centers for the gods of Moab and Sidon. One of the tenets of worshipping the god of the Ammonites, Molech, was the ritual of child sacrifice (Jeremiah 32:35). The sacrificing of children was grossly offensive to devout Jews. Solomon himself stated, "Children are a heritage of the Lord" (Psalms 127:3).

The people became more restless due to further abandonment of God's commandments and increased taxation to fund government building projects. In times past, the Israelites had willingly and freely given so much gold, silver, and raiment to build the tabernacle that God instructed Moses "to restrain the people from bringing any more offering to the sanctuary" (Exodus 36:5-7 NASB). Under Solomon, however, the increased taxation was not to build up the temple of God but to construct facilities for worshiping these foreign gods. As Solomon's life drew to a close, the Lord permitted Solomon's adversaries to interrupt the peaceful reign Solomon previously enjoyed. Neighboring rulers became more bold and brought conflicts into the twilight of Solomon's reign. These military challenges to Solomon were permitted because God was angry with Solomon for not wholeheartedly following the laws of God (1 Kings 11:9-13 NASB).

Upon Solomon's death, Prince Rehoboam was made king. The new king-to-be was aware of a certain degree of tension in Israel. Rather than staying in the capital of Jerusalem where the temple was situated, Rehoboam went out to Shechem to be anointed and proclaimed king. Shechem was thirty miles due north of Jerusalem in the heart of one of the largest tribal allotments of real estate. This land belonged to the tribe of Manasseh, one of the most populous tribes. By being anointed at Shechem, Rehoboam was attempting to curry favor with the people. Undoubtedly, King Rehoboam was aware that previously Jeroboam sought to challenge Rehoboam's father, King Solomon. Jeroboam soon learned of Solomon's death and returned to Shechem from Egypt to meet the new king. Jeroboam's agenda was to discuss the oppressive forced labor and heavy taxation which he supervised under King Solomon's reign.

Jeroboam spoke to King Rehoboam and stated the obvious: "Your father made our yoke heavy, now lighten our burden and we will serve thee." Rehoboam told Jeroboam and the other Israelites to give him three days to consider their request. The new king was forty years old and wisely sought the counsel of his father's elderly advisors. These older counselors urged the young king to be benevolent to the people and "speak good words to them." The old men predicted if Rehoboam will be kind to the Israelites then they will serve King Rehoboam "forever." Afterward the king sought the advice of his contemporaries—in other words, the younger men. These younger men were assertive and advised King Rehoboam to tell the people, "King Solomon's tax burden you thought was onerous was actually light and as your new king, I will add to your tax burden." Upon the arrival of the third day, King Rehoboam met with Jeroboam and the other Israelites, but the immature young King Rehoboam followed not the advice of the older men, with "kind words," but spoke harshly to the people. His pronouncement was one of further taxation and increased oppression. At this point, the ten northern tribes rebelled against the reign of King Rehoboam, rejecting the heritage of King Rehoboam's father, Solomon, and grandfather, David (1 Kings 12:4-16). The lineage of David (Judah) and only one other tribe remained under the authority of Rehoboam. Scholars have yet to resolve whether this second tribe was the tribe of Simeon or Benjamin. To date, no definitive answer has been forthcoming, but probably it was the tribe of Benjamin.

Judah and this other tribe from the southern region became the nation of Judah. The ten northern tribes became the Israelites and selected Jeroboam as their leader. They will later be deported to Assyria. The new residents of the territory of the ten northern tribes were mostly heathen clans from provinces of Assyria. These intermarried people groups will be carried off in defeat some two hundred years later. The Jews hated the Samaritans because of their rebellion, their intermarrying with foreigners, their golden calves, the idols, and the two alternative worship centers. Nevertheless, when the new king, Rehoboam, raised an army to attack the rebels of the ten northern tribes, God rebuked Judah and Benjamin for going to war against their "brothers." Just as King Rehoboam in Jerusalem was uncertain of the Jews' loyalty to him, the new king of Israel, Jeroboam, also was not too confident about the loyalty of those ten rebelling tribes. He established his capital at Shechem, the very town where Rehoboam had been crowned king of all Israel. This town in the hill country was the place where Jacob had bought land (1 Kings 12:4-16), dug a well, erected his altar, and where Joseph's bones were finally buried five hundred years after his death (Joshua 24:32). It was also where Joshua had given his farewell address (Joshua 24:1-15 NASB). In addition, this is where Jesus will confront the woman at Jacob's well nearly one thousand three hundred years later (John 4:5-6). In making his capital at Shechem, Jeroboam attempted to create a foundation for the new nation that would rival Jerusalem. However, in Israel's blessing of his twelve sons, God had vowed that the kings chosen by God would come from Judah's descendants (1 Chronicles 5:2). Jeroboam could not have been from the ultimate kingly line, for he was an Ephraimite and not from the tribe of Judah.

A second decision Jeroboam made was to fashion two golden calves to compete with the golden Ark of the Covenant in the temple in Jerusalem. When the people had worshiped the single golden calf in the Sinai Desert, three thousand people were killed as punishment (Exodus 32:28). Nevertheless, two golden calves were created and Jeroboam declared, "Behold thy gods, O Israel, which brought thee up out of Egypt." In other words, Yahweh was given no consideration in His provision for His people. Jeroboam was afraid that if the people went to Jerusalem to sacrifice, they would be persuaded to return and follow Judah's king, Rehoboam. Jeroboam decided to place one golden calf in the far north of Israel at Dan. The other golden calf was placed in the far south of Israel at Bethel, only twelve miles from Jerusalem (1 Kings 12:24-29 NASB). Once Jeroboam made the two golden calves and erected the cult worship centers, he appointed many lower class non-Levites as priests.

The result of Jeroboam's appointment of lower class non-Levites to the priesthood was a mass exodus of the true Levite priests from the northern tribes southward into Judah (2 Chronicles 11:13-17). These newly arriving Levitical priests from the northern tribes made Judah stronger, thereby making Rehoboam stronger as Judah's leader. In its specificity, the Bible tells the reader precisely how long Judah and Rehoboam were strong—three years. Verse 17 concludes with the reason for King Rehoboam and the nation of Judah's waxing strong: "For three years they walked in the way of David and Solomon." We see the formula for God's plan to unfold. The result of Levitical priests' guidance of the king and the population led to a strong king and a strong nation. It was not as if God had hidden the law. The people knew the law. Rehoboam only had to follow his father Solomon and his grandfather, David. Despite their failures, enough of God's ways were still available to the people to grow strong as a nation of only two tribes, while the ten northern tribes' alliance deteriorated further into depravity. This toleration of idol worship, with the two golden calves and multiple other religions, was unacceptable to God.

It is important to know Israel's King Jeroboam appointed priests from among the lowest of the people to perform functions at the two worship centers and other shrines (1 Kings 12:31). Why is it important? Because 1 Kings 12:31 specifies that these priests were not of the genealogy of Levi. Both Ezra and Nehemiah demonstrated the importance of holiness and genealogy for the priesthood. Ezra 7:1-6 shows Ezra could list his genealogy for seventeen generations, all the way back to the consecrated high priest, Aaron, despite the nation's seventy years in Babylonian slavery five hundred miles from the Promised Land.

One final note about King Rehoboam needs to be mentioned. Previously, we saw Nahshon, Moses, Aaron, and Bezalel were all close relatives. From among six million Israelites, King Rehoboam's choice of a wife was not random. Rehoboam's favorite wife was named Maachah, who was "of fair countenance" (2 Samuel 14:27). In the two previous verses from 2 Samuel 14, we see that her beauty, in part, had come from her grandfather, Absalom, and her great-grandfather, David. Thus, King Rehoboam, a grandson of David, married his second cousin who was a great-granddaughter of King David (1 Kings 15:2).

Genealogy of Rehoboam

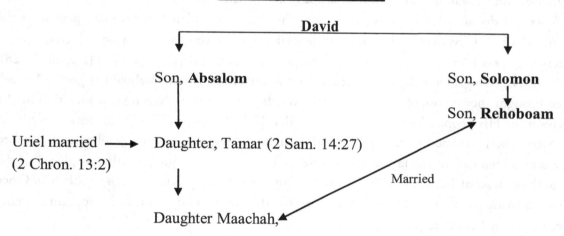

From this marriage will come nineteen rulers of Judah. *All but two of these kings are in the direct lineage of Jesus.* Of the seventeen Judean kings in Jesus's heritage, only nine are called "good" by the Bible. *None of the twenty rulers of the northern kingdom were ever called "good," and none were in the lineage of Jesus.* Samaria and Judah split into separate nations; the books of First and Second Kings follow the exploits of the kings from both nations. The history of Samaria (Israel) ceases in 2 Kings 17, when the Assyrians capture Samaria. *Second Kings 18 onward, including almost all of 1 and 2 Chronicles, is only about the nation of Judah.* Once again, the attention devoted to Judah and its kings is an exhibition of the dedication to verify the Messianic lineage of Jesus. Later, Jesus states that the kingdom will be taken from the Jews (Matthew 21:43) and given to the Church (Acts 13:46).

What did we learn about Rehoboam?

1. Rehoboam succeeded Solomon as King. Although he was forty years old, he was inexperienced and immature.
2. His poor responses to the people caused the ten northern tribes to rebel and form the northern kingdom of Samaria.
3. No dynasty in Samaria was very confident, as Samaria had over five dynasties in its only two-hundred-year existence.
4. After Rehoboam's reign, eighteen of his descendants served as Judah's king, with sixteen of these kings being direct ancestors of Jesus.
5. As a nation, Judah had only one dynasty which existed for three hundred fifty years, one hundred fifty years longer than Samaria.

Rehoboam's Relatives

Name	Relationship	APPROXIMATE Dates
Abraham	Great-grandfather, 13 generations removed	±2000 BC
Boaz	Great-grandfather, 3 generations removed	±1200 BC
Ruth	Great-grandmother, 3 generations removed	±1200 BC
Jesse	Great-grandfather	±1050 BC
David	King, Grandfather	1000 BC
Bathsheba	Queen, Grandmother	1040 BC
Solomon,	King, Father	980 BC
Jehoshaphat	King, Great-grandson	870 BC
Hezekiah	King, Great-grandson, 9 generations removed	730 BC
Josiah	King, Great-grandson, 12 generations removed	640 BC
Zerubbabel	Governor, Great-grandson, 16 generations removed	550 BC
James	Great-grandson, 27 generations removed	AD 30
Jude	Great-grandson, 27 generations removed	AD 30
Jesus	Great-grandson, 27 generations removed	AD 30

Chapter 22

Jehoiada

> And Jehoiada made a covenant between the Lord and the King and the people,
> that they should be the Lord's people. (2 Kings 11:17)

We now come to the darkest period of Judah's three-hundred-fifty-year existence. King Jehoshaphat was a good king for Judah, leading the nation to great riches and honor (2 Chronicles 17:3-6). He also took joy in the ways of God and expelled the sodomites from Judah (1 Kings 22:46). King Jehoshaphat was the great-great grandson of King Solomon (Matthew 1:7-8). It appears Solomon was the king's hero, for he followed some of King Solomon's precise actions from five generations earlier. Specifically, King Jehoshaphat built ships at Ezion-Geber, just as King Solomon had (1 Kings 9:26-28; 22:48). The mission of these ships was to "go to Ophir for gold," just as Solomon had done. However, Jehoshaphat's ships were "broken" in the exact same port of Ezion-Geber from which Solomon's ships had embarked on their profitable ventures to Ophir. Not only did the good king try to duplicate the successful commercial activities of King Solomon, he also desired to politically reunite Israel and Judah, with a goal to reclaim the zenith of power and influence that the united Israel had reveled in some ninety years earlier during his great-great grandfather's reign.

Because of this desire to reunite Israel, Jehoshaphat went from Jerusalem to the northern kingdom to visit the Samaritan King Ahab (1 Kings 22:2). This visit with Ahab appears successful, for Jehoshaphat signed a peace treaty with Ahab (1 Kings 22:44). In reality, King Ahab was an evil king, for Scripture declares, "He did evil in the sight of the Lord more than all that were before him" (1 Kings 16:30-31). Ahab was not concerned about the history of apostasy exhibited by the prior seven kings of Israel, for he had chosen Jezebel to be his wife, a princess and daughter of King Ethbaal from Sidon in the land of the Phoenicians. King Ethbaal's very name included the name of his god, "Baal." Jehoshaphat's signing of this peace treaty with the northern kingdom of Samaria was a fatal mistake. Almost immediately, God denounced Jehoshaphat's commercial partnership with Samaria (2 Chronicles 20:36-37 NASB). For nearly one hundred years thereafter, Judah will suffer mightily from this alliance Jehoshaphat signed with Samaria. Jehoshaphat was trying to emulate Solomon's reign, but it would have been prudent if he had also noted Solomon's failure and its consequence when Solomon made a pact with the Pharaoh and married Pharaoh's daughter. Subsequently, Solomon's foreign wives turned his heart toward their foreign gods. Ahab did the exact same thing by wedding Jezebel, a princess from Sidon, the

Phoenician capital immediately to Samaria's north. At that time intermarriage was considered good political strategy. However, spiritually, it violated the first of God's Ten Commandments, "Thou shall have no other gods before Me." Ahab already had shown a bent toward evil when he married the wicked Jezebel, who worshiped Baal and not Yahweh. After marrying Jezebel, Ahab's kingdom became even more evil and estranged from God. King Jehoshaphat had a son named Prince Jehoram. King Ahab and his Queen, Jezebel, had a daughter, Princess Athaliah, and a son, Prince Joram. Is it any surprise, then, in this era of politically arranged marriages that Prince Jehoram of Judah, became the husband of Jezebel's daughter, Princess Athaliah of Samaria? Upon Jehoshaphat's death, King Jehoram and Queen Athaliah began their reign (1 Kings 22:50; 2 Kings 8:16-18 NASB). The term "their reign" is appropriate because King Jehoram followed not after Yahweh, but after the apostate kings of his wife's family. It appears the wicked Jehoram did not need much encouragement from Queen Athaliah to be evil. Upon succeeding his father, Jehoshaphat, as King of Judah, Jehoram promptly assassinated his six brothers and all of their sons (2 Chronicles 21:2-17). As a result, God raised up enemies against Jehoram. Nevertheless, God continued to remember His covenant with David and his descendants that they will always have a king to sit upon the throne of Judah.

Meanwhile, in the northern kingdom, Ahab and Jezebel continued their fervent worship of Baal. Ahab had strategically married the daughter of the Phoenician king, Ethbaal, in the kingdom immediately to the north. Ahab and Jezebel's daughter, Athaliah, was married to the king of Judah, King Jehoram, their neighbor immediately to the south. Politically and strategically, Ahab and Jezebel had a perfect situation. There was just one problem. As it says in the conclusion of 1 Kings and in 2 Kings 2-7, God raised up the prophet Elijah to confront the sins of Ahab and Jezebel. This spiritual confrontation climaxed when the prophet Elijah defeated the four hundred fifty priests of Baal and four hundred priests of Ashtoreth on Mt. Carmel (1 Kings 18:19-38 NASB). Visibly, God rejected the reign of the evil Ahab and Jezebel. Ahab died fighting the Syrians, and his son Ahaziah succeeded his father as king in the northern kingdom. Following an accidental fall, he died after reigning ten years. King Ahaziah had no son and Ahab's second son Joram was made Samaria's king. (Joram is also known as Jehoram in several passages.)

At God's direction, Jehu, a former soldier in Ahab's army, was anointed king of Israel, first by Elijah and later by Elijah's successor, Elisha, to replace Ahab and his two sons. Upon being appointed Israel's king, Jehu promptly sought out King Joram and assassinated him (2 Kings 9:24). After he assassinated Ahab's second son, Jehu began a search for Ahaziah, king of Judah (the grandson of Ahab by Ahab's daughter Athaliah). When he found the king of Judah, Jehu also killed Ahaziah. (The assassinated King Joram of Samaria, the son of Ahab and Jezebel, was the brother to Queen Athaliah of Judah. Although some scholars view Joram as the uncle of Ahaziah, most believe Joram and Ahaziah were brothers-in-law.)

Concurrently, in the southern kingdom, King Jehoram and Queen Athaliah had a son named Prince Ahaziah. In addition, Jehoram had a daughter named Princess Jehosheba by a wife unnamed in Scripture.

Are you confused yet? Do not be discouraged. Within a decade, Israel experienced three kings while Judah was under the reign of two kings. To add further confusion, these two kingdoms, Judah and Samaria, had also intermarried.

To summarize, in the northern kingdom, Ahab married Jezebel, who encouraged Samaria's abandonment of God with increased worship of Baal and outright apostasy. Ahab and Jezebel's daughter, Athaliah, married the king of the southern kingdom of Judah, Ahaziah. Wicked Athaliah encouraged her husband to kill all his potential rivals, his six brothers and all their sons. With such rampant apostasy and sinfulness, God called Elijah to anoint a soldier from Ahab's army, Jehu, to be the next king of the northern kingdom and to blot out the reign and dynasty of Ahab and Jezebel and their two sons, Ahaziah and Joram (2 Kings 9:7-8 NASB). Afterwards, Jehu also assassinated a second king, King Ahaziah, the king of the southern kingdom. Samaria, the northern kingdom, and Judah, the southern kingdom, were in turmoil due to the elimination of their respective kings, who were both assassinated by Jehu. The deaths of Samaria's Joram and Judah's Ahaziah occurred in about 841 BC. In the nations of Samaria and Judah, confusion reigned supreme with all of the wars, varying alliances, sibling murders, killing of nephews, and intermarrying. Not only Samaria but also Judah were suffering from turmoil due to their worship of foreign gods. The following chart shows the royalty of the three kingdoms.

THREE KINGDOMS

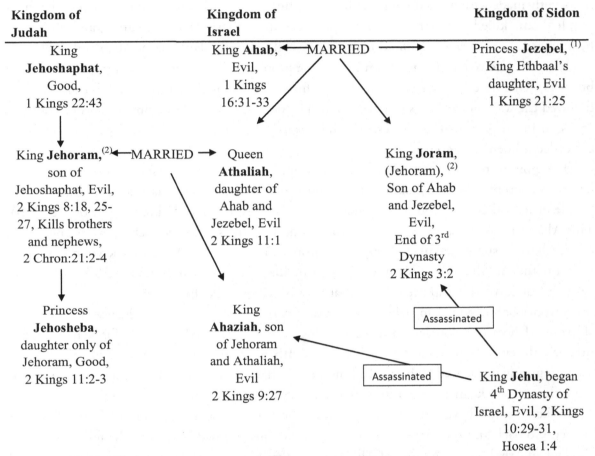

Kingdom of Judah	Kingdom of Israel	Kingdom of Sidon

King **Jehoshaphat**, Good, 1 Kings 22:43

King **Ahab**, Evil, 1 Kings 16:31-33 ◄—MARRIED—► Princess **Jezebel**, [1] King Ethbaal's daughter, Evil 1 Kings 21:25

King **Jehoram**, [2] ◄—MARRIED—► Queen **Athaliah**, daughter of Ahab and Jezebel, Evil 2 Kings 11:1

son of Jehoshaphat, Evil, 2 Kings 8:18, 25-27, Kills brothers and nephews, 2 Chron:21:2-4

King **Joram**, (Jehoram), [2] Son of Ahab and Jezebel, Evil, End of 3rd Dynasty 2 Kings 3:2

Princess **Jehosheba**, daughter only of Jehoram, Good, 2 Kings 11:2-3

King **Ahaziah**, son of Jehoram and Athaliah, Evil 2 Kings 9:27

Assassinated

Assassinated

King **Jehu**, began 4th Dynasty of Israel, Evil, 2 Kings 10:29-31, Hosea 1:4

(1) Queen Jezebel, through her daughter Athaliah's arranged marriage to King Jehoram, became a great-great grandmother into the lineage of the Royal Seed, the Messianic dynasty of Judah. *Wicked Jezebel was a great-grandmother, thirty-five generations removed, to Jesus, James, and Jude.*

(2) Note the chart has *two* kings that are named Jehoram—one, the son of Jehoshaphat, reigned in Judah, and the other, the son of Ahab, was king of Israel. *Both* reigned for about ten years from 852 BC. Two kings with the same name, who were brothers-in-law (or uncle and nephew), reigned concurrently in two adjoining kingdoms. Do you think there was ever any confusion in the two throne rooms during this decade? For simplicity's sake, the author uses "Joram" as the alternate name for King Jehoram of Samaria.

Besides the intermarrying, another source of confusion is created by the names. The preceding chart shows nine persons. Six of the nine names begin with the letter *j* and the three remaining names begin with the letter *a*. Spend a few minutes studying this chart. Look up the references provided below each name. These few minutes will be worthwhile very soon. After Jehu killed Joram, king of Israel (Samaria), Jehu directed his fury toward Joram's nephew (or brother-in-law), Ahaziah, king of Judah (2 Kings 9:23-24). The peace treaty good King Jehoshaphat of Judah innocently made with wicked King Ahab ten to fifteen years earlier had bad results. Jehoshaphat's son, Jehoram, killed all his brothers and nephews (and all Jehoshaphat's sons and grandsons) when he followed the apostate religion of his wife, the evil Athaliah, daughter of Ahab and Jezebel.

Jehoram received a message from Elijah, the prophet. Elijah accused the king of slaying his brothers, who were better than himself (2 Chronicles 21:13-19). In addition, because he had followed the ways of the kings of Israel, he will be defeated by the Philistines in battle, losing all his assets in the palace, all his wives, and all his sons. Then, Elijah predicted that he would suffer a dreaded ailment and eventually die.

Two points are worth noting here. First, notice 2 Chronicles 21:17 states, "so that there was never a son left him—save Jehoahaz, the youngest of his sons." A few verses later, we read that the people of Jerusalem rose and made Jehoram's youngest son, Ahaziah, king (2 Chronicles 22:1). This Ahaziah was the same son we just read about, known as Jehoahaz. Jehoram's youngest son of all, Ahaziah, succeeded his father on the throne. Unfortunately, Ahaziah, the youngest son of Jehoram and Athaliah was heavily influenced by his mother (2 Kings 8:26 NASB). And as we have already learned, Scripture records that he was evil, just like his parents.

It is obvious how good King Jehoshaphat's peace treaty with Ahab directly influenced Jehoshaphat's oldest son, Jehoram. Before Jehoram became king, he was influenced to do evil, for he had married Athaliah, the evil daughter of Jezebel. Jehoram and Athaliah had a son they named Ahaziah. Ahaziah was also greatly influenced by his wicked mother. He likewise was an evil king. It would be nice to think that this wickedness would stop after the generations of Jehoram, but it did not.

In fact, we now have arrived at the darkest moment of Judah's three-hundred-forty-five-year history. Go back and review the family tree chart we just studied. Now read the following verse: "And when Athaliah, the mother of Ahaziah, saw that her son was dead, she arose and destroyed all of the seed royal" (2 Kings 11:1).

Let us consider the situation for a moment. God makes provision for Noah during the flood. Thereafter, God's power and authority prevents Nimrod from building a tower to God.

In Genesis 49:10, Jacob blesses his son Judah, saying, "The scepter should not depart from Judah."

From Abraham, over one thousand years has passed. Pharaoh was defeated at the Red Sea. Moses had got the slave Nahshon, the carrier of the Royal Seed, out of Egypt via the Exodus. Under Joshua's command, the walls of Jericho collapsed. Rahab and Ruth each birthed a special son, each one the sole carrier of the Royal Seed in his generation. As a lad, David slew the giant Goliath, and was anointed king by Samuel. As King David, he secured most of the Promised Land. Consequently, after the Abrahamic Covenant one thousand years earlier, God made a new covenant with David in which he promised the seed of David would always sit on the throne of

Judah. David's son, Solomon, who had been raised up as the world's wealthiest and wisest king in history, erected a magnificent, gold-studded temple to the glory of Yahweh. Do we really think then, that this one woman, Queen Athaliah, somehow manages to single-handedly defeat God? That Athaliah can thwart God's plan that has been unfolding through the lives of Adam, Noah, Jacob, Judah, Nahshon, Rahab, Ruth, David, and Solomon?

Is this how the story ends? After forty-three generations and some two thousand years, is this how the story ends? No!

Now the Queen Mother Athaliah, daughter of Ahab and Jezebel, shows her true wickedness. After Jehu slew her brother, the evil King Jehoram of Samaria, Jehu also murders her son, King Ahaziah of Judah. Athaliah then adopts the strategy of her dead husband, King Jehoram. The widowed Queen's thirst for power is deadly. Recall when Athaliah's husband, Jehoram, killed all of his six brothers and their sons? Jehoram deliberately removed any rivals to his position as king except for his own sons and grandsons. Athaliah, this vile Phoenician Princess, had become Queen Mum of Judah. *She kills her own grandsons* in her thirst for power. The *only female ruler of Samaria or Judah* in three hundred fifty years was Athaliah.

Second Kings 11:1 represents the darkest, darkest hour of Judah's history.

King Jehoram had multiple wives. Review the Three Kingdoms family tree chart. Notice, Jehoram had a daughter, Princess Jehosheba, by a wife that was not Athaliah. Perhaps this wife was one of the ones carried off by the Philistines in battle, or maybe she died by the time this event occurred. Both King Ahaziah and Princess Jehosheba were children of King Jehoram but had different mothers. The following is an updated chart of King Jehoshaphat's family tree after Ahaziah was killed by Jehu.

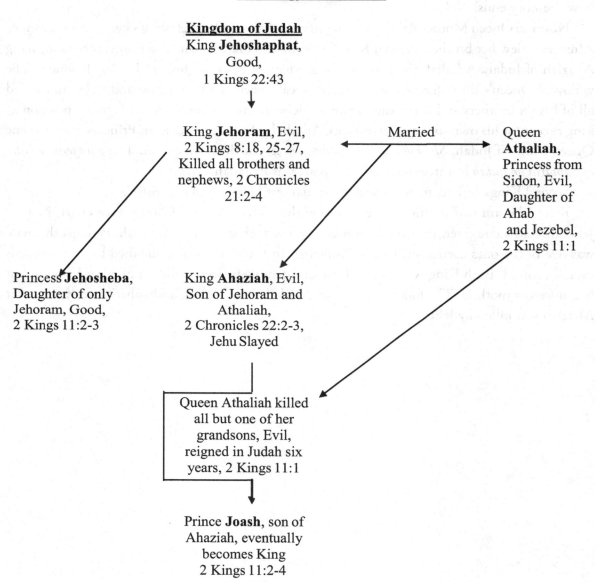

Genealogy of Jehosheba

Kingdom of Judah
King **Jehoshaphat**,
Good,
1 Kings 22:43

King **Jehoram**, Evil,   Married   Queen
2 Kings 8:18, 25-27,   **Athaliah**,
Killed all brothers and   Princess from
nephews, 2 Chronicles   Sidon, Evil,
21:2-4   Daughter of
                                           Ahab
                                           and Jezebel,
                                           2 Kings 11:1

Princess **Jehosheba**,   King **Ahaziah**, Evil,
Daughter of only   Son of Jehoram and
Jehoram, Good,   Athaliah,
2 Kings 11:2-3   2 Chronicles 22:2-3,
                             Jehu Slayed

Queen Athaliah killed
all but one of her
grandsons, Evil,
reigned in Judah six
years, 2 Kings 11:1

Prince **Joash**, son of
Ahaziah, eventually
becomes King
2 Kings 11:2-4

King Jehoram, although described as "evil" for following his mother's ways, did manage to do a couple of good things. For example, he contributed to the hallowed things in the temple treasury. However, Jehoram's most notable achievement concerned his daughter, Jehosheba. The King orchestrated an arranged marriage between his daughter and a man named Jehoiada. Finally!!!

Jehoiada was the high priest who lived to be one hundred thirty years old (2 Chronicles 24:6, 15). It appears the high priest, Jehoiada, was approximately ninety years old when this arranged marriage occurred. We have arrived at the moment of truth: what made high priest Jehoiada and his princess-wife, Jehosheba, so special? Once Athaliah's husband Jehoram was anointed king, he murdered his siblings and nephews. After the Queen Mum determined her son was dead, Athaliah similarly destroyed the royal seed (2 Kings 11:1). Athaliah then proclaimed herself Queen of Judah.

The very next verse, verse 2, is priceless.

> "But Jehosheba, the daughter of King Jehoram, sister of Ahaziah, took Joash, the son of Ahaziah and stole him from among the King's sons, which were slain; and they hid him, even him and his nurse, in the bed chamber from Athaliah so that he was not slain" (2 Kings 11:2).

God triumphed again! Jehosheba was subjected to her father's idolatrous practices, yet she chose to place her trust in Yahweh. Undoubtedly, living in the royal palace was a hard life for this young woman. Her stepmother, Athaliah, daughter of the wicked Jezebel had led Jehosheba's father, Jehoram, and her half-brother, Ahaziah, away from the ways of Yahweh and toward the worship of Baal.

Fortunately for all mankind, Princess Jehosheba and her husband, high priest Jehoiada, remained true to God. It was providential protection that kept Queen Athaliah from noticing one of her grandsons had not been murdered at her command. This was not the only instance in Scripture where a lady of the royal family was married to the high priest. (Elisheba, daughter of Amminadab, from the royal Messianic line had been the wife of the very first high priest, Aaron). With good reason, the princess undoubtedly feared for her life, as did the high priest. If the Queen would destroy her own grandsons, it was readily apparent, without a moment's notice, she would eliminate any stepdaughter hindering her plans. Furthermore, Athaliah had no regard for the authority of the high priest, especially when he was thwarting her schemes.

Consider for a moment the situation. Jehosheba and Jehoiada were in extreme danger daily, even hourly. Yet, they had to appear as if nothing was wrong. Continually the princess kept her composure when present at state functions and royal family events. The palace intrigue had to be one of anxiety and perpetual stress. Frequently there was the need of moving the young Prince Joash and his nurse around in the palace. The queen had access to all of her kingdom and that included every square foot of the royal palace. All the servants, cooks, nurses, guards, maids, soldiers, and advisors were continually in and out of the palace complex. How would you explain a baby's unexpected cry in some remote corner of the palace? How about the disappearance of extra food? What was the routine for washing young Joash's diapers and small-size clothing at the palace? Where were his toys, games, and clothing stored? Where did the young lad play? Did he have any friends his age? If he did, that was dangerous because friends could expose Joash and jeopardize his very survival.

(Possibly one excuse for the evidence of a child around the palace might have been Jehosheba and Jehoiada's own son, Zechariah, provided he was the approximate age of Joash. If the two boys were contemporaries, then that would present other difficulties and stresses.)

Jehosheba and Jehoiada are to be recognized as outstanding heroes in God's plan. This couple dealt with moment-to-moment palace intrigue for not just a day or a month but for six years (2 Chronicles 22:12). The difference between 2 Chronicles 22:12 and 2 Kings 4:1 points to Prince Joash being one year old when he was taken into hiding. When King Ahaziah's sole remaining survivor, Prince Joash, became seven years old, his uncle, high priest Jehoiada, summoned the captains, rulers, and men in positions of authority over the palace and temple—temple guards, soldiers, Levites, and priests (2 Kings 11:4-12). These leaders were then introduced to the young Prince Joash.

The high priest had six long years to contemplate his strategy. The palace and temple guards maintained a round-the-clock continual presence guarding the temple-palace complex. Whenever there was a changing of the guard, the number of men normally on duty would double. Jehoiada instructed the leaders to maintain a double number of guards. One-third were positioned at the palace with the other two thirds of the guards near the temple environs. Apparently, the total number of guards was also doubled on the Sabbath. Thus, there are twice the number of guards on duty due to the Sabbath day and double the number of guards on duty at a changing of the watch. In essence, the number of guards was quadrupled. All these guards were equipped with weapons from the royal armory. Even the priests and Levites were furnished with weapons (2 Chronicles 23:6-9).

The increase in temple attendants on the Sabbath would not have seemed unusual, but normal. A large audience also would help to document the truth of Jehoiada's proclamation. The high priest introduced the seven-year-old Prince Joash as his father's rightful successor to the throne of Judah, placing upon the youngster's head the royal crown of Judah and placing a scroll of the law in his hands. In placing the scroll of the law in now-King Joash's hand, the high priest Jehoiada was being obedient to Moses's writings in Deuteronomy,

> "And it shall be when he sitteth upon the throne of his kingdom that he shall write
> him a copy of this law in a book out of that which is before the priests, the Levites:
> And it shall be with him and he shall read therein all the days of his life: that he may
> learn to fear the Lord his God, to keep all the words of this law and these statutes to
> do them, that his heart not be lifted up above his brethren" (Deuteronomy 17:18-20).

Once Athaliah heard the commotion outside the palace, she came to the temple compound. At one of the pillars near the entrance to the temple stood King Joash. Once she spied her new king, Athaliah's response bordered on humorous. She tore her clothes and cried, "Treason! Treason!" (This from the lady who had murdered all but one of her royal grandsons!) The high priest had instructed the guards to seize Athaliah, but not to kill her in the temple area. She was captured shortly thereafter and slain in the palace.

After Israel split, the northern kingdom of Israel (Samaria) had twenty kings, while the southern kingdom of Judah had nineteen kings and one queen: Athaliah.

The most likely author of 1 Kings and 2 Kings is the prophet Jeremiah. In these two books, the reigns of virtually *all* of the thirty-nine kings from Samaria and Judah are summarized and deemed good or evil. However, Jeremiah does not even acknowledge the six-year reign of Athaliah on the throne of Judah. The silence in Scripture is deafening. Jeremiah only mentions Athaliah to explain how Joash became king.

After the death of the Queen, the brave high priest made a three-way covenant between the Lord, the king, and the people (2 Kings 11:17). As a result of the *restoration of the seed* of David to the throne of Judah, the people rejoiced and demolished the house of Baal and killed its priests. Once again, the people's trust in Yahweh was affirmed. When the one-thousand-year old covenant with Abraham was in doubt, or when the one-hundred-fifty-year-old covenant with David was in doubt, God gloriously produced a single royal heir to continue the royal covenant that he had made with King David.

The following chart will help to explain the complex relationships in young King Joash's family.

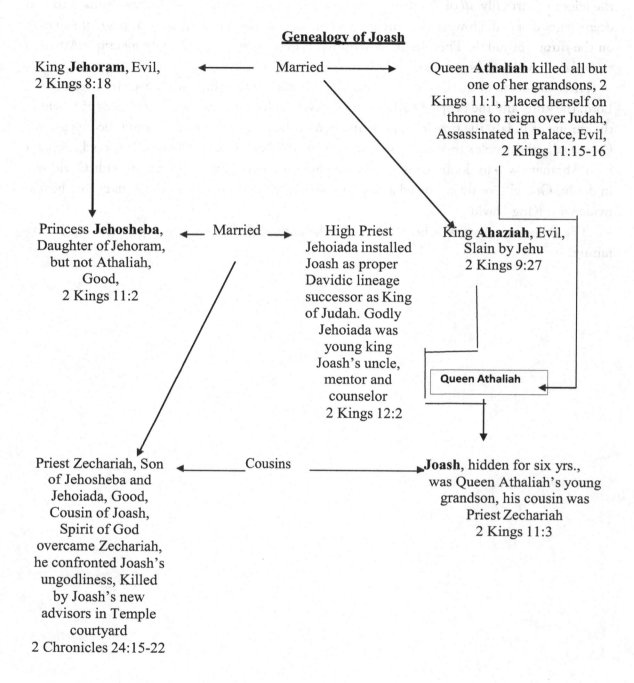

Genealogy of Joash

King **Jehoram**, Evil,
2 Kings 8:18

Married

Queen **Athaliah** killed all but one of her grandsons, 2 Kings 11:1, Placed herself on throne to reign over Judah, Assassinated in Palace, Evil, 2 Kings 11:15-16

Princess **Jehosheba**, Daughter of Jehoram, but not Athaliah, Good, 2 Kings 11:2

Married

High Priest Jehoiada installed Joash as proper Davidic lineage successor as King of Judah. Godly Jehoiada was young king Joash's uncle, mentor and counselor 2 Kings 12:2

King **Ahaziah**, Evil, Slain by Jehu 2 Kings 9:27

Queen Athaliah

Priest Zechariah, Son of Jehosheba and Jehoiada, Good, Cousin of Joash, Spirit of God overcame Zechariah, he confronted Joash's ungodliness, Killed by Joash's new advisors in Temple courtyard 2 Chronicles 24:15-22

Cousins

Joash, hidden for six yrs., was Queen Athaliah's young grandson, his cousin was Priest Zechariah 2 Kings 11:3

Do not be confused in reading of the life of Joash because King Joash's alternate name was Jehoash. (Joash will be used for continuity and for simplicity's sake.) The child-king was blessed in that his uncle was the high priest Jehoiada who became the trusted holy advisor to the young King Joash. Jehoiada wisely guided the young king, who owed his very life to his uncle. The high priest recommended the rebuilding of the temple. Previously, Athaliah's followers had removed most of the holy things from the temple and used them in the house dedicated to Baal. King Joash guided the people to bring offerings to rebuild the temple to Yahweh. The renewed temple was decidedly inferior to Solomon's temple because no silver or gold were used in its reconstruction (2 Kings 12:13 NASB). As long as the high priest lived, he gave sound wisdom and guidance to King Joash and the nation of Judah prospered.

After Jehoiada's death, the thirty-seven-year-old king found less Godly advisors. High Priest Jehoiada and Jehosheba had a son, Zechariah, who became a priest. Once his father had died, the young priest confronted the people in the royal court regarding their falling away from God. As high priest, Jehoiada demanded the guilty Queen Athaliah not be killed at the temple. As she fled, she was apprehended and killed in the palace. Unfortunately, King Joash had no such respect for the temple. When Joash's advisors killed Zechariah, the King's cousin, in the temple, Zechariah was stoned to death in the very spot Zechariah's father, Jehoiada the high priest, had forbade the killing of wicked Athaliah (2 Kings 11:15; 2 Chronicles 24:7, 21 NASB). It is most likely that this Zechariah is the same person Jesus is referring to in Matthew's gospel when He says:

> "That upon you may come all the righteous blood shed upon the earth, from the blood of righteous Abel unto the blood of Zechariah, son of Berechiah, whom you slew between the temple and the altar" (Matthew 23:35).

Both Abel and Zechariah were Jesus's relatives. Abel was Jesus's great uncle seventy generations removed, and Zechariah was a cousin twenty-three generations removed.

A couple of conclusions are appropriate. The Bible tells us Zechariah was holy for the Spirit of God was upon him (2 Chronicles 24:17-27). Priest Zechariah was a first cousin of King Joash, as Zechariah's mother, Jehosheba, was a half-sister to Ahaziah. (King Jehoram was the father of both Jehosheba and Ahaziah.) If Joash and Zechariah were near the same age, it is possible that as lads, Joash and Zechariah were playmates and played together around the temple-palace complex. Yet Joash did not punish the murderous counselors who killed the son of the high priest who had saved Joash's life.

Recall how King Rehoboam also ignored King Solomon's older advisors, resulting in the division of Israel into Samaria and Judah. Likewise, King Joash followed his younger advisors after Jehoiada's death to his own regret, as his own servants would later assassinate him (2 Kings 12:20 NASB). The high priest Jehoiada "stood in the gap" along with his royal wife to preserve the Royal Seed. For all practical purposes, the high priest was king for three decades as he advised the young Joash, yet the Bible never offers the slightest hint of Jehoiada's possible abuse of his position or authority in any way. As a result, Jehoiada was awarded a most unique distinction.

Although he was high priest, *he was buried among the kings of Judah* (2 Chronicles 24:16). Some of the evil kings were not buried in the Valley of the Kings, but the holy, faithful Jehoiada was buried amidst the kings of Judah (2 Chronicles 21:20, 28:27). Jehosheba is mentioned nowhere else in the Bible outside of 2 Kings 11:1-2 and 2 Chronicles 22:11. Nevertheless, this heroine risked her life for six years to help fulfill God's promise to King David nearly two hundred years earlier.

Joash's son, Amaziah, succeeded his father. War soon resulted between Samaria and Judah. Judah was defeated, and once again, the temple and palace were robbed of their gold and silver vessels (2 Chronicles 25:24). Subsequently, rivalry and resentment between Samaria and Judah persisted for the next one thousand years.

Now it is clear why Matthew chose to skip three generations of Judah's kings. Matthew skipped Ahaziah (Joash's father), Joash, and Amaziah (Joash's son). Of course, Athaliah was ignored as well. Matthew returned to Jesus's genealogy with Uzziah, the grandson of Joash. By the time of Jesus, Judah's contempt for Samaria was so intense that Jews traveling between Galilee and Judah would walk along the east bank of the Jordan River rather than enter the land of Samaria. This would necessitate walking a detour of up to forty miles around Samaria. This contempt was based on the ten tribes' earlier abandonment of Judah. Sometime later, Samaria even attacked Judah. These same rebels made two worship centers with twin gold calves rather than come to the temple in Jerusalem. (Now, we can better understand the disciples' disbelief when Jesus walked right into Samaria and stopped a harlot of Shechem in order to engage her in a midday conversation at the most public place of all, the community water well, dug earlier by Jacob (John 4:5-11 NASB)).

High priest Jehoiada and his wife, Princess Jehosheba, are very important for they had preserved the Royal Seed of her family in order for her great-nephew, twenty-three generations removed, to be the Messiah, the King of Kings, Jesus.

What did we learn about Jehoiada?

1. King Jehoshaphat signed a peace treaty with King Ahab of Samaria.
2. King Ahab strengthened alliances with his neighbor to the north, King Ethbaal of Sidon, by marrying Ethbaal's daughter, Princess Jezebel, making her Ahab's queen.
3. The two prophets, Elijah and Elisha, were in continual confrontations with the wicked Ahab and Jezebel.
4. Good King Jehoshaphat selected his oldest son, Prince Jehoram, as king.
5. Once Jehoram became King of Judah, he killed all his brothers and nephews because they were potential rivals to challenge Jehoram's right to the throne. He strengthened his political alliances by wedding Ahab and Jezebel's daughter, Princess Athaliah, the princess of Samaria.
6. Jehoram had a daughter by an unnamed wife, the good Princess Jehosheba, whom the king arranged to marry the good high priest, Jehoiada.

7. King Jehoram and his wicked queen, Athaliah, had a son, King Ahaziah, who was evil. Through their common father, King Jehoram, King Ahaziah was a half-brother to Princess Jehosheba.

8. Jehu assassinated both King Jehoram of Israel and King Ahaziah of Judah. Thereafter, Jehu claimed the throne of the northern kingdom for himself, and he left Judah in turmoil. Jehu's reign started Samaria's fourth dynasty.

9. Once the Queen Mum, Athaliah, learned the new king of Samaria, Jehu, had killed her son, King Ahaziah of Judah, she promptly killed all her grandsons and claimed the throne of Judah for herself. She was Judah's only reigning queen in four hundred years.

10. High priest Jehoiada and his wife, Princess Jehosheba, snatched their nephew, Prince Joash, the youngest son of Ahaziah, from certain death by his grandmother, Athaliah. The high priest and Princess hid their one-year-old nephew for six years in the temple-palace complex, possibly with their own son, Zechariah.

11. When Prince Joash was seven, his uncle, high priest Jehoiada, announced a coup. The usurper, Athaliah,was taken away from the temple.The queen was assassinated shortly thereafter in the palace.

12. High priest Jehoiada served faithfully as a spiritual mentor and worthy counselor to the lad, King Joash, for decades.

13. High priest Jehoiada and Princess Jehosheba's son, Zechariah, also became a priest.

14. Because of his exemplary service to the nation of Judah and to King Joash, high priest Jehoiada was buried with Judah's kings.

15. Without the guidance of Jehoiada, King Joash turned to younger advisors who led King Joash and Judah away from Yahweh and toward idols and foreign gods, such as Ashtoreth.

16. The young priest, Zechariah, confronted his cousin, King Joash, and the king's advisors about their turn from Yahweh. Joash permitted his assistants to stone to death the good priest in the temple courtyard precisely where Joash's uncle, high priest Jehoiada, told the priests not to kill Joash's grandmother, the wicked Athaliah. Thus, Jehoiada's nephew, King Joash, allowed the stoning of Jehoiada's son, the priest Zechariah, who was also King Joash's first cousin.

17. With the despicable actions of Athaliah in this chapter, we see why the probable author of 1 and 2 Kings and 1 and 2 Chronicles, Jeremiah, recorded only the bare facts of her six-year tenure and does not even acknowledge her as evil. Essentially, all other thirty-nine kings of Israel and Judah were deemed evil or good in Scripture. Not so with the wicked Athaliah. The Bible is mute on her reign.

18. The extreme depravity of Judah at this time offered ample evidence for Matthew's genealogy of Jesus to skip completely Ahaziah, Joash, and Amaziah. Technically, in a listing of reigning monarchs, Athaliah would be between her son, Ahaziah, and her sole-surviving grandson, Joash. However, Matthew simply ignores these three kings and Athaliah, as well.

Jehoiada's Relatives

Name	Relationship	APPROXIMATE Dates
Jehosheba	Princess (Judah): Wife	840 BC
Zechariah	Priest (Judah): Son	800 BC
Jehoshaphat	King (Judah): Grandfather in-law	870 BC
Jehoram	King (Judah): Father in-law	850 BC
Ahaziah	King (Judah): Brother in-law	841 BC
Athaliah	Queen (Judah): Step-mother in-law	840 BC
Joash	King (Judah): Nephew	835 BC
Amaziah	King (Judah): Great-nephew	796 BC
James	Great-nephew, 23 generations removed	AD 30
Jude	Great-nephew, 23 generations removed	AD 30
Jesus	Great-nephew, 23 generations removed	AD 30

Chapter 23

Shealtiel and Zerubbabel

On that day, declares the Lord of Hosts, will I take you Zerubbabel, son of
Shealtiel, my servant, declares the Lord, and I will make thee as a signet ring; for
I have chosen you, declares the Lord of Hosts. (Haggai 2:23 NASB)

Previously, we studied the twenty kings of Israel and the nineteen kings of Judah. Now, let us
study the following chart of Judah's final kings.

Last 9 Kings of Judah

Last Nine Kings of Judah	Type of Reign	Royal Seed Lineage?
Ahaz	Evil	Yes
Hezekiah	Good	Yes
Manasseh	Evil	Yes
Amon	Evil	Yes
Josiah [1]	Good	Yes
Jehoahaz	Evil	No
Jehoiakim [2]	Evil	Yes
Jehoiachin	Evil	Yes
Zedekiah	Evil	No

The following notes should be helpful.

1. Josiah was a unique king of Judah. First, he was prophesied by name to be king three
   hundred years before he was born (1 Kings 13:2 NASB). Second, not only did he serve
   Judah as king, but three of his sons were also kings: Jehoahaz, Jehoiakim, and Zedekiah.
   No other king of Judah had three sons reign as king. The Bible declares all three of

Josiah's sons were evil. Jehoiakim's son Jehoiachin (Josiah's grandson) also served as king. Although Jehoahaz and Zedekiah were kings of Judah, the Royal Messianic lineage was through their brother Jehoiakim's son, Jehoiachin. Jehoiachin was eighteen years old when the Babylonian king Nebuchadnezzar installed Jehoiachin as king (2 Kings 24:8 NASB). His reign lasted all of three months. Nevertheless, it was long enough for Scripture to record his reign as being evil, just as had been those of his father and uncles. Part of the confusion surrounding Jehoiachin has to do with his name. The Bible records two additional names for Jehoiachin—Coniah (Jeremiah 22:28) and Jeconiah (Matthew 1:11). For simplicity, only the name "Jehoiachin" will be used.

2. We saw how Matthew chose to ignore Queen Athaliah's action in usurping the throne, and that Matthew skipped over the reign of Athaliah's son Ahaziah, her grandson Joash, and her great-grandson Amaziah. Lastly, Matthew's genealogy also skips over Jehoiakim (Matthew 1:11), with the genealogy of Jesus going from good king Josiah to his grandson, Jehoiachin.

At least a portion of God's disdain for King Jehoiakim occurred when the King cut up the scroll inspired by God and recorded by Jeremiah. Jehoiakim cut the scroll into pieces and threw the remnants into a fire (Jeremiah 36:11-26 NASB). Jehoiakim died with Jeremiah expressing the Lord's contempt for Jehoiakim as king because Judah had forsaken the covenant God had made with Abraham, Jacob, Isaac, and David. Upon Jehoiakim's death, Jeremiah recorded Yahweh's instructions: "They shall not lament for him, saying 'Our Lord' or 'Ah, his glory.' He shall be buried with the burial of a donkey, dragged and cast forth beyond the gates of Jerusalem" (Jeremiah 22:9, 18-19).

Once Jehoiachin was placed on his father's throne by Nebuchadnezzar, Jeremiah recorded further harsh words about Jehoiachin.

> "As I live, saith the Lord though Jehoiachin, the son of Jehoiakim, king of Judah, were the signet ring upon my right hand, yet would I pluck thee thence, and I will give thee unto the hand of them that seek thy life . . . even into the hand of Nebuchadnezzar, king of Babylon...And I will cast thee out, and thy mother that bear thee into another country where you were not born; and there shall you die . . . Is this man, Jehoiachin, a despised, broken idol? Is he a vessel wherein is no pleasure? Wherefore are they cast out? *He and his seed, and are cast into a land which they know not?* . . . Thus saith the Lord. Write you this man childless, a man shall not prosper in his days, *for no man of his seed shall prosper sitting upon the throne of David and ruling anymore in Judah*" (Jeremiah 22:24-26, 28, 30; emphasis added).

To be perfectly clear, Jehoiachin was not without sons. In fact, we know Jehoiachin had seven sons, yet none of Jehoiachin's seven sons were ever to be king of Judah (1 Chronicles 3:17-18). The kingdom of Judah reached a sad, sad conclusion. Yes, God had a grand plan to bring Abram from southern Turkey and change his name to Abraham and establish a covenant with him, vowing a promised land, a new nation, and even a new people. Then God was silent for four hundred thirty years while the Israelites sojourned in Egypt.

Six hundred years after Abraham, following the Exodus, the covenant was affirmed; God provided for His people as the children of Yahweh began to secure the Promised Land.

After the additional four-hundred-fifty-year period of the judges passed, Samuel anointed Saul as king. Later, God directed Samuel to anoint David as king. Subsequently, this began a *four-hundred-year reign* of the dynasty of David, fulfilling the Davidic Covenant through twenty-one kings, with *nineteen of these kings carrying the Royal Seed of Judah.* At the end of the reign of Jehoiachin, God declared the conclusion of the Royal Seed sitting on the throne of Judah. In three raids between 605 BC and 586 BC, King Nebuchadnezzar conquered and humbled Jerusalem. King Nebuchadnezzar carried to Babylon four thousand six hundred members of the Royal Family of Judah (Jeremiah 52:28-30). Specifically mentioned in Scripture are the princes, queen mother, the queen, and the king himself (2 Kings 24:14-15, Jeremiah 24:1 and Daniel 1:3). (Notice the Scripture does not mention any of the princesses, just the princes. This is a strong hint emphasizing that the princes and kings all point toward the Messiah.) Some eight thousand other craftsmen, carpenters, officers, and mighty men were also taken to Babylon (2 Kings 24:16). When we studied the Exodus, we saw a census had recorded a population of six hundred thousand soldiers. To the six hundred thousand soldiers, we must add the remaining population of babies, children, women, and the elderly. A total population of 2 to 3 million is a reasonable estimate. Seven hundred years had passed since the Exodus. Barring any major plague, the population had grown further. The ten- to twelve thousand Jews carried to Babylon were just the royal family and the skilled tradesmen. These twelve thousand carried to Babylon were out of a population of perhaps four million or more in Judah. These twelve thousand taken to Babylon were less than one-half of 1 percent of the nation's entire population. Jeremiah makes this abundantly clear in 2 Kings 24:14, "None remained save the poorest sort of the people of the land." Obviously, Nebuchadnezzar carried off Judah's first family and the intelligentsia. In addition, the Babylonian king plundered the temple and the king's palace, removing the gold and treasures (2 Kings 24:13; 2 Chronicles 36:18 NASB). After removing all the precious items remaining, Nebuchadnezzar burned the temple and demolished the palace walls (2 Chronicles 36:19 NASB). Jeremiah was the prophet God left in Judah to record all this destruction at the hands of the Babylonian army. The devastation was because the people of Judah polluted the temple, disregarded the prophets from God, and rejected the message of God.

Ultimately, God's compassion wore thin—so thin, until there was no longer a remedy (2 Chronicles 36:14-16 NASB). The priest Ezekiel was a contemporary of Jeremiah. While Jeremiah eventually left Judah and was carried to Egypt (Jeremiah 44:1), Ezekiel was among the choice captives taken from Judah to Babylon (Ezekiel 1:1-3 NASB). God raised up Ezekiel to proclaim His truth in Babylon after the captives had been in exile for five years. The book of Ezekiel was written in Babylon (Iraq). It was not pertinent to the nation of Israel, but only to the Jews held captive in Babylon.

"Thus saith the Lord God; 'Although I have cast them far off among the heathen and although I have scattered them among the countries, yet will I be to them as a little sanctuary'" (Ezekiel 11:16).

Since the temple was destroyed in Jerusalem, a new worship center was invented in Babylon—the synagogue. This little sanctuary, the little holy place, is to be the synagogue.

Recall how Israel blessed his twelve sons in Egypt when he proclaimed, "The scepter shall not depart from Judah." In the prior verse, Israel calls his fourth son "a lion." The lion has been a symbol of kingship for thousands of years. In Ezekiel 19:1-2, the prophet laments for the princes of Israel. Over the next several verses, Ezekiel mentions a lioness (Judah) and her various young lions eventually being captured and brought to Babylon in chains. Ezekiel concludes this chapter with the following verse,

"And fire is gone out of a rod of her branches, which have devoured her fruit so that she hath no strong branch to be a scepter to rule. This is a lamentation and shall be for a lamentation" (Ezekiel 19:14).

When Nebuchadnezzar conquered Jerusalem, the royal kingship of the Davidic dynasty came to an end. The lion of Judah was in chains in far-off Babylon. Although Jehoiachin had seven sons, no strong "branch" was qualified to be king of Judah. The scepter which Jacob (Israel) proclaimed would never leave the sons of Judah was now declared to have no strong branch to be a scepter. The Davidic lineage of kings in Judah ends with Jehoiachin being carried off in chains to Babylon.

Being the thorough scholar, Jeremiah concludes 2 Kings with four verses about King Jehoiachin's life in Babylon. At the end of King Jehoiachin's life, there are two points we need to consider. First, Nebuchadnezzar appointed another ruler over the people left behind in Israel, Gedaliah (2 Kings 25:22-26). The remnant of the Royal Seed remaining in Israel assassinated this ruler, who had been Josiah's scribe (2 Kings 22:8), and the remaining royal family scurried to Egypt for safety. Second, after thirty-seven years in captivity, the new king of Persia released Jehoiachin from prison and gave him royal privileges for the remainder of his life. In the past few years, archaeologists have discovered ration tablets inscribed with Jehoiachin's name showing Jehoiachin's receipt of royal food from the King's table. *The royal dynasty of David came to an end.* Nevertheless, Jeremiah continued recording the lineage of David's descendants in far off Babylon, still anticipating the Messiah. The nation of Judah had no branch to reign; the scepter which Israel proclaimed would never leave the sons of Judah now had "no strong branch to be a scepter."

Recall 1 Chronicles 3 is about David's sons. Beginning in verse 15 of 1 Chronicles 3, Ezra documents the sons of Josiah. The royal dynasty of David's descendants was over. *Nevertheless, 1 Chronicles 3:15-19 continues the genealogy of David's descendants even when they were exiled to Babylon.* Now, the members of the Royal Family were slaves in Babylon, yet Ezra continued to record their kingly royal heritage (1 Chronicles 3:1-24 NASB). Also, recall the keeping of the genealogy while slaves in Egypt for four hundred thirty years. First Chronicles 3:24 concludes with

David's final recorded descendant, Anani, who lived during the time of Malachi (approximately 430 BC). This was about five hundred years after David's death in 970 BC. For five centuries after David's death, the Jews continued to anticipate *his descendant coming as the Messiah.*

In the genealogy of Babylonian slaves, Jehoiachin's grandson, Zerubbabel, is mentioned in 1 Chronicles 3:19. We are now introduced to one of the most mysterious, intriguing characters in the entire Bible. The lineages recorded in Matthew and Luke diverge between David's two sons, Solomon and Nathan. These two distinct genealogies continue separately for about twenty generations over a period of almost four hundred years. Matthew 1:12 states, "Shealtiel begat Zerubbabel." But in Luke 3:27, Zerubbabel is listed as "son of Salathiel." Naturally, the question becomes: who was this Zerubbabel? One issue concerns Zerubbabel's very name. Some Bible students view the name as of Hebrew origin. Others conclude the etymology of the name to be Assyrian or Babylonian. Remember, numerous scholars do not even agree that Matthew's account follows Jesus's earthly father Joseph's heritage, while Luke records Mary's lineage. Yet, in Matthew 1:12 and Luke 3:27, it appears that these two unique family trees that were separated twenty generations and four centuries earlier *now become intertwined once again.* Likely, "Shealtiel" and "Salathiel" were the same person and the father of Zerubbabel. Now that presents new questions. A second topic Bible students have posed is: were Shealtiel and Salathiel one and the same person? As with Zerubbabel's name, one possibility is that Shealtiel was considered a Hebrew name, while Salathiel was viewed as a Greek translation of this same Hebrew name. Even if we accept Shealtiel and Salathiel as one and the same, still a third issue arises. Zerubbabel appears to be exiled King Jehoiachin's grandson (see 1 Chronicles 3:17-19). Matthew and Luke both recorded Zerubbabel's father as this Shealtiel (or Salathiel). Read 1 Chronicles 3:17-19 closely. Verse 19 stated that one Pedaiah was the father of Zerubbabel, with Salathiel mentioned in verse 17, and Pedaiah in verse 18. A possible resolution of this third issue would be as follows: Jehoiachin's son Assir had a daughter, making her Jehoiachin's granddaughter. This unnamed granddaughter married Neri in the lineage of Mary (via Nathan). Possibly, Shealtiel (Salathiel) was the son of this marriage. If Shealtiel died without fathering any sons, then Pedaiah, Shealtiel's brother, must have married the widow. Pedaiah and the widow then had a son they named Zerubbabel.

This situation was not unique. The story of Judah and Tamar, as we saw earlier, first presented the institution of Levirate marriage. Later in the account of Ruth and Boaz, we saw the successful consummation of such a Kinsman-Redeemer marriage. The purpose of the substitute male relative was always to maintain the deceased husband's lineage. Shealtiel might have been the actual father of Zerubbabel, or Pedaiah, as Kinsman-Redeemer, could have been the biological father of Zerubbabel with the deceased Shealtiel actually being the biological uncle of Zerubbabel.

Yet a fourth issue surrounds Zerubbabel. The prophet Haggai repeatedly affirmed Zerubbabel as the son of Shealtiel. Remember Jeremiah declaring the signet ring would be "plucked" away from Jehoiachin? Now, as we read the verse that opened this chapter, Haggai 2:23, we find that the signet ring will be given to Zerubbabel. Haggai's mission was encouraging the people to complete the construction of the second temple under Zerubbabel's guidance, as Zerubbabel had been appointed governor of Judah (Haggai 1:1; 14 (NASB). Although Zerubbabel was King Jehoiachin's descendant and probable great grandson, upon returning from Babylonian captivity to Jerusalem, he was always called "governor of Judah" and was never called "King."

A fifth issue is found in the Book of Ezra. Ezra the prophet wrote about all the gold and silver temple items being returned to Jerusalem by Cyrus, the King of Persia, with instructions for them to be placed within the second temple, once it was constructed. The caravan leader was "Sheshbazzar, the Prince of Judah" (Ezra 1:8)." In chapter 5, Ezra said Cyrus had given "unto one whose name was Sheshbazzar, who he had made governor." Two verses later, Ezra stated Sheshbazzar also laid the foundation of the temple. Then this Sheshbazzar just disappeared from Scripture. The most reasonable explanation of reconciling the name Sheshbazzar and Zerubbabel can be found in the Babylonian policy of changing old Hebrew names to new Babylonian names, such as the changes made in the names of Shadrack, Meshach, and Abednego. Their friend, Daniel, had his name changed to Belteshazzar. Note as evidence the similarity in word construction of Sheshbazzar and Belteshazzar. One logical explanation for these names - Sheshbazzar and Belteshazzar - is that these were the probable Babylonian names of Zerubbabel and Daniel, respectively. Nevertheless, many scholars today believe Sheshbazzar was followed by a different man named Zerubbabel, as the leader of the returning exiles.

The most fascinating of all Old Testament prophets who mentioned Zerubbabel has to be Zechariah. In Chapter 4 of the book bearing his name, Zechariah recorded his fifth vision. The vision was a word from the Lord addressed through Zechariah to Zerubbabel. The vision expressed the notion that, "Not by might, nor by power, but by My spirit, saith the Lord of Hosts, shall Zerubbabel reign." Zerubbabel's kingly ancestors had used might and power, but henceforth, Yahweh was going to use His Spirit. Because Zerubbabel, at God's direction, laid the foundation of the second Temple, the vision concluded with two "anointed ones" who were to be at the entrance to the temple. Most Bible scholars conclude these two anointed ones were to be Zerubbabel, governor of Judah, and Jeshua, the high priest who returned from Babylon with Zerubbabel. Once again, we see a pairing of the administrative governing role with the priestly role. We saw these twin roles in the tribes of Judah and Levi. Later was the pairing of Moses and Aaron. Further on, the high priest Aaron had married Elisheba, sister of Nahshon, who was in the lineage of the Royal Seed. More recently, it was Princess Jehosheba, sister of King Ahaziah, who married Jehoiada, the high priest.

As for those two olive trees and the candlestick Zechariah mentions in his Old Testament writings (Chapter 4:11-14, NASB), read this New Testament verse:

> "These are the two olive trees and the two candlesticks standing before the god
> of the earth" (Revelation 11:4).

The Garden of Eden and its river, the twelve tribes surrounding the tabernacle in the Sinai Desert, the Tree of Life in the garden - all will be in the future New Jerusalem. And now we see two olive trees and the golden lampstands from Zechariah 4 reappear in Revelation 11.

In Zechariah 6, Yahweh, using Zechariah as a prophet, encourages the second temple to be completed. In the later verses of chapter six, the Lord instructs Zechariah to use silver and gold to fashion an elaborate crown to place upon the head, not of Zerubbabel, the Governor, but upon the head of the high priest Jeshua (Zechariah 6:11, NASB). What is momentous is that Jeshua is the high priest who was crowned with the distinctive crown. Finally, after *thousands of years* of the separate roles for the king and the priest, the roles were united in the being of *just one person, Jeshua*. Although Aaron wore a crown as the first high priest (Exodus 29:6), Melchizedek is the only prior example of one individual serving as both King and Priest – way back in Genesis 14.

After having viewed some of the major issues surrounding the life of Zerubbabel, it is time to study his accomplishments as Judah's lone governor. Zerubbabel's greatest accomplishment as Governor of Judah is his erection of Jerusalem's second temple. Zerubbabel's Temple area was about the same size as Solomon's Temple complex (i.e. one half to two thirds the size of a football field). Moses called upon Bezalel to fashion the Sinai tabernacle tent. Next, David provided a tent to house the Ark of the Covenant in Jerusalem. Eventually, King Solomon was commissioned by God to construct the first temple on Mount Moriah. This first temple stood from about 965 BC to its destruction by Nebuchadnezzar in 586 BC. Judah's first temple served God's chosen people for almost four hundred years with twenty of David's descendants serving as king of the nation. Nebuchadnezzar had carried the royal family captive into Babylon. In approximately 537 BC, the Persians conquered the Babylonians. Cyrus, the great king of Persia, granted permission for some of the Jewish exiles to return to Jerusalem seventy years after their first captivity (2 Chronicles 36:21; Jeremiah 25:11-12; and Daniel 9:2). King Jehoiachin was brought to Babylon in chains about 586 BC. Seventy years later, King Cyrus sought Jehoiachin's descendants out from among the exiles. Zerubbabel was likely the great grandson of captured King Jehoiachin. Cyrus appointed Zerubbabel as Governor (not King) of Judah to lead a caravan of returning exiles back to Judah.

Pause a moment to read Ezra 1:4 and 8-11. Some Bible students have termed this entourage *"The Second Exodus."* Note in verse 4 the phrase "silver, gold, goods, cattle, and free will offerings." Turn in your Bible and read Exodus 12:35-38: "They (the Israelites) asked of the Egyptians jewels of silver and jewels of gold and raiment." Skip a few verses down in Exodus and read, "even very much cattle." Against Pharaoh's will, but under Moses' leadership, the Egyptians willingly gave the Israelites "silver, gold, raiment, cattle, flocks, herds and whatever they requested." Almost one thousand years later, at Cyrus' direction, the Persians gave the Jews "silver, gold, goods, beasts and a free will offering."

In addition, Cyrus made certain that the five thousand four hundred gold and silver articles previously taken by Nebuchadnezzar from the Jerusalem temple seventy years earlier were returned to Jerusalem under the new governor, Zerubbabel. About twelve thousand members of Judah's royal family with select craftsmen and mighty men were taken to Babylon. Seven decades later, over forty thousand returned to Judah. The next few verses list the number of horses, mules, camels, and donkeys making the journey under Zerubbabel's command. Read Lamentations chapters 1 and 2 to see the challenge Zerubbabel faces when he arrives at Jerusalem.

"How lonely the city sits in solitary that was full of people. She is like a widow" (Lamentations 1:1).

"The Lord has afflicted her for the multitude of her transgressions. Her children are gone into captivity before the enemy" (Lamentations 1:5).

"The Lord is righteous: While I have rebelled against His commandments: ... My virgins and young men are gone into captivity" (Lamentations 1:18).

"... And God hath violently taken away His tabernacle... He has destroyed His places of assembly: The Lord hath caused the solemn feast in Sabbath to be forgotten in Zion and hath despised in the indignation of His anger, the king, and the priest" (Lamentations 2:6).

"The Lord has cast off His altar. He has abhorred His sanctuary. He hath delivered into the hands of the enemy the walls of her palaces... The Lord has determined to destroy the wall of the daughter of Zion" (Lamentations 2:7-8).

Nebuchadnezzar had pillaged the temple and palace. Then he burned the limestone structures. In conclusion, the Babylonian king demolished the buildings down to the retaining wall, the wall holding in place the embankment of the Temple Mount. All that remained was the western retaining wall of the Temple Mount. (This retaining wall is today Jewry's *most holy site* - it is the Wailing Wall in Jerusalem).

It was under these conditions and to this site that Zerubbabel led the forty thousand under his command. While some had chosen to remain in Persia, the returnees found a daunting task at Mount Moriah. Even so, Zerubbabel and the high priest, Jeshua, managed to get worship initiated once again at the temple site.

In the second year of their return, Zerubbabel managed to get the foundation in place. Local adversaries soon troubled the Jews such that construction of the second temple was stopped (Ezra 4:4-5). King Cyrus was succeeded by King Darius, and the prophets Haggai and Zechariah rose up to encourage the people to overcome the adversaries and obstacles to finishing the second temple. Haggai delivers a word from the Lord to Zerubbabel and Jeshua, "Is it time for you, oh ye, to dwell in your paneled houses and the temple to lie in ruins?" Haggai dated his ministry to "the second year of Darius, the King, in the sixth month" (Haggai 1:1-4 NASB). Concurrently, a second prophet, Zechariah, dated his ministry as, "In the eight month, in the second year of Darius" (Zechariah 1:1 NASB).

The nation of Judah and Governor Zerubbabel had two prophets simultaneously encouraging and exhorting the people onward. About seventy years after the first temple had been destroyed, around 516 BC, the second temple was dedicated. Most likely, the second temple approximated the size of the original temple. The first temple had been about one hundred seventy-five feet long, with a width of eighty feet, and rising to a height of just over fifty feet. The second temple became known as Zerubbabel's temple.

But the former slaves did not build anywhere near as magnificent a temple as Solomon's first temple. From a pure material standpoint, the second temple was substantially less glorious than Solomon's temple. However, what especially was missing from the second temple was the Ark of the Covenant and God's glory (Jeremiah 3:16). Recall earlier, how God had dwelt among His people above the Ark of the Covenant, between the cherubim in an area known as the Mercy Seat. As all of Israel continued to sin, God finally removed His Spirit from residing above the Ark (Ezekiel 10:18-19 NASB).

According to the Bible, the Spirit of God never returned to this second temple. Not only was Zerubbabel's temple not as magnificent as Solomon's temple, but the central features of the first temple, the Ark of the Covenant, and God's Spirit, were absent. While exiled in Babylon, the people of Judah were unable to travel to the temple in Jerusalem or focus their worship on the Ark of the Covenant in the Holy of Holies. And even if they could have somehow traveled to Jerusalem, it would have been for naught. Nebuchadnezzar had leveled the temple to the ground, and the Ark had disappeared at the hands of either the Jewish priests or the Babylonian soldiers. As noted earlier, the Jews' synagogue was "invented" in Babylon when the captives could no longer get to the temple.

With only the improvised synagogues, the exiles in Babylon clung ever more tightly to the ancient writings of Moses and the more contemporary writings of Ezekiel and other prophets while they were prisoners in Babylon. Once the exiles returned to Judah, they listened more intently to the words of Haggai, Ezra, Nehemiah, and Zechariah and the scrolls of Scripture began to replace the Ark in prominence.

(After five hundred years of focus on the synagogue, the scrolls, and tradition, the Jews could not bring themselves to shift their focus from their traditions to the Messiah when He began His ministry.)

This decidedly inferior temple, empty of the Holy of Holies' single most important item, the Ark, will serve the people as Zerubbabel's temple from about 515 BC until the master builder, King Herod, effectively razed it around 20 BC. Although inferior, Zerubbabel's temple served the Jews for approximately four hundred ninety-five years. Solomon's temple served the people only four hundred years.

Herod's temple was much larger than Solomon's or Zerubbabel's temples. The structure itself was three-and-one-half times the size of the two prior temples. Once Herod rebuilt the entire Temple Mount area, it is estimated to have been fifteen to sixteen times larger than Solomon's temple. This third temple, Herod's temple, would take from 20 BC to AD 64 to construct. All of Jesus's worship in the temple would be in this temple of Herod's that was being built and remodeled *continuously* during Jesus's entire life. Jesus *never* worshiped in a tabernacle, tent, or temple built by His ancestors. Furthermore, Jesus never worshiped in a completed temple. Herod's temple took a total of eighty-four years to remodel and build. Once completed, it functioned only six years. Herod's temple was obliterated by the Roman General, Titus, in AD 70. Zerubbabel's temple, the most basic of Judah's three temples, also had the longest life at nearly five hundred years before it was razed by Herod. The following chart will express a comparison of the tabernacle and the three temple complexes.

Tabernacle, Temples, and Touchdowns

Tabernacle	1/4 - 1/3 size of football field
Solomon's temple	1/2 - 2/3 size of football field
Zerubbabel's temple	1/2 - 2/3 size of football field
Herod's temple	15 times size of football field

Recall Jeremiah's indictment of King Jehoiachin's lineage—not one of his seven sons or their descendants will ever be King of Judah (Jeremiah 22:30 NASB). In some murky manner, Zerubbabel was a grandson or great-grandson of Jehoiachin, but Jeremiah's prophecy was that no descendant of Jehoiachin's would ever sit as king on the throne of Judah. Zerubbabel was appointed governor of Judah, but he was never a *king*. The Davidic line of kings ended, just as the judges were no more, once Samuel, the last judge, at God's direction, anointed the first king, Saul. The gold and silver crown was placed, not on Zerubbabel's head, but upon the head of the high priest, Jeshua. After almost one thousand five hundred years with a governing authority (whether a prince, a judge, a king, or a governor) and a spiritual authority (whether a priest, a prophet, a seer, a holy man, or a high priest), the two roles were finally united into the personhood of just one man, the high priest Jeshua.

Mostly this book has shown two types of lineage. The first has been of the Royal Family, the kings, queens, princes, and princesses. Second, the Bible also shows the importance to God of the lineage of spiritual heritage and purity of His priestly servants. Jeshua served initially as high priest and is now wearing a gold crown. Similarly to the kings, Jeshua also can document his own priestly lineage for nearly one thousand two hundred years, from approximately 1700 BC to 536 BC. During this period, some twenty-three generations of Jeshua's family served Israel as high priest. The following chart establishes Jeshua's heritage. Also notice Jeshua's uncle is the priest Ezra, who probably authored most of the books of 1 and 2 Chronicles and Ezra.

Genealogy of Jeshua

Abraham (Matthew 1:2)
▼
Isaac
▼
Jacob (Israel)
▼
Levi (1 Chronicles 6:1)
▼
Kohath (Ezra 7:1-5)
▼
Amram
▼
Aaron – Moses- Miriam (1 Chronicles 6:3)
▼
Eleazar
▼
Phineas
▼
Abishua
▼
Bukki
▼
Uzzi
▼
Zerahiah
▼
Meraioth
▼
Amariah
▼
Ahitub
▼
Zadok
▼
Ahimaaz
▼
Azariah
▼
Johanan
▼
Azariah (High Priest, in Solomon's Temple, 1 Chronicles 6:10)
▼
Amariah
▼
Ahitub
▼
Zadok
▼
Shallum
▼
Hilkiah
▼
Azariah
▼
Seraiah

_____

▼   ▼
Ezra ◄brothers ►**Jehozadak** (High Priest at Babylonian Captivity, 1Chron. 6:15, Ezra 7:1-6)
▼
Jeshua (High Priest with Zerubbabel Nehemiah 12:26)
▼
Joiakim
▼
Eliashib (Contemporary of Nehemiah, Nehemiah. 12:10)
▼
Joiada
▼
Johanan
▼
Jaddua (High Priest at time of Alexander the Great, Nehemiah 12:22)

Compare Jeshua's lineage with Ezra's lineage near the end of chapter 24. Also see Ezra 7:1-5

What have we learned about Zerubbabel?

1. Josiah had three wicked sons who each became king of Judah. One of Josiah's three wicked sons, King Jehoiakim, had a son named Jehoiachin, who succeeded his father as king of Judah.

2. Jehoiachin reigned only three months, but Scripture reveals his brief reign was evil.

3. God elevated the Babylonian king, Nebuchadnezzar, to humble Judah and Jerusalem due to their repeated sins. Nebuchadnezzar plundered the temple and the palace of the gold, silver, precious things, and possibly the Ark of the Covenant and carried all the items seven hundred miles away to Babylon (northern Iraq).

4. One example of the religious rebellion of the Jews concerns the land. The Israelites failed to follow Yahweh's instruction to permit the land to lie fallow every seven years. They ignored this statute for nearly five centuries. The captivity in Babylon lasted seventy years, long enough for the land to enjoy its Sabbath's rest (Leviticus 26:33-35). Seventy years times one year of rest for every seven years equals four hundred ninety years.

5. God called Nebuchadnezzar "My Servant" to accomplish Yahweh's will (Jeremiah 25:9). God used Jeremiah the prophet to record, "When seventy years are accomplished, then I will punish the King of Babylon and that nation for their iniquity." Part of this punishment is that King Nebuchadnezzar later had a mental breakdown (Jeremiah 25:12 and Daniel 4:19-37).

6. Jeremiah proclaimed that none of Jehoiachin's seven sons would ever sit as king of Judah. Furthermore, Jehoiachin would be led in chains to Babylon, where he would die more than three decades later.

7. Nebuchadnezzar crushed Judah and took nearly five thousand members from the royal family into Babylonian captivity.

8. During the Jews' seventy-year captivity, Babylon was conquered by Persia.

9. Cyrus the Great of Persia was compelled to arrange for Jews to rebuild the temple in Jerusalem under Zerubbabel's leadership.

10. The last king of Judah who was a carrier of the Royal Seed, Jehoiachin, had a grandson (?) named Zerubbabel. Cyrus appointed Zerubbabel as governor of Judah and not as king, although Scripture places him in the direct lineage of the Royal Seed.

11. At the urging of Haggai, Zechariah, and others, Judah's second temple was completed after twenty years of on-again, off-again construction under Zerubbabel's leadership.

12. The Ark of the Covenant removed from Solomon's temple by Nebuchadnezzar or the priests was never recovered. However, as we learned earlier, in Revelation, John saw the Ark of the Covenant in the heavens.

13. Zerubbabel and the high priest Jeshua, were leaders of the second Exodus from Persia, much as Moses and his brother Aaron were joint leaders of the first Exodus from Egypt.

14. After four hundred years and twenty kings in the lineage of David, the Davidic dynasty was concluded, although Scripture continues the genealogy of the First Family as slaves in the land of Babylon.

15. Scripture and tradition were so emphasized and exalted in Judah that they became the replacement for the lost Ark of the Covenant. By the time of Jesus, various sects arose that emphasized different points of view concerning the words of God and tradition. These groups were known as the Pharisees, Herodians, Zealots, Sadducees, and so on. A fifth group, the Essenes, rejected most of this worship of tradition and Jewish commentary about the Law and withdrew into the Judean desert near the Dead Sea.

Zerubbabel's Relatives

Name	Relationship	APPROXIMATE Dates
Abraham	Great-grandfather, 31 generations removed	±2000 BC
Boaz	Great-grandfather, 21 generations removed	±1200 BC
David	Great-grandfather, 18 generations removed	±1040 BC
Solomon	Great-grandfather, 17 generations removed	980 BC
Jehoshaphat	Great-grandfather, 13 generations removed	875 BC
Josiah	Great-great-grandfather	640 BC
Jehoiachin	Last Royal Seed king of Judah; grandfather	580 BC
Nahum	Great-grandson (?), 8 generations removed	650 BC
Salathiel	Father? – Same as Shealtiel	625 BC
Shealtiel	Father? – Same as Salathiel	625 BC
Pedaiah	Father? – Brother of Shealtiel?	625 BC
Joseph	Great-grandson, 8 generations removed	20 BC
Mary	Great-granddaughter, 17 generations removed	15 BC
Jesus	Great-grandson, 18 generations removed	AD 30

Chapter 24

The Others

> And I will bring forth a *seed* out of Jacob and out of Judah an inheritor of my mountains; and mine elect shall inherit it, and my servants shall dwell there. (Isaiah 65:9, emphasis added)

This study of the Royal Seed of Israel cannot devote a chapter to every single one of the one hundred three direct carriers of the Royal Seed. The Bible is mostly silent about one-half of Jesus's ancestors, except for simply listing their names in the genealogy of Jesus. Consequently, this book is limited to only select members of the Royal Family. Many very important and famous Biblical characters have been ignored in this book. For example, men such as Gideon, Samson, Paul, and Peter have not been mentioned, not because they are unimportant, but because they are not from the lineage of Israel's Royal Family. This chapter includes only a sample of individuals linked to the family of the Royal Seed. One subject is good King Hezekiah. The other seven individuals, aside from being connected to the Royal Family, all have something in common. These seven are Joshua, Isaiah, Zephaniah, Nahum, Daniel, Zechariah, and Ezra. None of these seven were kings, yet, in some way, each is connected to the Royal Seed. What these seven have in common is their names are all memorialized as the names of books of the Bible.

The ninth subject is not a single person at all but a group of men. From one hundred three male carriers of the Royal Seed, Mary and Joseph had thirty-six common ancestors. Twenty-nine were ancestors of only Joseph. That leaves thirty-eight ancestors peculiar to only Mary. We will consider most of Mary's ancestors as a group.

Joshua

The chapter about Judah presented a chart, noting the frequency the twelve tribes of Israel are mentioned in the Bible. The names of Judah, Levi and Ephraim occur *eight hundred more times* than the other nine tribes combined. Because Joseph was separated from his family, his father Israel gave him a blessing of material prosperity (Genesis 49:26; Deuteronomy 33:16-17; 1 Chronicles 5:1-2). Israel blessed the younger of Joseph's two sons, Ephraim, before his older brother Manasseh, saying the "younger brother shall be greater than he" (Genesis 48:17-22). The three most prominent tribes of Judah, Levi and Ephraim each received a specific blessing.

The "al" Blessings

Recipient	Roy-al Blessing	Spiritu-al Blessing	Materi-al Blessing
Tribe	Judah	Levi	Ephraim
Reference	Genesis 49:9-10	Exodus 7:1-2	1 Chronicles 5:1-2

Recall Nahshon had been chosen by Moses as the "prince" from the tribe of Judah to lead the procession of Israelites through the Sinai wilderness. At the encampment, it was Judah to the east, Reuben on the south, Ephraim on the west, and Dan to the north completing the perimeter. The tribe of Levi always camped inside the four other groups.

Just as Nahshon was appointed to lead Judah and Aaron was to head the Levites, the "prince" from the tribe of Ephraim was a man named Elishama. Elishama was the grandfather of the mighty Joshua, a military commander and author of the book of Joshua. He gives only a brief reference to his father Nun, but the Bible student can discover Joshua's lineage in 1 Chronicles 7:20-28. These leaders – Nahshon from Judah, Aaron from the Levites and Elishama from Ephraim were contemporaries. Furthermore, Nahshon and Aaron were brothers-in-law and Elishama was their cousin, nine generations removed.

Joseph requested he not be buried in Egypt (Genesis 50:24-26), just as his father Israel had earlier requested (Genesis 49:29-33; 50:2, 13), and four hundred years later, during the Exodus, Moses took the bones of Joseph as they traveled. Joseph was the father of Ephraim. Moses' capable aide, Joshua, was a descendant of Ephraim. The old man Moses had first sent Joshua out as one of the twelve spies into the Promised Land (Exodus 33:11), and Joshua and Caleb returned the only two positive reports. Later, Moses commissioned Joshua to command the Israelites in defeating the Amalekites (Exodus 17:8-10).

After God showed Moses the land that He will give to the Israelites, Moses asked God to appoint a successor to lead the Israelites in conquering Jericho and some thirty kings in Canaan. God chose Joshua because he was filled with God's spirit (Numbers 27:16-23).

We see the military commander, author and spirit-filled leader, Joshua, was a cousin of Jesus via Joseph from some ten generations earlier (1 Chronicles 7).

Near the end of Joshua's life, the tribe of Ephraim received their allotment of the Promised Land. At last, Joshua interred his ancestor Joseph's bones in the very territory awarded to Joseph's descendants four hundred years after Joseph's death (Joshua 24:29-32).

Joshua's genealogy is found in 1 Chronicles 7:20-28. Also see Numbers 1:10.

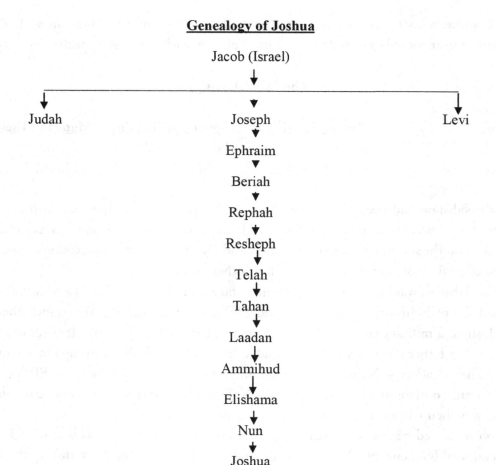

Genealogy of Joshua

Jacob (Israel)

Judah   Joseph   Levi

Ephraim

Beriah

Rephah

Resheph

Telah

Tahan

Laadan

Ammihud

Elishama

Nun

Joshua

Isaiah

Isaiah was a prophet who served as advisor to four of Judah's kings. He moved easily between the priesthood and the kings. His ministry was to the educated, the wealthy, and the "bluebloods" of Judah. He wrote one of the longest books in the Old Testament. He prophesied the coming of the Messiah seven hundred years into the future. Isaiah prophesied further into the future than any Old Testament prophet. In Isaiah's own words,

> "And there shall come forth a shoot out of the stem of Jesse and a Branch shall grow out of his root and the spirit of the Lord shall be upon him . . . the wolf shall dwell with the lamb and the leopard shall lie down with the kid . . . and the lion shall eat straw like the ox" (Isaiah 11:1-2, 6-7).

Compare Isaiah 13:10 with Revelation 18:1 and 21:23. Further, compare Isaiah 13:19 and Revelation 17:5 and 18:10. If Isaiah was not of the Royal Family, how could he have been so well educated, a worthy writer, comfortable around wealth and power, articulate in his communication, and having the respect of priests and kings alike? Certainly he was called of God, but a very probable and logical explanation is that Isaiah was somehow related to the Royal Family of Judah. Scripture never states that Isaiah was a member of the Royal Family. But if he was, that could explain his living in Jerusalem, his education, his having time to write, and his ease in being among priests and kings. Ancient tradition declares Isaiah was a cousin to King Uzziah, but no Biblical text supports this.

One final point concerning Isaiah: when the clay jars containing the Dead Sea Scrolls were discovered in 1947 at Qumran, the most complete and most famous scroll found was a copy of the Old Testament book of Isaiah, which became known as the Great Isaiah Scroll. Scholars have estimated *this particular copy of Isaiah was approximately one hundred years old when Jesus was born.* Upon careful inspection and comparison of the ancient scroll with today's Bible, some scholars have concluded as much as ninety-five percent of today's Bible text of Isaiah should be deemed consistent with this ancient scroll. Much of the five percent difference has to do with transcribing errors and misspelling. This is a huge vindication of God's word standing true over the centuries and millenniums and should be a source of comfort to modern man.

Hezekiah

Of the forty or so kings of Israel and Judah, Hezekiah was considered special.

> "He [Hezekiah] trusted in the Lord God of Israel; so that after him was none like him among the kings of Judah, nor any that were before him. He cleaved to the Lord and departed not from following Him, but kept His commandments, which the Lord commanded Moses" (2 Kings 18:5-6).

A major accomplishment of Hezekiah's reign was the construction of an aqueduct tunnel to supply Jerusalem with water from outside the walls of the city. This third-of-a-mile-long tunnel was the very one used during World War I by the British General Allenby to capture the Temple Mount from the hands of the Ottoman Empire after a five-hundred-year occupation. Amazingly, Allenby, under intense international pressure to preserve the site, never fired a shot in securing the area. In more recent times, archaeologists have discovered a cornerstone confirming this tunnel was built exactly as the Bible stated during Hezekiah's reign (2 Kings 20:20).

While Hezekiah's son, Manasseh, and grandson, Amon, were evil, Hezekiah's great grandson was the good King Josiah. Josiah was king during Israel's last great period of prosperity. Matthew 1:9-11 affirms these four kings of Judah are in Jesus's lineage.

Zephaniah

The prophet Zephaniah quickly states his genealogy. He lists five generations of his family, and then answers who is king of Judah (Josiah), and who is the king's father—all in one verse! Zephaniah was the great-great-grandson of good king Hezekiah (Zephaniah 1:1). Zephaniah attacked the deities of his great-great-uncle, King Manasseh, who was Hezekiah's son. While Hezekiah was Judah's most spiritual king, earlier Jeremiah recorded Manasseh as being the most evil king of all (2 Kings 21:9-12). Manasseh was so bold as to even erect two altars to worship the "heavenly host" in the very courtyard of the Jewish temple. Zephaniah, as a member of the Royal Family, should be remembered for his boldness in proclaiming God's message. When he publicly condemned the princes and the king's children, he was indicting his own siblings, cousins, and other royal family members.

Daniel

Like Zephaniah, Daniel declares himself to be a member of Judah's Royal Family (Daniel 1:3-6). The Book of Daniel is set in Babylon where Daniel was held captive. Daniel was probably a teenager when he was led away from Jerusalem by the Babylonian army. Once he arrived in Babylon, it is likely he endured becoming a eunuch (2 Kings 20:16-18; Isaiah 39:5-7; Daniel 1:1-3, 5, 7, 11, 18). At the conclusion of his writings, the prophet was in his eighties. The focus of Daniel is on prophecy, both of his immediate future and of the end times. Daniel's writings and the book of Revelation have *more references* to the Antichrist and end times than any other two books in the entire Bible.

One insight we gain from Daniel is mentioned by no other biblical writer, for Daniel declares, "Wisdom was given me" (Daniel 2:28, 30).

> "And the king should do according to his will: And he shall exalt himself and to magnify himself above every god and shall speak unusual things against the God of Gods and shall prosper . . . neither shall he regard the god of his fathers, nor the desire of women, nor regard any god but he shall magnify himself above all" (Daniel 11:36-37).

Some students of the Bible believe the passage, "Neither shall he regard the god of his fathers" suggests the Antichrist will be of Jewish heritage. Also, the phrase "nor the desire of women" may infer the Antichrist will be a homosexual. The other characteristics of the Antichrist are mentioned by numerous writers of the Bible, but Daniel is alone and unique with these two comments regarding possible bits of information concerning the Antichrist.

Finally, compare these two prophecies—one mostly from the book of Daniel and the other mostly from Revelation.

THE TWO PROPHECIES

70 YEAR PROPHECY	70 WEEK PROPHECY
70 Year Babylonian Captivity	**70 Week Church Age**
Old Testament Period	New Testament Period
Reference: Daniel 9:2	Reference Daniel 9:24
Nebuchadnezzar – a King of Kings	Jesus - the King of Kings
Daniel 2:37	Revelation 17:14
Punishment of Judah's Sin	Punishment of World's Sin
By hand of Ancient Babylon	Led by Babylon, the Great Harlot
Daniel 9:11	Revelation 18:2
Restore Jerusalem	Create New Jerusalem
Daniel 9:25	Revelation 21:1-2
Leader: Prince Zerubbabel	Leader: Prince of Peace, Jesus
Ezra 1:8 – 2:2	Isaiah 9:6

As we conclude Daniel's story, ponder Daniel 9:25. Daniel the prophet is obviously a member of Judah's Royal Family, and Zerubbabel, as Jehoiachin's grandson, also belongs to Judah's Royal Family. In this verse, he sets the time for the end of the present age at seventy weeks. The seventy weeks leading to the Messiah began upon the restoration of the temple in Jerusalem under Zerubbabel, as the appointed governor of Judah. His task was to rebuild the temple. As the great grandson (?) of King Jehoiachin, Zerubbabel is of the Royal Seed. We see that Daniel and Zerubbabel are related, as both men are members of Judah's Royal Family. But, most important of all, somehow, some way, they are both related to Jesus.

Zechariah

Zechariah was a man with a slight chance of being a member of the Royal Seed of Israel, but he was the most Messianic of all the Minor Prophets. Zechariah's ministry began after the conclusion of Daniel's writing and coincided with Zerubbabel's return to erect the second temple in Judah. He was the grandson of a chief priest, yet Zechariah was also a prophet (Zechariah 1:8;

Nehemiah 12:4-16). Zechariah possibly had a heritage from his family of priests faithfully serving Yahweh in the temple and being in frequent contact with the Royal Seed of Judah. His emphasis on finishing the temple, and his being a co-worker with Zerubbabel, who definitely was in Jesus's lineage, heightens our expectations. And finally, if Zechariah was related to the lineage of Jesus, that could help us to better understand his visions looking five centuries into the future with an emphasis on Messianic prophecy and Jesus's coming as the long anticipated Messiah.

Ezra

About 539 BC, King Cyrus of Persia appointed Zerubbabel to be governor of Judah. Zerubbabel led a contingent of Jews to Jerusalem to rebuild the temple. The foundation was laid around 535 BC, but for approximately fifteen years, the work ceased, due partially to political intrigue. With the chastising by the prophet Haggai and the encouragement of the prophet Zechariah, the temple was finally completed in 516 BC.

Some eighty years later, a second caravan led by Ezra set out to Jerusalem from Persia. When Ezra arrived, the temple was nearly eighty years old. But the people, the priests, and the Levites serving the Jews were not obedient in following the Mosaic Law. Of particular concern to the leaders was "the Holy Seed have mingled themselves with the people of those lands: the hands of the princes and the rulers have been chief in this trespass" (Ezra 9:1-2 NASB). A time of spiritual revival was now at hand. Ezra sought a return to the laws recorded by Moses and implemented by Aaron. Ezra observed the people intermarrying with the non-Israelites. Ezra knew one of the chief causes in the fall of Israel had been King Solomon marrying many foreign wives, with the result that his heart was turned from Yahweh to build temples for his wives' multiple foreign gods (1 Kings 11:1, 6-9). Ezra was distraught. After the punishment by God of a seventy-year captivity in Babylon (Iraq), the people were still continuing in the ways of Solomon from four hundred years earlier. Ezra realized the people had learned nothing from Israel's subjugation by the cruel Babylonians. Ezra was granted authority to encourage the people to return to the Law of Moses. Furthermore, Ezra was selected to appoint officials for the land and to mete out punishment (Ezra 7:6, 14, 21 NASB).

Ezra's objectives were to encourage and to guide the citizens toward holiness and obedience, all with King Cyrus's blessing. The prophet Jeremiah implored the citizens of Judah to repent. "Thus saith the Lord, stand ye in the ways and see and ask for the old paths" (Jeremiah 6:16 NASB). As a leader, Ezra set an example. Ezra's message returned to the writings of Jeremiah and became one of "ask for the old paths."

In Ezra chapter 7, the scribe finally introduces himself. His introduction is his genealogy. Ezra's father, Seraiah, was the high priest before Nebuchadnezzar's victories (2 Kings 25:18). In addition to Ezra, Seraiah had a second son named Jehozadak. Jehozadak was the high priest carried into Babylonian captivity (1 Chronicles 6:14). Furthermore, his nephew is Jeshua who returned with Zerubbabel. Once Ezra's ancestry is connected to Levi, it is certain that Aaron's great-grandfather is Israel (Jacob). Ezra confirms not only his relationship to his father, Seraiah, as high priest, and his brother, Jehozadak, as high priest, but also seventeen generations earlier to the very first high priest, Aaron. Furthermore, Ezra anchors his heritage to Jacob (Israel) and, by inference, to Isaac, to Abraham, to Noah, and eventually to Adam. Ezra confirms he is a scribe/priest related to the Royal Seed, the Messianic line of Jesus. By documenting his heritage to the Royal Seed, Ezra's ultimate purpose is to document his authority as a spokesman for Yahweh.

As Aaron's great-grandson, twenty generations removed, Ezra was a cousin to the Messianic line. The following chart will present Ezra's genealogy from Ezra chapter 7. A comparison of Ezra 7 with 1 Chronicles 6 notes the absence in Ezra 7 of six of Ezra's ancestors. Most likely, this is a transcription error. Turn back to the chart "Genealogy of Jeshua" and notice Meraioth's son is Amariah, according to 1 Chronicles 6. In Ezra 7, after Meraioth, the next high priest is Azariah. The similarity between the two names, Amariah and Azariah, is obvious.

Genealogy of Ezra

Abraham (Matthew 1:2)
▼
Isaac
▼
Jacob (Israel)
▼
Levi (1 Chronicles 6:1)
▼
Kohath (Ezra 7:1-5)
▼
Amram
▼
Aaron – Moses – Miriam
▼
Eleazer
▼
Phineas
▼
Abishua
▼
Bukki
▼
Uzzi
▼
Zerahiah
▼
Meraioth
▼
? ▼
? ▼
? ▼
? ▼
? ▼
? ▼
Azariah (High Priest, Solomon's Temple, 1 Chronicles 6:10 & Ezra 7:10)
▼
Amariah
▼
Ahitub
▼
Zadok
▼
Shallum
▼
Hilkiah
▼
Azariah
▼
Seraiah
▼
Ezra ◄ brothers ► **Jehozadak** (High Priest at Babylonian Captivity 1 Chron. 6:15; Ezra 3:2)
▼
Jeshua

See 1 Chronicles 6:1-15 NKJV. Note six names are missing in Ezra's genealogy from Ezra 7. Nevertheless, Ezra and High Priest Jehozadak have the same ancestors for fourteen generations after Abraham and have the same ancestors for eight generations after the High Priest Azariah. Whether this gap was lost in translations over the centuries or merely skipped by Ezra, there is not a definitive answer.

Nahum

Of the numerous Bible persons we have studied, Nahum probably has the most dubious claim to potentially being a member of Israel's Royal Family. Nahum possibly grew up in Galilee at Capernaum ("village of Nahum"). Other scholars feel that his childhood may have been spent south of Jerusalem. Unlike most of the prophets, Nahum only gives us a one-verse biography. Furthermore, he is quoted nowhere else in Scripture. We have almost no data on his life.

So why include Nahum in a book about Jesus's family heritage? Two slim threads may tie Nahum to Jesus. First, he may have been born in Galilee at Capernaum, near where Joseph and Mary lived in Nazareth. Second, in Luke's account of Mary's genealogy, nine generations prior to Mary is the only other reference to a "Nahum" in the entire Bible (Luke 3:25 NASB). It does not appear to fit in the correct time period, since there are only nine generations between Nahum and Mary over a six-hundred-year span; yet the fact remains, this is the only other time in the entire Bible the name "Nahum" is mentioned after Nahum 1:1. The prophet Nahum possibly is an ancestor of Mary, the mother of Jesus.

Mary's Ancestors

As we learned previously, of Jesus's one hundred three earthly male ancestors, little has been said about the thirty-eight forefathers unique to Mary's family. The two most prominent, however, we have already discussed. One is Solomon's older brother, Nathan, and twenty-nine generations after Nathan, a Nahum appears in Mary's lineage. The subsequent thirty-six remaining forefathers of Mary just blend into Judah's history. None, as far as we know, were kings, or priests, or prophets. Furthermore, the Bible records no evidence of any of these men being connected, casually or intimately, with the Royal Seed, the Royal Family of Judea. Of the almost twenty kings in Jesus's heritage, all are in the lineage of Solomon and none from Mary's lineage through Nathan. The great majority of the men in Mary's lineage are mentioned only one time in the entire Bible, and that is in Luke chapter 3, where Luke records the likely genealogy of Mary. The Bible is silent on most of Mary's forefathers.

However, one potential relative of Mary deserves *very special* consideration – Salome. By studying Matthew 4:21; Matthew 27:56; Mark 15:40; and John 19:25-27, it seems reasonable to conclude Salome was the sister of Mary. Obviously, then she is the aunt of Jesus. Salome was the wife of Zebedee and the mother of James and John; therefore, Salome's sons were not only part of Jesus's "inner circle" (along with Peter), but also Jesus's first cousins. That Salome would ask her nephew if her sons could sit at the right and left sides of Jesus's throne seems less bold (Matthew 20:20-24). Jesus's last command was for His cousin, John, to take care of Mary after Jesus's death. James was martyred soon after Jesus's death (Acts 12:2). In contrast, John lived a long life and appears to have authored the Gospel of John, the books of First, Second, and Third John, as well as Revelation.

What did we learn about these other relatives?

1. For some people in the Bible, their relationship to the Royal Family of Israel is undefined, vague, or doesn't exist.
2. In eternity, believers will be surprised to learn how other Biblical characters considered minor persons today in the Messianic lineage will be vital, significant individuals in the family of God.
3. The purpose of this chapter was to offer some possibilities as to other potential members of the lineage of the Royal Seed.

The "Others" Relatives

Name	**Relationship**	**Reference**
Isaiah	Cousin to King Uzziah	(tradition)
Hezekiah	Related to all of Judah's kings	1 & 2 Kings
Zephaniah	Great-great-grandson King Hezekiah	Zephaniah 1:1
Daniel	Uncertain but member of Royal Family	Daniel 1:3, 6
Zechariah	Uncertain	?
Ezra	Priest, scribe, brother of High Priest Jehozadak	1 Chronicles 6:1-15
Nahum	Uncertain	Nahum 1:1, Luke 3:25
Mary's Ancestors	Forefathers of Mary	Luke 3:23-38

Chapter 25

John the Baptist

> For I say unto you, among those that are born of women, there is not a greater
> prophet than John the Baptist: but he that is least in the kingdom of God is greater
> than he. (Luke 7:28)

Zerubbabel and Jeshua returned to Jerusalem about 535 BC in order to restore the worship of Yahweh and to construct a second temple. Once the foundation was laid, there were fifteen years of no further progress. Eventually, in approximately 516 BC, Zerubbabel completed the erection of the second temple. In 458 BC, Ezra came to Jerusalem trying to encourage the citizens to return to holiness and to spark a religious revival (Ezra 7:10 NASB). However, just as Solomon married foreign wives and later served foreign gods, the locals continued this practice. Ezra pronounced a decree for the Israelite men to divorce their foreign wives (Ezra 10:1-2 NASB). By 444 BC, Nehemiah's administrative skills helped the population complete the wall around the temple and Jerusalem. About 435 BC, the Old Testament's last prophet, Malachi, began his ministry in this environment. Malachi preached a return to the relationship of the covenant between God and his people (Malachi 3:1). To make his message plain, Malachi declares, "For I am the Lord, I change not" (Malachi 3:6).

But, this passage is probably not the most important verse from God's point of view. The very last verses of Malachi, the very last verses of the Old Testament are probably what God wants us to remember.

> "Behold, I will send you Elijah, the prophet before the coming of the great and
> dreadful day of the Lord, and he shall turn the heart of the fathers to the children
> and the heart of the children to their fathers, lest I come and smite the earth with
> a curse" (Malachi 4:5-6).

Many scholars feel, as these verses attest, that John the Baptist and Jesus are the only two prophets to be the subject of prophecy themselves (see also Mark 9:13).

After Malachi, then . . . then . . . God was silent for four hundred years. Just as God was silent for four hundred thirty years between the end of Genesis and the beginning of Exodus, God once again grew silent.

World events had not quieted down. In fact, quite the opposite occurred. A century after Malachi, Alexander the Great came from Greece (Macedonia) and went through Israel to establish Alexandria, Egypt. Thereafter, Alexander conquered Persia. Upon his death, Israel was subject to Egyptian rulers once again, and later, Israel experienced Syrian domination for decades.

During this time, the mathematician Pythagoras lived (520 BC), as did the philosophers Socrates (470 BC) and Plato (427 BC). About this same time, the Parthenon was erected in Athens (440 BC). As Nehemiah was completing the walls around the temple in Jerusalem, (444 BC), the Greeks were building the Parthenon in Athens. To the west of Israel, the Roman Republic gradually began to assert its power around 300 BC. In the east, about 250 BC, India witnessed the rise of Ashoka, one of India's foremost emperors. Ashoka was the first emperor to actively promote the worship of Buddhism concurrently with the establishment of his Maurya Dynasty. Buddha died about 400 BC, with Ashoka erecting a final tomb around 250 BC. From Europe and Persia-India, Roman, Greek, and Buddhist influence began to be noticed in Israel, via the traders' caravans. In 166 BC, the Jews revolted under the leadership of the Maccabees. Two years later, the Roman military, led by General Pompey, conquered Jerusalem, and Roman-appointed leaders began ruling over the people of Israel. In 40 BC, Herod the Great became the first of his clan to be appointed by Rome as the leader of Israel and its chief tax collector.

It is not surprising, with all this turmoil and conflict, that the Jews splintered into several different groups. First, the Pharisees desired to separate from the Greco-Roman influence in the land. To cope with their oppression, they created new rules, oral law, and rabbinic commentary. Second, the Sadducees were members of the High Priesthood and Jerusalem's "upper crust." Essentially for them, the position of high priest was an alternative political system available to the best politicians and those citizens with the most power. Third, the Herodians were the wealthy Jews whose desire was to maintain their status-quo. A fourth group was the Zealots. They lived in northern Israel near the Sea of Galilee. Their focus was on Judah, first, last, and always. A sub-clan of the Zealots was known as the Sicarii, who carried daggers to kill their overlords by stealthily removing a dagger from the folds of their garments and silently killing any Roman, especially when in a loud, noisy crowd. A fifth sect was the Essenes, whom we will study shortly.

Amid these political upheavals, a remnant remained dedicated to serving Yahweh. Earlier, Aaron and his direct descendants were selected by God to be the priestly leaders. Fellow Levites assisted, but Aaron's descendants ranked above the Levites. Later, King David divided Aaron's descendants into twenty-four sections to minister in the temple. Each of the twenty-four divisions ministered in the temple one week every six months. Obviously, some sections were selected to minister for four additional weeks to make up for the shortfall in weeks of scheduled service. (Two occasions per year multiplied by twenty-four sections would have provided priests for only forty-eight weeks per year.) In about 4 BC, the eighth section, or lot, was assigned to the household of Abijah.

First Chronicles chapter 24 notes the priestly duties were first assigned to these twenty-four chief priests. Of these chief priests, note in particular 1 Chronicles 24:10, where the chief priest is named Abijah. Abijah's clan faithfully served in the temple for almost five hundred years. In 586

BC, Nebuchadnezzar pillaged and burned the temple. Abijah's clan remained faithful to Yahweh, even in Babylonian exile for almost one hundred years. We know this, because in approximately 444 BC, Nehemiah brought priests back from Babylon to serve once again in the temple. The priests and Levites returning with Zerubbabel included Abijah's clan. The clan members are even named in verse 17. Also named is Iddo, father of prophet-priest and author Zechariah.

Now, hit your fast-forward button four hundred forty years into the future. Read Luke 1:5-7. These verses tell us Zechariah is of the clan of Abijah and his wife, Elizabeth, is of the daughters of Aaron. Hence, both Zechariah and Elizabeth are Levites. These two elderly descendants of Levi are still faithfully serving Yahweh. It was rare for a priest to be selected to serve in the temple. Because there were twenty-four divisions, only two priests from each division would serve annually in the temple. Some scholars have estimated at this time the population of each division was about seven hundred fifty priests. If a division's population was seven hundred fifty men with only two serving annually, a priest might *never* have the honor to serve even one week in the temple during in his *entire life*. In other words, of eighteen thousand priests, only fifty-two would be selected annually. Simply put, one priest out of every three hundred would be chosen annually. On this occasion, the elderly Zechariah was selected to serve for the division of Abijah. Undoubtedly, it would have been an emotional time for the old priest.

After four hundred years of silence by the Lord, and without warning, the Archangel Gabriel appears in the temple to this aging priest named Zechariah!

> "There was in the days of Herod . . . a certain priest named Zechariah of the division of Abijah, and his wife was of the daughters of Aaron, and her name was Elizabeth. And they were both righteous before God, walking in all the commandments and ordinances of the Lord, blameless, and they had no child, because Elizabeth was barren and they both were now well stricken in age" (Luke 1:5-8).

The Archangel Gabriel suddenly appears standing at the right side of the altar of incense. This altar was located immediately in front of the veil before the Ark of the Covenant (Exodus 30:6 NASB). The Archangel announces that God has heard Zechariah and Elizabeth's prayers, and that they will have a son, whom they are to name "John." Gabriel also forecasts the child's mission in life.

> "And he shall go before him in the spirit and power of Elijah, to turn the hearts of the fathers to the children" (Luke 1:17).

After four hundred years of silence, the last words of the Old Testament penned by Malachi had just become some of *the very first words of the New Testament* (Malachi 4:5-6). Gabriel announces that the couple will birth a son. Zechariah and Elizabeth's son, John the Baptist, was the last of the Old Testament prophets and the first of the New Testament prophets. Zechariah and Elizabeth's advanced ages only serve to heighten the expected miracle, just as we saw earlier in the account of the birth of Abraham and Sarah's miracle baby boy, Isaac. Malachi's last words were "Behold, I will send you Elijah, the prophet . . . and he shall turn the hearts of the father to the children."

Elijah was one of God's more unusual prophets. First, he wore unusual clothing (2 Kings 1:8 NASB). Second, Elijah tended to live in caves rather than in dwellings built by man (1 Kings 19:9 NASB). Zechariah would have known Elijah wore these strange garments and chose to live in caves. Zechariah would also recall the days of Elijah were times of contention with Ahab and Jezebel. Elijah had faithfully challenged the wicked Ahab and Jezebel in the northern kingdom eight hundred years earlier (1 Kings 17:1; 18:1 NASB).

Although Elijah lived 800 years earlier, the last words from God via the prophet Malachi were now over 400 years old. Nevertheless, these final words were familiar to the aged priest Zechariah. Those days were similar to the times of Zechariah, which were tumultuous as well. The period when Zechariah lived was a period of upheaval. Now Herod the Great rules under the auspices of the ever-dominant Roman Empire.

Then without warning, in Zechariah's improbable, once-in-a-lifetime entrance into the Holy of Holies, the Archangel Gabriel suddenly appears and converses with the old, faithful priest. Gabriel states the son born to Zechariah and Elizabeth will be great, from God's viewpoint. He will drink no wine or any form of alcohol, and he will be filled with the Holy Spirit, even in his mother's womb (Luke 1:13-16 NASB). The Godly priest exhibited his humanity by not believing the Archangel. As result, Zechariah is unable to speak until after his son was born. Elizabeth became pregnant and stayed inside her house for several months.

Six months later, eighty miles to the north, this same archangel, Gabriel, suddenly appears to a young girl in Nazareth. Just as Gabriel told Zechariah to "Fear not," he also tells this young girl, "Fear not." Gabriel announces to Mary she will birth the "son of the Most High." Mary questions Gabriel, who informs Mary her aged cousin (or relative), Elizabeth, is six-months pregnant. Scripture states Mary hurriedly leaves the area near the Sea of Galilee in the north of Israel and journeys southward toward the home of Elizabeth in Judah. As soon as Mary arrives, the baby in Elizabeth's womb is "filled with the Holy Spirit" and jumps for joy (Luke 1:44 NASB). Zechariah and Elizabeth were excited that she was pregnant, and now the babe in the womb is excited. The cause of this excitement was after four hundred years of silence, "the Lord God of Israel . . . hath visited and redeemed His people, and remembered His covenant with Abraham" (Luke 1:67-75 NASB). Mary praises God, "He spake to our fathers, *to Abraham, and to his seed forever*" (Luke 1:55 NASB).

The young Mary stayed with her older relative, Elizabeth, for three months, or until just before or just after John's birth (Luke 1:56 NASB).

John the Baptist's elderly parents were probably dead by the time John grew to adulthood. He lived in the desert, waiting on his call from God (Luke 1:80). His life in the wilderness had been foretold by Isaiah (Isaiah 40:3-5; Luke 3:4 NASB). Perhaps John settled in the desert with the Essenes, the sect who preserved the Dead Sea Scrolls. At the Essenes' village, Qumran, several baptismal pools still exist in this very dry, arid, desert land—one of the driest places on Earth. Yet, water was used freely to baptize their converts on the shore of the Dead Sea, an area where fresh water was almost priceless. Of the various sects in Jesus's day, the Essenes were the only sect never condemned by Jesus.

It was near Qumran, just a few miles from the Jordan River, where John's ministry began. John the Baptist, as did Elijah, wore clothing atypical for his time—clothes of camel's hair with a leather belt (2 Kings 1:8, and Matthew 3:4). His food was locusts and honey. Locusts (the insect) were an acceptable food under Levitical law (Leviticus 11:22). If "locust" infers fruit from a type of tree, John the Baptist may have possibly been a vegetarian (Matthew 11:18). Since he was to drink no wine or have any type of contact with grapes or cut his hair, he may have been a Nazarite (2 Kings 1:8; Matthew 3:4). If John was indeed a Nazarite, he had a similar lifestyle to Samson and Samuel, both of whom were Nazarites (Numbers 6:1-8). Many of the rituals and procedures of the Nazarites were *very similar* to the duties of the high priest. Previously, we saw the high priest Jehoiada anoint the young lad Joash as King. Therefore, it appears John's baptism of Jesus in the Jordan River was the true Levitical High Priest anointing the true King of Kings.

A COMPARISON OF TWO PROPHETS

Elijah	**John the Baptist**
Rough clothing	Camel's clothing
Leather belt	Leather belt
Lived in cave	Lived in desert
Hairy	Camel's hair (Zech. 13:4)
Diet - bread and water (1 Kings 19:6)	Diet - locusts and honey (Num. 6:1-8
Very little meat, possible vegetarian	Matthew 3:4; Luke 1:15)

Jesus Himself called his relative, John the Baptist, a type of Elijah (Matthew 11:14; 17:11). Gabriel foretold the same (Luke 1:17). Even the public felt John the Baptist was Elijah (Mark 6:15). Elijah was a foreshadowing of John the Baptist, and John the Baptist was a foreshadowing of Jesus.

After his father Zechariah was filled with the Holy Spirit, he shared the purpose of John's message: "To give knowledge of salvation unto His (God's) people by the forgiveness of their sins, whereby the dayspring . . . dawn . . . (Jesus) from on high hath visited us to give light to them that sit in darkness and in the shadow of death" (Luke 1:67; 77-79).

Even this pronouncement from Zechariah contains a hint as to John living among the Essenes. Along with the Dead Sea Scrolls, various commentaries were found at Qumran. One of these texts is named "The War of the Sons of Light Against the Sons of Darkness." Again, read the verse above. Notice in the passage "dayspring," "dawn," "to give light," "sit in darkness," "shadow of death." Observe all the references to "light" and "dark." These concepts of light versus dark were typical of Essenes' thought about holiness and sin.

As John the Baptist began his ministry, the people came down to the Jordan River from Jerusalem twenty-five miles to the west to hear John's message. His message was, "Repent, confess your sin, be baptized in the Jordan River" (Matthew 3:2; 6-7). Even the wealthy and powerful Pharisees and Sadducees came to hear John. In his messages, John the Baptist was blunt and minced no words, even calling the Pharisees and Sadducees "vipers." John also preached that he was not Elijah and would not be worthy to even unloose the coming Messiah's sandals (John 1:27).

John was given a sign to know when the Messiah would come to him—the Spirit of God will descend from heaven like a dove and rest upon the man. The first step in anointing a priest was the washing followed by the anointing (Exodus 29:4-7; 2 Kings 11:12). Jesus had walked ninety miles from Galilee to the Jordan River to be baptized by John. Traditionally, high priests were washed and consecrated at the entrance to the tabernacle. However, John the Baptist, as a type of "high priest," washed Jesus not in corrupt Herod's Temple in Jerusalem, nor was Jesus washed by the vile high priest Caiaphas. (Within three years, it would be this same Caiaphas who would call for Jesus's death.) No, Jesus was "washed" by a type of true and holy Elijah, his relative John the Baptist. And this ceremony took place not in the temple, but in the Jordan River (Exodus 29:4, 30:18-21, 40:12; Hebrews 10:22).

Was John stunned to see the Spirit land on his "cousin"? After all, since Mary had become pregnant shortly after Elizabeth, John was only about six months older than Jesus. Had he ever met Jesus? Jesus lived in Galilee, and Qumran was ninety miles away. Did John already know his relative is the long-awaited Messiah? Once John baptized Jesus and the Holy Spirit came upon Jesus, the Messiah's ministry began. Within a brief time, Jesus's disciples were baptizing more people than John the Baptist (John 4:1).

In the same direct, bold manner in which John condemned the Pharisees and Sadducees, he later condemned Herod Antipas for marrying his sister-in-law, Herodias, because it violated Old Testament law. To appease his new wife Herodias, Herod Antipas imprisoned John. At Herod's birthday party, his wife's daughter, Salome, who was Herod's grandniece *and* stepdaughter, performed a seductive dance which won Herod's favor. She was granted permission to ask for up to one-half of anything in Herod's kingdom. Upon consultation with her mother, Salome asked for John the Baptist's head, ending his life.

With the conclusion of John's life, we see more clearly God's plan, stated by none other than Jesus himself, John's very own relative. Jesus tells us the law, the prophets, and the prophecy had concluded with the coming of John: "for all the prophets and the law prophesied until John" (Matthew 11:13). This passage fulfilled and confirmed the very last verses of Malachi 4:4-6, the very last verses of the Old Testament. Furthermore, Jesus remarked that this man who belonged to the Royal Family was a close relative of Jesus himself. "Verily, I say unto you, among them that are born of women, there hath not risen one greater than John the Baptist" (Mathew 11:11).

Here's a question. Since John was of the seed of Abraham, was the greatest of all humans, was the "High Priest" who baptized Jesus, was a member of the Royal Family, and was a close relative of the Royal Seed himself, will John the Baptist be the "best man" at the wedding feast of the bridegroom and the church?

> "Let us be glad and rejoice and give honor to Him: for the marriage of the Lamb is come and his wife hath made herself ready, and to her was granted that she should be arrayed in fine linen, clean and white. For the fine linen is the righteous acts of the saints" (Revelation 19:7-8).

> "And I, John, saw the holy city New Jerusalem coming down from God out of heaven, prepared as a bride adorned for her husband . . . and there came unto me one of the seven angels . . . saying come hither and I will show the bride, the Lamb's wife" (Revelation 21:2,9).

> "And the Spirit and the bride say 'Come' and let him that heareth say 'Come' and let him that is athirst come and whosoever will, let him take the water of life freely" (Revelation 22:17).

Two Levites, Zechariah and Elizabeth, became the parents of John the Baptist. In a sense, John the Baptist was a Levite priest. He announced the coming of the Messiah from the tribe of Judah and baptized his cousin Jesus as the Messiah. Jesus is the culmination of the Royal Seed. Once again, the tribes of Levi and Judah intersected in God's plan, just as they had one thousand seven hundred years earlier.

What have we learned about John the Baptist?

1. After a second four-hundred-year period of silence, God abruptly spoke through the Archangel Gabriel to the elderly priest Zechariah in the temple.
2. John the Baptist's life fulfilled Malachi's final words from four hundred years earlier.
3. John was of the seed of Abraham and Levi. He was probably born six months before Jesus's birth and was beheaded by Herod Antipas not too many months before Jesus's crucifixion. Clearly, these two "cousins" were born approximately at the same time and died in close proximity as well. However, John's initial ministry preceded Jesus's by a relatively short period.
4. John was probably an Essene living near where the Dead Sea Scrolls were found in 1947. He preached near Qumran and baptized in the Jordan River. He wore crude, rough clothing of camel hair with a leather belt, similar to Elijah. His hair was likely uncut,

and he refrained from anything having to do with grapes. In many ways, this Nazarite description of John is similar to the special restrictions also observed by the high priests.

5. John baptized Jesus in the Jordan River, beginning Jesus's ministry.
6. Jesus declared no man was greater than John the Baptist.
7. John's position, in effect, may have been one of the high priest's anointing the King of Kings, not in the temple, but in the Jordan River. Aaron's ministry began after his consecration by his brother, Moses, and Jesus's ministry began after His baptism by His "cousin," John the Baptist.

John the Baptist's Relatives

Name	Relationship	APPROXIMATE Dates
Adam	Great-grandfather, 64 generations removed	?
Abraham	Great-grandfather, 44 generations removed	±2000 BC
Levi	Great-grandfather, uncertain generations	±1700 BC
James	Cousin? (Relative) Luke 1:36; Galatians 1:19	AD 30
Jude	Cousin? (Relative) Luke 1:36; Jude 1	AD 30
Jesus	Cousin? (Relative) Luke 1:36	AD 30

Chapter 26

Jesus

> Then shall the *king* say unto them on His right hand, Come you blessed of My Father, inherit the *kingdom* prepared to you from the foundation of the world. (Matthew 25:34; emphasis added)

> The time is fulfilled, and the *kingdom* of God is at hand: repent ye and believe the gospel. (Mark 1:15; emphasis added)

> Now the parable is this: *the seed is the word of God.* (Luke 8:11; emphasis added)

> And the *word was made flesh* and dwelt among us, and we beheld His glory, the glory of the only begotten of the Father, full of grace and truth. (John 1:14; emphasis added)

I hope the reader will find this chapter unique. It will provide little commentary to read, but offer different ways to view Jesus. This chapter will provide alternative ways to consider the majesty, the royalty, the power, the holiness, and the authority that can be assumed only by Jesus. Yes, Jesus is the Royal Seed. Much as a gem cutter will carefully examine a rough diamond numerous times before ever striking the first blow, it is now time to consider some of the brilliant attributes of the Savior's authority, glory, holiness, and power.

Much time has been spent studying Old Testament genealogies. *After Matthew and Luke offer their New Testament genealogies of Jesus, lists of genealogies no longer appear.* Why not? Because the journey has arrived at its destination—the Royal Seed of Israel. Jesus is the ultimate in royalty—the King of Kings. Because of the numerous characteristics of Jesus, authors of the Bible have ascribed over two hundred fifty names to Him.

In modern times, man has lost this sense of awe, power, honor, glory, and sovereignty due Jesus as the King of Kings. That was not true in the sixteenth and seventeenth centuries, when men were subject to earthly kings. We can observe the awe, respect, and honor shown in hymn titles from that era for the King of Kings. For example: "Jesus Shall Reign Where'er the Sun" (written by Isaac Watts around 1725); "All Hail the Power of Jesus's Name" (circa 1781), "Come, Thou Almighty King" (circa 1766); "O Worship the King" (written by Josef Haydn's brother, Michael Haydn, circa 1803), and "Rejoice! The Lord is King" (written by Charles Wesley, circa 1777).

This chapter will view the King of Kings' unique qualities from twelve different dimensions. Why twelve? According to the Book of Revelation, in the New Jerusalem we can expect twelve gates, twelve angels, twelve tribes, twelve foundations, twelve apostles, twelve pearls, and the Tree of Life with twelve fruits. Because of this focus on the number twelve in the New Jerusalem, twelve different perspectives are presented about Jesus and His royal claim to the title—King of Kings.

I. Princes and a Princess

Typically, a king's role was preceded by his being a prince. The Bible makes the following distinctions and pronouncements about four of Jesus's forefathers and one of His great-grandmothers.

PRINCELY TITLES

Name	Reference
Abraham	"Thou art a mighty prince among us" – Genesis 23:6
Sarah	Called "Sarai" 'princess' (Hebrew) – Genesis 17:15
Jacob	"Shall no more be called Jacob, but Israel, for as a prince, hast thou power with God" – Genesis 32:28
Nahshon	"Prince of the children of Judah" – 1 Chronicles 2:10
David	"David, a prince among them" – Ezekiel 34:24 NASB

These four princes are all direct ancestors of Jesus. The Scriptures called these men "prince" some eight hundred years before there was even a kingdom! In Abraham's case, *he was called a prince* some two thousand years before Jesus's ministry. Abraham and Jacob were both called "prince" prior to the Israelites' four-hundred-thirty-year sojourn in Egypt as slaves! Nevertheless, these Israelites diligently kept genealogical records for over four hundred years while they were slaves in Egypt. Fourteen months after the Exodus, Moses followed God's instructions and declared Nahshon a "prince" (Numbers 1:16-18). God had already devised a master plan of royalty and kingship for his Son way back, even before Creation. Later Isaiah entitles Jesus the "Prince of Peace" (Isaiah 9:6). In the New Testament, Paul describes Jesus as "Prince of Life" (Acts 3:15) and "Prince and Savior" (Acts 5:31). The fact God's children were slaves for four hundred thirty years in Egypt or seventy years in Babylon did not alter God's master plan for a Royal Family to secure the Promised Land and to be ruled by the King of Kings.

Isaiah, Daniel, and Paul all acknowledged Jesus as Prince. In Isaiah and Daniel's writings, these declarations of the Messiah being a Prince were seven hundred and five hundred years, respectively, before Jesus was even born. Paul, the bold evangelist of the New Testament, confirmed the princely titles of Jesus expressed by Isaiah and Daniel. As a former Pharisee, Paul could be counted on to adequately study genealogy and correctly apply titles. In Acts 23:6 and 26:5, this "Pharisee of Pharisees" even states his own genealogy. Isaiah was likely a member of the Royal

Family, and Daniel definitely was. Isaiah, Daniel, and Paul were prominent Jews, and all would have been cautious about making any sort of statements, especially any type of written statements. Nevertheless, all three authors were bold in declaring Jesus a prince.

JESUS AS PRINCE

Title	Reference
Messiah	Daniel 9:25 NASB
Prince of Peace	Isaiah 9:6 NASB
Prince and Savior	Acts 5:31 NASB
Prince of Life	Acts 3:15 NASB
Prince	Daniel 9:25 NASB

II. Royal Kings and a Governor

Not only does Jesus's royal heritage include four princes and a princess, it also includes nineteen kings. After King David, every succeeding king in Judah also had served as a prince.

THE KINGS OF JESUS'S LINEAGE

Name	Reference
David	2 Samuel 2:4
Solomon	1 Kings 2:12
Rehoboam	1 Kings 12:6
Abijam	1 Kings 15:1
Asa	1 Kings 15:9
Jehoshaphat	2 Chronicles 20:35
Jehoram	2 Kings 8:16
Ahaziah	2 Kings 8:25
Joash	2 Kings 11:2
Amaziah	2 Kings 14:9
Uzziah	2 Chronicles 26:1
Jotham	2 Kings 15:32
Ahaz	2 Kings 16:10
Hezekiah	2 Kings 19:1
Manasseh	2 Kings 21:11
Amon	2 Kings 21:24
Josiah	2 Kings 22:3
Jehoiakim	2 Kings 23:34
Jehoiachin	2 Kings 24:6

Recall, of Judah's twenty-one kings, only two of Josiah's sons were not in Jesus's lineage (Jehoahaz and Zedekiah). After twenty-one kings, Judah fell to the Babylonian ruler, Nebuchadnezzar. Later, Babylon fell to Persia, and the Persian ruler, Cyrus, deemed Judah to be a province of Persia. He appointed the great-grandson of Jehoiachin, Zerubbabel, to serve as governor of the vassal state.

When Matthew was emphasizing Jesus's lineage, he was reminding his readers—this man, Jesus, has a heritage from before there even existed an Israel. During Solomon's time, when Israel attained its height of glory and power, Jesus had a heritage. When Judah was a distinct, separate nation, Jesus had a heritage among nineteen of the twenty-one kings who ruled Judah. During Judah's days as a vassal state of Persia, when Judah's lone governor, Zerubbabel, was in charge, he too, was an ancestor of Jesus. Jesus's qualifications to be king include in His heritage, one princess, four princes, a governor, and nineteen kings. With such a pedigree, who would be more qualified to serve as king!

Jeremiah prophesied that no heir of Jehoiachin would ever sit as king of Judah (Jeremiah 22:28-30). By adoption, Jesus is in the regal lineage of Jehoiachin, for Joseph was of the house and lineage of David (Luke 2:4 NASB). Although Jesus is an offspring of David, it is not through Solomon's kingly line, but through Solomon's older brother, Nathan, and the lineage of Mary, that Jesus validates His reign as King of Kings (Genesis 3:15).

Three of the Gospel writers use the term "Son of David" when describing Jesus—and Jesus truly is the Son of David (Matthew 9:27; Mark 10:47; Luke 18:38). Forty one generations occur between King David's time and Jesus's life. In tracing the lineage of Jesus from David's son, Nathan, to Mary, notice *none* of these forty men ever served as a king in Israel or Judah. When Matthew, Mark, and Luke describe Jesus as the Son of David, he truly is. Not biologically, but via Nathan's lineage. *One thousand years after David, Jesus is the very next king*! That is why, when Jesus terms himself as the "Offspring of David" in the last chapter of the Bible, Jesus is indeed the successor Monarch to the reign of King David (Revelation 22:16). Jesus's claim to the title King of Kings is strengthened by His genealogy. No one else has such a heritage of patriarchs, tribal leaders, four princes, a princess, a governor, two forefathers who served as kings of united Israel, and nineteen forefathers who all served as kings of Judah. The following are twenty-five regal titles used by Bible authors to describe Jesus as a king. Truly Jesus is the King of Kings.

JESUS AS KING

Title	**Reference**
1. King	Matthew 21:5
2. King of Kings	Revelation 17:14; 19:16
3. King over all Earth	Zechariah 14:9
4. King of Nations	Revelation 15:3
5. King of Glory	Psalm 24:7-16
6. King of Jews	Matthew 2:2, 27:37; Mark 15:26; Luke 23:38
7. King of Israel	John 1:49
8. King of Zion	Psalm 2:6; Zechariah 9:9; John 12:15
9. Head over all	Colossians 2:10
10. Head over all things	Ephesians 1:22
11. Head of everyman	1 Corinthians 11:3
12. Head of Church	Ephesians 5:23; Col. 1:15
13. Head	Ephesians 4:15; Col. 2:19
14. Ruler	Matthew 2:6
15. Ruler of Kings of the Earth	Revelation 1:5
16. Ruler in Israel	Micah 5:2
17. Sovereign	1 Timothy 6:15
18. Scepter from Israel	Numbers 24:17
19. Leader and Commander	Isaiah 55:4
20. Lawgiver	Isaiah 33:22
21. Blessed and only sovereign	1 Timothy 6:15
22. Judge of the Living and Dead	Acts 10:42
23. Judge Israel	Micah 5:1
24. Son of the Most High	Luke 1:32
25. Son of the Gods	Daniel 3:25

III. Royal Priest and Prophet

Upon completion of the Exodus, while the Israelites were camped safely in the edge of the Sinai Desert, God gave Moses important instructions and directions. When Moses made his first visit up Mount Sinai, God called for the Israelites "to be a peculiar treasure unto God." Immediately thereafter, God's call to His chosen people was, "You shall be unto me a kingdom of priests and a holy nation" (Exodus 19:6). In the very next chapter, Exodus 20, God speaks unto Moses the Ten Commandments. Read now these verses from Revelation.

> "And Jesus Christ, who is the faithful witness . . . and the Prince of the kings of the earth . . . and washed us from our sins in His own blood. And hath made us kings and priests unto God" (Revelation 1:5-6).

"And hast made us unto our God, kings and priests and we shall reign on the earth" (Revelation 5:10).

Once again, we see the *kingdom* and the *priests* from the Old Testament Book of Exodus manifested in the New Testament Book of Revelation. Now it is certain, Jesus is not only to be a king. He is also to be a priest.

Writing from Babylon, the prophet Ezekiel states why the Israelites have become captives. The Israelites disobeyed God's laws and even the high priests had become corrupt.

> "*Her priests* have violated my law and have profaned mine holy things: they have not distinguished between the holy and the unholy, neither have they showed difference between the unclean and clean and have hid their eyes from my Sabbath, and I am profaned among them. *Her princes* in the midst thereof are like wolves tearing the prey . . . And *her prophets* have seen false visions and divining lies" (Ezekiel 22:26-28; emphasis added).

And just two verses later, we read,

> "And I sought for a man among them . . . that should make a hedge and stand in the gap, before me, for the land, that I should not destroy it; but I found none" (Ezekiel 22:30).

Five centuries later, Scripture documents the rampant disregard for holiness even among high priests. During the trials of Jesus, Caiaphas and Annas were more politicians than they were high priests. Although the priesthood had changed over the centuries concerning the law, Jesus said He had come to change "not one jot or tittle, but to fulfill" the Old Testament law (Matthew 5:18).

Once the priesthood of Aaron became corrupt, God raised up a new seed of a different priestly order. In Genesis, Abraham worshiped the king-priest-prophet Melchizedek. The new high priest

Jesus is a return to this older order of Melchizedek that existed centuries before Aaron was born. Not only would Jesus be a king and a high priest, but He was also to be a prophet. In Ezekiel 22:26, God seeks just one man to "stand in the gap." God now has that one man in the person of Jesus as the King-High Priest-Prophet from the order of Melchizedek.

JESUS AS PRIEST

Title	Reference
High Priest	Hebrews 3:1; 4:14; 6:20; 7:26
Priest	Hebrews 5:6, 7:17-21
Rabbi	Matthew 26:25, 49; Mark 9:5, 11:21; John 1:38-39
Rabboni	Mark 10:51; John 20:16

JESUS AS PROPHET

Title	Reference
Prophet	Luke 24:19
Prophet	Acts 3:22-23

The following two charts will exhibit the priests from the order of Aaron and the priests from the order of Melchizedek. Verses from 1 Chronicles 6:1-15 and Nehemiah 12:1-22 declare a genealogy of 32 generations of high priests from the Levitical priesthood of Aaron.

Jeshua was the high priest who was crowned with the gold and silver crown, uniting for the first time the priesthood and the proclamation of the coming Messiah.

The Genealogy of the High Priests from the Order of Aaron

Abraham (Matthew 1:2)
▼
Isaac
▼
Jacob (Israel)
▼
Levi (1 Chronicles 6:1)
▼
Kohath
▼
Amram
▼
Aaron – Moses- Miriam (1 Chronicles 6:3)
▼
Eleazar
▼
Phineas
▼
Abishua
▼
Bukki
▼
Uzzi
▼
Zerahiah
▼
Meraioth
▼
Amariah
▼
Ahitub
▼
Zadok
▼
Ahimaaz
▼
Azariah
▼
Johanan
▼
Azariah (High Priest, in Solomon's Temple, 1 Chronicles 6:10)
▼
Amariah
▼
Ahitub
▼
Zadok
▼
Shallum
▼
Hilkiah
▼
Azariah
▼
Seraiah
▼
Ezra ◄ brothers ► Jehozadak   (High Priest taken captive to Babylon, 1 Chron. 6:15, Ezra 3:2; 7:1-6)
▼
Jeshua (High Priest-Returned with Zerubbabel)
▼
Johoiakim
▼
Eliashib (Contemporary of Nehemiah, Nehemiah. 12:10)
▼
Joiada
▼
Jonathan (Elephantine Papyrus)
▼
Jaddua (High Priest at time of Alexander the Great, Nehemiah 12:22, approximately 333 BC)

In contrast to the thirty-two generations of high priests in the Aaronic Priesthood, the older, superior order of Melchizedek lists only two priests.

The Genealogy of the High Priests from the Order of Melchizedek

Melchizedek   Genesis 14:18-20; Hebrews 7:1-3

  ▼

Jesus   Hebrews 5:5-10

IV. Royal Ancestors

There's yet another method to determine kingship—who are the king's relatives? The authors, Jeremiah, Ezekiel, Hosea, Isaiah, John, Moses, Matthew, Mark, Paul, Daniel, and Luke all include relatives of Jesus in their description and naming of the Messiah. From Genesis to Jude, the theme of the Bible is Jesus. The story of the sixty-six books of the Bible is the story, from Adam through seventy-six generations to Jude, about how each generation is related to the Messiah. Then the very last book, Revelation, shows Jesus in all His glory and proclaims His regal authority (Revelation 22:16). Jesus is the commander leading His mighty army to eternal victory.

Descriptions of Jesus

Title	Reference	Author
Son of Joseph	John 6:42	John
Adam	1 Corinthians 15:45	Paul
Branch of David	Jeremiah 33:15	Jeremiah
David	Jeremiah 30:9; Ezekiel 37:24; Hosea 3:5	Ezekiel, Hosea
Seed of David	Romans 1:3; 2 Timothy 2:8	Paul
Heritage of Jacob	Isaiah 58:14	Isaiah
Lion from the tribe of Judah	Revelation 5:5	John
Mighty one of Jacob	Isaiah 49:26	Isaiah
Offspring of David	Revelation 22:16	Jesus
Rock of Israel	Isaiah 30:29	Isaiah
Root of David	Revelation 22:16	Jesus
Root of Jesse	Isaiah 11:10; Romans 15:12	Isaiah, Paul
Son of Mary	Mark 6:3	Mark
Stem of Jesse	Isaiah 11:1	Isaiah
Son of David	Matt. 9:27; Mark 10:47; Luke 18:38	Matthew, Mark, Luke
Star from Jacob	Numbers 24:17	Moses
Son of the Father	2 John 3	John
Son of God	Matthew 4:3, 8:29	Matthew
Son of Man	Matthew 8:26	Matthew
Son of the Most High	Luke 1:32	Luke
Son of the Gods	Daniel 3:25	Daniel

As this chart exhibits, names of eight different relatives of Jesus are used in the descriptive titles of Jesus—Adam, David, Jacob, Jesse, Judah, Israel, Mary, and Joseph. These eight ancestors' names were used by twelve different authors of the Bible to assist in describing and documenting the authenticity of their relative, Jesus, to be king. Two of these twelve authors, Isaiah and Daniel, are also probably ancestors of Jesus. And even Jesus describes Himself by connecting His heritage to a relative, "I am the root and offspring of David" (Revelation 22:16 NASB).

Another term used to describe Jesus is "Son of God." Seventeen different individuals or groups identify Jesus as the Son of God. On ten occasions, believers acknowledge Jesus as God's son. Even more convincing are the seven individuals or groups of *unbelievers* who recognize Jesus as the Son of God.

DECLARE JESUS AS SON OF GOD

Gergesene demoniacs	Matthew 8:29
Disciples	Matthew 14:33
Peter	Matthew 16:16
High Priest Caiaphas & Council	Matthew 26:63; Luke 22:70
Roman Centurion	Mark 15:39
Mark	Mark 1:1
Angel Gabriel	Luke 1:35
Devil	Luke 4:3
Capernaum demons	Luke 4:41
John the Baptist	John 1:34
Nathanael	John 1:49
Jesus	John 3:18; Revelation 2:18
Jews	John 19:7
John	John 20:31
Ethiopian eunuch	Acts 8:37
Paul	Acts 9:20; 2 Corinthians 1:19
Apollos?	Hebrews 4:14

V. Royal Builders

Another technique used to confirm leadership of a nation is to consider who built the nation's primary structures. Today, four thousand five hundred years after Cheops erected his Great

Pyramid at Giza, we still acknowledge his kingship, not so much by his governance while Pharaoh, but for his ability to construct such a building as his own tomb. The following is a detailing of the master builders of Israel. *Up until Herod, every major structure or fixture* used in the worship of Elohim was built by a royal ancestor of Jesus.

Royal Builders of the Tabernacle, Tent, and Temples

Name	Duty	Member Royal Family	Reference
Bezalel	Built Tabernacle	Yes–cousin	Exodus 31:2
David	Erected Jerusalem Tent	Yes-Great grandfather	1 Chronicles 15:1
David	Collected Temple Materials	Yes-Great grandfather	1 Chronicles 29:1-3
Solomon	Built first Temple	Yes-Great grandfather	2 Chronicles 2:1
Zerubbabel	Built second Temple	Yes-Great grandfather	Ezra 6:15
Herod	Built third Temple	No	John 2:20

VI. Faith Hall of Fame

Almost every people group has some sort of collection or recognition of its most outstanding members. The unknown author of Hebrews in chapter 11 includes what we call today the Hall of Fame of Faith. As examples of their faith, the author of Hebrews deems sixteen different individuals in the Bible worthy of mentioning by name. Each of these sixteen names is preceded with the phrase, "by faith." Of these sixteen Bible heroes, no less than eight of them were Jesus's direct ancestors. Another two or three of them can easily be traced via Biblical genealogies to membership in the Royal Family. Names with a *"D"* are the direct Messianic ancestors of Jesus, according to Matthew 1 and Luke 3. Scripture also provides genealogical connections to the Messianic line for Abel, Joseph, Moses, and Samuel. These are marked with an *"F"* for Family.

FAITH HALL OF FAME

Abel - F
Enoch - D
Noah - D
Abraham - D
Sarah - D
Isaac - D
Jacob - D

Joseph - F

Moses - F

Rahab - D

Gideon

Barak

Samson

Jephthah

David - D

Samuel – F

The Bible confirms that *twelve* of sixteen heroes in the Faith Hall of Fame are relatives of Jesus.

VII. Books of the Bible

Have you ever considered, of the sixty-six books in the Bible, how many of these books in their titles include the names of one of the members of the Royal Family of Israel? Ten of the people listed below are relatives of Jesus and the Royal Family. Nahum is also a possible eleventh relative.

Book	**Named In**
Ruth	Matthew 1:5
Song of Solomon	Matthew 1:7
Daniel	Isaiah 39:7
Nahum *	Luke 1:25
Zephaniah	Zephaniah 1:1
Isaiah	Isaiah 6:1, 13
James	Galatians 1:19
Jude	Jude 1
Ezra	2 Kings 25:18; Ezra 7:1
1 & 2 Samuel	1 Chronicles 6:33
Joshua	1 Chronicles 7:20-28

*Outside the book of Nahum, Luke 1:25 is the only reference to a person named "Nahum." Ten of the sixty-six books of the Bible (or over 10 percent) are named for a relative of Jesus. Furthermore, Psalms, Proverbs, and Ecclesiastes are still other books penned by Jesus's ancestors, David and Solomon.

Twenty-two books of the sixty-six in the Bible were authored by either direct descendants of Jesus or the author, in some manner, is related to Jesus. About one third of the Bible was written by, or named for, Jesus's ancestors.

The following chart will more precisely list the Bible's authors who are family members of Israel's Royal Family.

BIBLE AUTHORS' RELATION TO THE ROYAL FAMILY OF JESUS

Author's Name	Relationship	Author of
David	Great Grandfather	Most of Psalms
Solomon	Great Grandfather	Proverbs
Solomon	Great Grandfather	Ecclesiastes
Solomon	Great Grandfather	Song of Solomon
Zephaniah	Cousin	Zephaniah
James	Half brother	James
Jude	Half brother	Jude
Moses	Cousin	Genesis
Moses	Cousin	Exodus
Moses	Cousin	Leviticus
Moses	Cousin	Numbers
Moses	Cousin	Deuteronomy
Samuel	Cousin	Judges
Samuel	Cousin	Ruth
Samuel	Cousin	1 Samuel
Ezra	Cousin	1 Chronicles
Ezra	Cousin	2 Chronicles
Ezra	Cousin	Ezra
Isaiah (?)	Relationship uncertain	Isaiah
Daniel (?)	Relationship uncertain	Daniel
Nahum (?)	Relationship uncertain	Nahum
Joshua	Cousin	Joshua

VIII. The Two Covenants

First Chronicles 2-4 and Matthew chapter 1 document Jesus as the rightful heir to the throne of King David forever. First Chronicles 6 and Hebrews chapters 3-9 document Jesus as the rightful heir to the position of High Priest forever. Around the Babylonian captivity (586 BC), the prophet Jeremiah revealed God's provisions for a new covenant.

> "Behold the days come, saith the Lord, that I will make a *new covenant* with the House of Israel and with the House of Judah. Not according to the covenant that I made with their fathers in the day that I took them by the hand to bring them out of the land of Egypt which my covenant they brake, although I was a husband to them, saith the Lord. But this shall be the covenant that I will make with the House of Israel: After those days, saith the Lord, I will put my Law in inward parts and write it in their hearts" (Jeremiah 31:31-33; emphasis added).

In other words, worship of God in the future will not be limited to the temple in Jerusalem but will expand to include minds and hearts throughout the entire saved world. God will put His Law into the elects' minds and write it into their hearts through the working of the Holy Spirit. Here is a comparison of God's Old and New Testament covenants.

<u>**Old Covenant**</u>	<u>**New Covenant**</u>
Numerous High Priests	Jesus, Only High Priest
Order of Aaron	Order of Melchizedek
Daily Sacrifices	One-time Sacrifice
Washed by Water	Washed by Blood
Animal Sacrifice	Messiah Sacrifice
Genealogy of Aaron	Genealogy of Jesus
Holy of Holies, Priest entered one time per year	Veil torn, Free access to everyone

IX. The Two Weddings

Jeremiah described God as a husband to the Jews, much like Jesus is bridegroom to the Church. Somehow, in some way, it appears, God will possibly be the husband to the Jews just as Jesus will be the husband of the Church. Earlier, the nation of Israel had committed adultery against God (Matthew 12:39). In James 4:4, the apostle challenges the members of the early Church to refrain from committing spiritual adultery against the Bridegroom.

THE TWO WEDDINGS

GOD		JESUS	
Jerusalem, Daughter of God Jews, bride of God	Micah 4:10 Isaiah 61:10	Best Man? John the Baptist	John 3:29
Thy maker is thine husband: thy Redeemer; the holy one of Israel	Isaiah 54:5-6	Church, bride of Jesus	Revelation 21:9
		Saved, wife of Jesus	Revelation 19:7
I am married to you, backsliding children…and I will bring you to Zion Betrothed thee unto Me forever	Jeremiah 3:14, 31:22 Ezekiel 16:32, 44-45 Hosea 2:5,19-20	Bridegroom, gift to bride Bride adorned	Revelation 21:2-10
Israel, wife of God, voice of the Bridegroom and voice of the bride	Jeremiah 33:11		

X. Characteristics of Jesus's Ancestors

FIRST MAN - Adam - Genesis 2:19

RICHEST KING WHO EVER LIVED-   Solomon – 1 Kings 10:23

OLDEST MAN WHO EVER LIVED* – Methuselah (969 years) – Genesis 5:27

SECOND OLDEST MAN WHO EVER LIVED* -Jared (962 years) - Genesis 5:20

GOD'S FRIEND – Moses – Exodus 33:11

SOUGHT AFTER GOD'S HEART – David – Acts 13:22

GATHERED MATERIALS FOR FIRST TEMPLE – David – 1 Chronicles 22:1-5

BUILT THE TABERNACLE – Bezalel – Exodus 31:2-11

THIRD OLDEST MAN WHO EVER LIVED* - Noah (950 years) - Genesis 9:29

BUILT FIRST TEMPLE – Solomon – 1 Chronicles 22:9-10

WISEST MAN WHO EVER LIVED – Solomon – 1 Kings 10:23

BUILT SECOND TEMPLE – Zerubbabel – Ezra 5:2

GREATEST PROPHET – Moses – Deuteronomy 34:10

SELECTED TENT FOR ARK IN JERUSALEM – David – 2 Samuel 6:17

FOURTH OLDEST MAN WHO EVER LIVED* – Adam (930 years) – Genesis 5:5

PURCHASED TEMPLE SITE – David – 2 Samuel 24:21

GREATEST MAN WHO EVER LIVED - John the Baptist – Matthew 11:11

HAS POWER WITH GOD – Jacob – Genesis 32:28

FRIEND OF GOD – Abraham – James 2:23

PLEASING TO GOD – Enoch - Hebrews 11:5

HEIR OF RIGHTEOUSNESS – Noah- Hebrews 11:7

MAN FOR WHOM NATION OF ISRAEL WAS NAMED – Jacob – Genesis 32:28

*The first-, second-, third-, and fourth-oldest men in all of history (i.e. Methuselah, Jared, Noah and Adam) are all ancestors of Jesus, the King who lives forever.

XI. The Thirty Relatives of Jesus

Scan this list of Jesus's relatives and consider how many sermons, Bible stories, or Sunday School lessons feature one of these ancestors of Jesus as the main character.

JESUS'S THIRTY RELATIVES

Name	Relationship	APPROXIMATE Dates
Adam	Great-grandfather	±4000 BC
Methuselah	Great-grandfather	?
Enoch	Great-grandfather	?
Noah	Great-grandfather	?
Abraham	Great-grandfather	±2000 BC
Isaac	Great-grandfather	±1900 BC
Jacob (Israel)	Great-grandfather	±1800 BC
Levi	Great uncle	±1750 BC
Judah	Great-grandfather	±1750 BC
Aaron	Great uncle	±1350 BC
Rahab	Great-grandmother	±1240 BC
Ruth	Great-grandmother	±1220 BC
Boaz	Great-grandfather	±1220 BC
Samuel	Cousin?	±1070 BC
Jesse	Great-grandfather	±1050 BC
David	Great-grandfather	1000 BC
Solomon	Great-grandfather	970 BC
Jehoshaphat	Great-grandfather	870 BC
Hezekiah	Great-grandfather	730 BC
Isaiah	Unknown?	720 BC
Josiah	Great-grandfather	640 BC
Zephaniah	Cousin	630 BC
Daniel	Unknown?	540 BC
Zerubbabel	Great-grandfather	540 BC
Ezra	Cousin?	460 BC
John the Baptist	Cousin?	AD 30
Mary	Mother	AD 30
Joseph	Stepfather	AD 30
James	Half-brother	AD 30
Jude	Half-brother	AD 30

XII. Jesus's Quotes and References to the Old Testament

Jesus confirms the validity of the Old Testament by His frequent use of Old Testament writings. For example, the following quotes and references by Jesus are Old Testament quotes noted by Matthew, author of the first book of the New Testament.

JESUS'S QUOTES	MATTHEW'S REFERENCE
Hosea	9:13
Malachi	11:10
Isaiah – R	13:14
	13:15
	15:7-9
	21:13
Zechariah	26:31
Moses – R	19:4-5
	19:18-19
David – R	21:42
	22:44
	27:46
Daniel – R	24:15

JESUS REFERS TO	MATTHEW'S REFERENCE
Solomon – R	6:29
	12:42
Moses – R	8:4
Abraham – R	8:11
Isaac – R	8:11
Jacob – R	8:11
John the Baptist – R	11:11
Elijah	11:14
	17:11
David – R	12:3
Jonah	12:39
	16:4
Noah – R	24:37

Matthew records Jesus quoting or referring to fifteen different Old Testament Bible characters. Moses and David are listed in both lists. The "*R*" highlights a known or likely member of Jesus's relatives. *Jesus was not just quoting or referring to generic Old Testament Bible heroes. Jesus was talking about his family, his ancestors.* In Matthew, of the fifteen individuals referenced or quoted by Jesus, *ten of these fifteen individuals are His ancestors.*

What did we learn about Jesus?

1. The Bible documents Jesus's heritage from Adam through seventy-six generations to Mary and Joseph.
2. Biblical authors attest to Jesus being King, Great High Priest, and Prophet.
3. His heritage includes kings, princes, princesses, a governor, and authors of some of the books of the Bible.
4. He is the Son of God.

Jesus's Relatives

Name	Relationship	Reference
James	Half-brother	Gal. 1:19
Jude	Half-brother	Jude 1
Mary	Mother	Mark 6:3
God	Son of God	Matthew 8:29
All Believers	By Adoption - Sons of God	John 1:12

Chapter 27

James and Jude

If ye fulfill the *royal law* according to the Scriptures, thou shalt love thy neighbor as thyself, ye do well. (James 2:8; emphasis added)

Keep yourselves in the love of God, looking for the mercy of our Lord Jesus Christ unto eternal life. (Jude 21)

In prior chapters, we have extensively studied the genealogy of Jesus and His ancestors. This chapter will investigate two of Jesus's contemporaries, both of whom were His siblings. Even in the New Testament, the Royal Family of Israel still is very important—over one-half of the New Testament is made up of the Gospels about Jesus's life plus the writings by His two brothers, James and Jude. The Scripture names Jesus's four half-brothers: James, Joseph, Simon, and Jude (Matthew 13:55; Mark 6:3, and Galatians 1:19). According to 1 Corinthians 9:5, after Jesus's resurrection, two of Jesus's brothers became missionaries. They took wives along with them on their missionary journeys. Jesus also had at least two half-sisters, although the Bible does not provide us with any names of the sisters. Obviously, Jesus was the oldest, and because of the virgin birth, His brothers and sisters would, technically, have been His half-brothers and half-sisters. Some students of the Bible have offered the idea that Joseph was much older than Mary, and that he fathered these other children before he was betrothed to Mary. In this scenario, Jesus would not have been the oldest child. Other scholars have postulated that Jesus was the only child ever birthed by Mary, so any other children would not have been Jesus's blood relatives. These conjectures seem unlikely, for at the crucifixion, James and Joseph (Joses) are listed as sons of Mary (Matthew 27:56; Mark 15:40). The most commonly accepted hypothesis of this "blended family" is that Jesus was the oldest, and the other children were all birthed by Mary, with Joseph as their father.

This chapter takes a closer look at two of Jesus's brothers, James and Jude. Why these two particular brothers? Because both are authors of New Testament books entitled with their respective names, the Book of James and, later, the Book of Jude.

JAMES

In any list of Jesus's siblings, James is always listed first. It seems logical that after Jesus, he was the next oldest male child. Scholars generally assign a date to the book of James around AD 42. If this is correct, the book of James is one of the very first New Testament books written. Some scholars believe after Jesus's death and resurrection, His followers felt His return was days or months away. After waiting a decade or so, James likely penned his book.

Another reason to consider an earlier date for the book written by James is its emphasis on purity of doctrine. In just five chapters, James gives over fifty instructions: "If any man lacks wisdom . . . ask of God" (James 1:5). "Are you willing to recognize . . . faith without works is useless?" (James 2:21). "From the same mouth come both blessings and curses. My brethren, these things ought not to be this way" (James 3:10). "Draw near to God, and He will draw near to you" (James 4:8). "Be patient" (James 5:7).

Initially, James supported his older brother's ministry. However, once the confrontation with the rabbis occurred at Nazareth, James seemed to distance himself (John 7:5 NASB). Did James wonder, *Maybe Jesus is even crazy?* (See Mark 3:21). After Judas betrayed Jesus, a replacement was sought among the followers of Jesus. At this time, James was still wary of his older brother and none of Jesus's brothers were selected as apostles. However, once the resurrection occurred, James was a changed man. We are all aware of Jesus's special appearance to the apostle we know as "doubting Thomas." Less well known is that among Jesus's brothers was a "doubting James." Specifically, James is named as receiving a special visit from the resurrected Jesus (1 Corinthians 15:7). Eventually, James became the head elder at the "mother church" in Jerusalem (Acts 12:16-17; 15:13).

In the book of James, the commands are bold, direct, pithy, statements. It is hard to misinterpret James's writings. His words may make us uncomfortable in his blunt, declarative style, but he is never vague. Just believing in the existence of God, he assures us, is inadequate. One must also have personal salvation, a personal faith. "You believe that God is one. You do well; the demons also believe and shudder . . . that faith without works is useless" (James 2:19-21 NASB).

James also returns to the early rebellion of Nimrod at Babel. In the Greek language, *gē* signifies sky, earth, water, and so on. But that is not the Greek word James uses in the fourth chapter of his writing; James selects the Greek word *kosmos*, which infers a natural order, a global system, or globalization. As we saw earlier, this path leads from Babel in Genesis to Babylon in Revelation.

"Do you not know that friendship with the world *(kosmos)* is hostility towards God? Therefore, whoever wishes to be a friend of the world *(kosmos)* makes himself an enemy of God" (James 4:4 NASB). Once James accepted Jesus as his personal savior, he was anxious, eager, and impatient for his brother's second coming to earth. James is particularly impatient about his brother's return toward the conclusion of his epistle (James 5:7-11). Maybe this is why, after ten years of waiting for Jesus's imminent return, James was inspired by the Holy Spirit to record his instructions in doctrine and how Christians should be living out their faith.

Two final, important thoughts concerning the book of James: First, James references Abraham, Isaac, and Rahab in chapter 2. *James is really referring to one of his great-grandmothers and to two of his great-grandfathers when he refers to Abraham, Isaac, and Rahab.* These three are not just heroes of the faith. No, these three are all ancestors of James himself! And then also in the second chapter, James instructs the believer to "fulfill the Royal Law." In other words, "Obey the law of the King." When we are submissive to the Royal Law, we are all promised, "Once he had been approved, he will receive the Crown of Life, which the Lord has promised to those who love Him" (James 1:12 NASB). James first saw loyalty exhibited in his resurrected brother Jesus's commitment to the Royal Family of Israel. James refers to three of his Messianic relatives, and he talks about keeping the Royal Law. In other words, he talks about the law of the king. The ultimate reward, James shares, is there will be the Crown of Life which will be given to everyone who loves and obeys his older brother's commandments. As a member of the Royal Family, James writes about his ancestors being heirs of the Kingdom, keeping the Royal Law, and receiving the Crown of Life.

JUDE

Jude is acknowledged as one of the youngest of Mary and Joseph's five sons. In Matthew 13:53, Jude is mentioned last among the brothers. In Mark 6:3, Jude is listed next to last, but before his brother, Simon. Jesus and James were the two most prominent of Jude's older brothers. If we assume James probably wrote his book sometime around AD 42, then as the youngest or next to youngest brother, Jude, probably authored the book bearing his name, maybe thirty years later, or about AD 72. Like his brother James, Jude spends much time in emphasizing the purity of doctrine in the church, but Jude adds another dimension, an emphasis on prayer.

Two things are noteworthy in Jude's brief book of only twenty-five verses. In the opening verse, he distinctly identifies himself by his relationship to Jesus and to James. Jude first connects himself to his two most prominent brothers. In verse 14, Jude *affirms Moses's account* and *Luke's genealogy of Mary* by stating "Enoch . . . the seventh from Adam." In just these twenty-five verses, while stressing purity of doctrine, and prayer, Jude *references two of his ancestors, Adam and Enoch*, from seventy-six to seventy generations earlier. In addition, Jude notes his two most recent relatives, his siblings, Jesus and James.

In the prior chapter concerning the Messiah, we saw that Jesus quoted or referenced ten of His ancestors from the Royal Seed. Previously, we noticed James mentioned Abraham, Isaac, and Rahab. By the time Jude concludes his writings, he lists two additional ancestors of Jesus, James, and himself. These two Royal Family ancestors are Adam and Enoch. Jude *confirms the validity of the ancient genealogy of Mary* coming via Adam and Enoch. James mentions Abraham, Isaac, and Rahab, while Jude mentions James, Adam, and Enoch. Jude and James help document the accuracy of Jesus's genealogy as recorded in Genesis chapter 5 and Luke chapter 3.

In Genesis chapter 5, Moses lists ten men by name. Although other sons and daughters were born to these ten men (Genesis 5:4, 7, 10, 13 etc.), only ten men are specifically named. *Luke 3:36-38 lists these same ten men in the exact sequence as ancestors of Jesus.* And, finally, Jude, as Jesus's half-brother, over two thousand years from Adam, affirms his ancestor Enoch was the seventh man from Adam (Jude 14 NASB). Three of the Gospel writers verified Jesus as the Messiah in the prior chapter. Also, the sign placed by Herod at the crucifixion in three languages declared Jesus to be "King of the Jews." In addition to the Gospel authors and Herod's pronouncement at the crucifixion, there are yet other witnesses documenting Jesus's earliest ancestors. Moses, Luke, and Jude are consistent in identifying Enoch as the seventh generation after Adam.

THREE WITNESSES

MOSES	LUKE	JUDE
Adam - Genesis 5:1	Adam - Luke 3:38	Adam - Jude 14
Seth - Genesis 5:3	Seth - Luke 3:38	# 2 Generation
Enosh - Genesis 5:6	Enosh - Luke 3:38	# 3 Generation
Cainan - Genesis 5:9	Cainan - Luke 3:37	# 4 Generation
Mahalalel - Genesis 5:12	Mahalalel - Luke 3:37	# 5 Generation
Jared - Genesis 5:15	Jared - Luke 3:37	# 6 Generation
Enoch - Genesis 5:18	Enoch - Luke 3:37	Enoch - Jude 14
Methuselah - Genesis 5:22	Methuselah - Luke 3:37	
Lamech - Genesis 5:25	Lamech - Luke 3:36	
Noah - Genesis 5:29	Noah - Luke 3:36	

In conclusion, the *Royal Seed* culminates in Jesus. Furthermore, two of Jesus's own brothers also emphasized their ancestry, the Royal Law, and the eternal Crown of Life, all centered on the King of Kings.

What did we learn about James and Jude?

1. James, half-brother of Jesus, likely the next oldest son, became head of the Jerusalem Church and wrote the Book of James.
2. Jude, half-brother of Jesus, likely the youngest or next-to-youngest brother, wrote the Book of Jude.

James' and Jude's Relatives

Names	Relationship	Reference
Joseph, Simon	Brothers	Matthew 13:55
Unnamed Sisters	Sisters	Matthew 13:56
Jesus	Half-brother	Galatians 1:19, Jude 1

Chapter 28

Holy Spirit

He commanded them that they should not depart from Jerusalem but wait for the promise of the Father. 'John baptized with water but you should be *baptized with the Holy Spirit*' . . . It is not for you to know times or epochs which the Father has fixed by His own authority; but you shall receive *power when the Holy Spirit* has come upon you and you shall be My witnesses, both in Jerusalem and in all Judea and Samaria and even the remotest part of the earth. (Acts 1:4-5, 7-8; emphasis added)

From shortly after Creation, Satan has repeatedly attempted to murder the carrier of the Royal Seed. If Satan had been successful, then God's plan of sharing the Holy Spirit with mortal man would have failed. Once Jesus conquered death, the two-thousand-year history of Satan's attempts to assassinate the carrier of the Royal Seed concluded. Once the Holy Spirit began indwelling millions of human beings as the Temple of God, the assassination attempts had failed. Study the following chart to observe God's provision of the Holy Spirit to protect God's Royal Plan from Satan. This chart documents two hundred fifty attempts by Satan to kill, to eliminate, and to extinguish the Royal Dynasty of the Father, of Jesus, and of the Holy Spirit.

Satan's Attempted Royal Assassinations- Old Testament

Victim	Perpetrator	Number of Attempts	Reference
Abel	Brother Cain; Abel righteous	1	Hebrews 11:4
Noah	Childless 500 years	1	Genesis 5:32
Abraham	Pharaoh attempted to kill	1	Genesis 12:12
Abraham	Battle Chedorlaomer	1	Genesis 14:17
Abraham	Abimelech attempted to kill	1	Genesis 20:11
Sarah	Barren 90 years	1	Genesis 16:1-6
Rebekah	Barren 20 years; Lord removed	1	Genesis 25:21
Jacob	Esau wanted to kill him over the birthright	1	Genesis 27:42-43
Tamar	Judah wanted to kill her for her adultery	1	Genesis 38:24
Salmon	If Jericho spy, King of Jericho tried to kill	1	Joshua 2:5

Victim	Perpetrator	Number of Attempts	Reference
Rahab	Harlot; hid Israelite spies	1	Joshua 2:12
David	Goliath	1	1 Samuel 17:50
David	Saul with javelin	1	1 Samuel 18:11
David	Dowry, 200 Philistines' foreskins	200	1 Samuel 18:27
David	Jonathan and servants	1	1 Samuel 19:1
David	Philistines	1	1 Samuel 19:8
David	Saul, second javelin	1	1 Samuel 19:10
David	First messengers	1	1 Samuel 19:11
David	Second messengers	1	1 Samuel 19:20
David	Third messengers	1	1 Samuel 19:21
David	Fourth messengers	1	1 Samuel 19:21
David	Philistines	1	1 Samuel 23:2
David	Saul	1	1 Samuel 23:14-15
David	Amalekites battle	1	1 Samuel 30:17-18
David	Philistines	1	2 Samuel 5:19
David	Moabites	1	2 Samuel 8:2
David	Hadadezer	1	2 Samuel 8:3
David	Syrians	1	2 Samuel 8:5
David	Syrians	1	2 Samuel 10:18
David	Ammonites	1	2 Samuel 12:29-30
David	Absalom	1	2 Samuel 15:13-14
David	Ahithophel	1	2 Samuel 17:21-22
David	Ishbi-Benob (Goliath's brother?)	1	2 Samuel 21:16-22
Ahaziah	King killed by Jehu	1	2 Kings 9:27
Grandsons	Killed by grandmother, Athaliah	1+?	2 Kings 11:1
Amaziah	King killed by his servants	1	2 Kings 14:20
Amon	King killed by his servants	1	2 Kings 21:23
Josiah	King killed in battle	1	2 Kings 23:29

Satan's Attempted Royal Assassinations – New Testament

Victim	Perpetrator	Number of Attempts	Reference
Jesus	Herod's attempt to use Wise Men	1	Matthew 2:12
Jesus	Herod killed baby boys – Joseph and Mary fled to Egypt	1	Matthew 2:13, 20
Jesus	Satan, wall of Temple	1	Matthew 4:6
Jesus	Pharisees	1	Matthew 12:14
Jesus	Chief Priests and Elders	1	Matthew 21:46
Jesus	Chief Priest, Scribes, and Elders	1	Matthew 26:4
Jesus	Judas	1	Matthew 26:47
Jesus	High Priest Caiaphas	1	Matthew 26:65-66
Jesus	Governor Pilate and the Crowd	1	Matthew 27:25
	Total Assassination Attempts	248 +?	

In seventy-six generations, there were at least two hundred forty-eight documented attempts to kill a member of the Royal Dynasty—*to stop the Royal Plan of God*. Plus, Satan made other assassination attempts. For example, Nahshon was protected during the crossing of the Red Sea (Exodus 14), Solomon's conflicts (1 Kings 11), Rehoboam's wars (2 Chronicles 12:15), Abijah's battle (2 Chronicles 13:17), etc. Do you know another royal dynasty that has survived at least two hundred forty-eight assassination attempts? So, we come to this realization. God: 248 victories, Satan: 0 victories. So, why is all this Old Testament genealogy so important today—and in particular, to me? After these two hundred forty-eight documented attempts by Satan to stop God's Master Plan, Jesus sent the Holy Spirit to lead His children to Heaven. When Jesus was resurrected from the dead, Satan was defeated.

Two conclusions: First, God and Satan both have perfect scores, God: 248 victories versus Satan 248 defeats. Second, we must remain on guard against the schemes of Satan. He is very persistent. This score sheet offers us hope, assurance, confidence, and encouragement to yield our wills unto Jesus through the workings of the Holy Spirit. Jesus is the perfect victor. The Spirit of God no longer dwells in a tabernacle; now the Holy Spirit dwells in every believer's heart. The temple of God no longer is a physical structure in the Sinai Desert or on the Temple Mount in Jerusalem. With the coming of the Holy Spirit after Jesus's ascension, the temple of God now dwells internally in every believer's being.

When we study the New Jerusalem of the future, we also see many similarities to the Garden of Eden in the past. Conveniently, in addition to the crystal river, the gold, and the Tree of Life from the Garden of Eden, we now see a fourth similarity: the Spirit of God from the Garden of Eden will also be in the New Jerusalem.

THE PAST AND THE FUTURE

Garden of Eden	**New Jerusalem**
Genesis 2:10 River	Revelation 22:1 Crystal River
Genesis 2:11-12 Gold of Havilah	Revelation 21:21 Streets of Gold
Genesis 1:2 Spirit of God	Revelation 22:17 The Spirit
Genesis 2:9, 3:22 Tree of Life	Revelation 2:7, 22:2, 22:14 Tree of Life

The *last occurrence* of the term "Holy Spirit" is in the book of Jude; there is *no reference to the Holy Spirit in Revelation.* The phrases *holy city, holy angels,* and *holy apostles* are mentioned in Revelation, and even the term "Holy, Holy, Holy" is contained there, but not "Holy Spirit." Why not? It is because the Book of Revelation tells us about the Rapture and the return of Jesus to earth. At that point, believers won't be comfortless or helpless. Scripture announces God will wipe away all tears, all death, all sorrows, all crying and all pain. Jesus, the Lamb, shall shepherd and lead His children for eternity (Revelation 7:17).

What did we learn about the Holy Spirit?

1. The Spirit of God moved from Old Testament dwelling in the Holy of Holies to New Testament dwelling in the hearts and souls of believers.
2. The Holy Spirit is the source of power, the third Person of the Godhead.

Relatives of the Holy Spirit

Name	**Relationship**	**Reference**
God	Father	Genesis 1:2
Jesus	Son	Matthew 8:29
All Believers	Indwelled	Acts 2:38, 5:32

Chapter 29

Heirs

> Ye have received *the spirit of adoption*, whereby we cry 'Abba Father.' The Spirit itself beareth witness with our spirit that we are the children of God. And if children, then heirs, heirs of God and *joint heirs with Christ* . . . within ourselves, *waiting for the adoption* . . . the redemption of our body. (Romans 8:15-17, 23, emphasis added)

> Now to Abraham and his *seed* were the promises made. He saith not and to seeds as of many, but as of one. And to thy *seed* which is Christ . . . And if ye be Christ's, then are ye Abraham's *seed and heirs* according to the promise . . . that we might receive the *adoption of sons.* (Galatians 3:16, 29 and 4:5; emphasis added)

> But as many received Him, to them gave He *power to become the sons of God,* even to them that *believe on his name.* (John 1:12; emphasis added)

> That being justified by His grace, *we should be made heirs* according to the hope of eternal life. (Titus 3:7; emphasis added)

Early on, we read in Genesis 15:2-3, Abraham is concerned about having no heir. In Hebrews 11:9-10, the writer of Hebrews returns to Abraham's anxiety about the lack of an heir and addresses Abraham's concerns.

The Book of Hebrews was written by a mysterious, unnamed author. However, in his epistle to Jewish Christians, the author immediately sets forth: "Whom He hath *appointed heir* of all things. . . Who being the brightness of His glory, in the express image of His person" (Hebrews 1:2-3; emphasis added).

Paul, writing to the Romans, makes a similar claim.

> "For the promise that He should be the *heir of the world was not to Abraham or to his seed through the law but through the righteousness of faith.* For if they which are of the law, be heirs, faith is made void and the promise made of non-effect" (Romans 4:13-14; emphasis added).

Consider John's comment about Jesus in John 6:42, where the author declares "Jesus the son of Joseph." In addition, notice when Jesus was twelve and teaching in the temple, Luke quotes Mary saying "thy father and I have sought thee" (Luke 2:42, 48). John and Luke both show Jesus completely, fully, adopted into Joseph's blended family. Just as Jesus was adopted into Joseph's blended family, believers are also adopted into God's blended family.

Just as Jesus was adopted into Joseph's family, all Non-Jewish believers are adopted as children into the family of God.

> "Ye have received the spirit of *adoption*, whereby we cry, 'Abba, Father.' The spirit itself beareth witness with our spirit that we are the children of God: and if *children*, then *heirs*; *heirs of God*, and *joint heirs with Christ*. If so, be that we suffer with Him, that we may be also glorified together" (Romans 8:15-17; emphasis added).

Did I read that correctly? Those who believe in Christ will be adopted as children of God and will be joint heirs with Jesus! Wow! A joint heir with Jesus! Ponder that thought for a few minutes.

For mankind, even to this day, to be heirs of a promise made two thousand years ago seems unrealistic. If God's covenant of a Promised Land to Abraham was fulfilled one thousand years after the promise was made, cannot God fulfill His promises to us today, two thousand years after the promises were first made? Although this promise is over two thousand years old, nevertheless, even in modern times, it is still valid and in force by the authority of God's power via the activities of the Holy Spirit.

For believers in Jesus to clarify their adoption, their status in God's family, read the following from Galatians: "And if you be Christ's, then are ye Abraham's *seed* and *heirs* according to the promise" (Galatians 3:29; emphasis added).

Paul continues in his letter to the Galatians,

> "But when the fullness of the time was come, God sent forth His son, made of a woman, made under the law. To redeem them that were under the law, that we might receive the *adoption* of sons" (Galatians 4:4-5; emphasis added).

When Paul wrote to the believers in Ephesus, he quickly got to the point of adoption: "That we should be holy and without blame before Him in love: Having predestinated us unto the *adoption* of children by Jesus Christ" (Ephesians 1:4-5; emphasis added).

Finally, when Paul wrote to Titus, he penned these words: "That then justified by His Grace, we should be made *heirs* according to the hope of eternal life" (Titus 3:7; emphasis added).

The subject of believers being adopted into the family of God is stated clearly in the books of Romans, Galatians, Ephesians, and Titus. Furthermore, once we are adopted into the family of God, we become heirs of God. The best part of all, as we read from Romans 8:17 a few minutes ago, "we become joint heirs with Jesus." To be a joint heir with Jesus, now that's exciting! No doubt we should be filled with joy, happiness, and enthusiasm. But wait, there's more! What will the believer's eternal destiny be like? I don't know, and neither does any human know, but I do know this: *the word "mansion" is used only once in the entire Bible*, and it is used by Jesus shortly before His crucifixion.

"In my Father's house are many *mansions*: If it were not so, I would have told you. I go to prepare a place for you. And if I go and prepare a place for you, I will come again and receive you unto myself, that where I am, there you may also be" (John 14:2-3; emphasis added).

It is with wide-eyed joy that we can trust Jesus for our adoption, our being heirs, our being joint heirs, and for our mansions. These mansions will undoubtedly be something to behold. Jesus is now busy in Heaven preparing mansions for all believers.

Upon our faith in Jesus, all believers, by adoption, are made royalty — members of the Royal Family of Israel. By being a member of the Royal Family of God, we are joint heirs with Jesus of all of God's blessings.

Thus, dear reader, we come to the end of this book but not to the end of our story. Recall all of those genealogical charts you have studied. Well, it's now time to update the family genealogy of Jesus.

The Genealogy of You

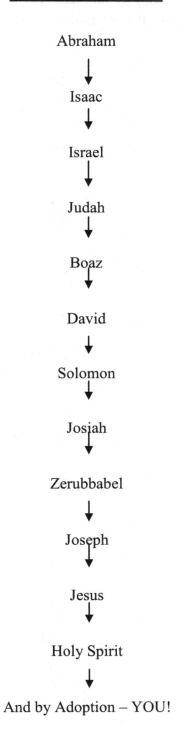

Abraham

Isaac

Israel

Judah

Boaz

David

Solomon

Josiah

Zerubbabel

Joseph

Jesus

Holy Spirit

And by Adoption – YOU!

To all who believe in Jesus and accept Him as their Savior, congratulations! You have been adopted into the Royal Family of Israel, the Royal Family of God. According to God's Holy Word, you are now royalty. See you in eternity at our mansions, as we exalt Jesus with our praises and serve Him as kings and priests in the Royal Family of God.

Notes

1. The genealogical chart, "The Royal Family of Israel" may be ordered from JFA, LLC by mailing a $30 check to Box 1751, Boone, NC 28607.
2. The Strongest Strong's Exhaustive Concordance of the Bible, Copyright ©2001 by Zondervan.
3. The Strongest Strong's Exhaustive Concordance.
4. Genesis 11:13 and 1 Chronicles 6:24 do not mention Cainan as the son of Arphaxad, but Cainan is mentioned in Luke 3:36 as son of Arphaxad and father of Salah.
5. Notice this pattern is similar to the 10 generations we saw in Genesis 5.
6. Willmington's Book of Bible Lists, H. L. Willmington 1876, Tyndale, pg. 118.
7. The Hebrew term for "Adam" is generic for "man" – nevertheless, the first ancestor of Jesus is Adam.
8. Willmington's Book of Bible Lists, pg. 92-93.
9. Encyclopædia Britannica Online, s. v. "Henrik Dam", accessed November 19, 2014, http://www.britannica.com/EBchecked/topic/150365/Henrik-Dam.
10. Strongest Strong's Concordance.
11. Strongest Strong's Concordance.

To better understand all the relationships in this book, the genealogical chart "The Royal Family of Israel" may be purchased for $30 from JFA, LLC at Box 1751, Boone, NC 28607.

Printed in the United States
By Bookmasters